	DATE DUE	

Representing God
in Washington

Representing God in Washington

The Role of Religious Lobbies in the American Polity

ALLEN D. HERTZKE

The University of Tennessee Press

KNOXVILLE

The paper in this book meets the minimum requirements of
the American National Standard for Permanence of Paper for
Printed Library Materials. ∞ The binding materials have
been chosen for strength and durability.

Library of Congress Cataloging-in-Publication Data

Hertzke, Allen D., 1950–
    Representing God in Washington.

    Bibliography: p.
    Includes index.
    1. Religion and politics—United States—History—
20th century.   2. Religion and state—United States—
History—20th century.   3. Lobbying—United States—
History—20th century.   4. United States—Religion—
1945-   .   5. United States—Politics and government—
1945-   .   I. Title.
BL65.P7H47   1988   322'.1'0973   87-15144
ISBN 0-87049-553-4

To my family,
Barbara, Patrick, and Simon

Contents

Tables

Preface

I am concerned in this study with the collective function of national religious interest groups in the American political system. My argument is that they play a unique representational role in the "pressure system," articulating the values of many non-elite citizens and modestly correcting the skewed nature of the lobby universe.

Because little has been written about the national religious lobbies, I have attempted to assess them in the broadest possible manner, incorporating as much elaborate texture as possible without compromising the clarity of the central argument. I did this because I believe Washington lobbying provides a telescopic view of religious political engagement in the United States. Thus, I have included considerable material on individual groups and leaders, in part to illustrate how the pluralism of American religion is manifested in political action. In addition, I have tried to document the ways in which the congressional system, as a strategic milieu, in turn shapes and constrains religious political "witness."

In reviewing the work of other scholars I found a disjointedness that seemed to explain why the subject has not been treated in this manner before. Interest group scholars have not paid much attention to religious interests, for example, while scholars of religion and politics have largely ignored the lobbies, concerning themselves instead with either philosophical and constitutional questions or mass attitudes and voting behavior. In addition, those few scholars who have dealt with representational issues have largely concentrated on a narrow band of religious groups without attention to broader interactive effects, leading them to underestimate the religious contribution to national representation.

Religious lobbies mirror the theological, organizational, ethnic, and regional diversity of American religion. In a sense, then, this study of religious groups is not only about Washington lobbying but will offer, I hope, insights into the deeper connections of religion to society and politics in America.

Acknowledgments

In tracing the evolution of this book, I am profoundly aware of the extent to which it is not alone my work but represents in a fundamental way the enormous contributions of others. This study began as a Ph.D. dissertation in political science at the University of Wisconsin-Madison. The three people most responsible for guiding the initial research were Leon Epstein, who served as my dissertation chairman, Booth Fowler, whose pioneering work on religion and politics paved the way for this study, and Graham Wilson, who suggested the focus on lobbies and the title. Leon and Booth, in particular, read numerous drafts of chapters, and I gained immeasurably from their insights and sage counsel. Significantly, they encouraged me from the beginning to write it like a book and not a dissertation. I also benefited from the suggestions of Richard Champagne, Cathy Johnson, and Robert Frykenberg, who read portions of the manuscript. Finally, I am indebted to the many professors and graduate students at Wisconsin who contributed immensely to my intellectual growth, and to the Wisconsin Alumni Research Foundation, which provided a travel grant to defray some of the expenses of my research trips to Washington, D.C.

The Carl Albert Congressional Research and Studies Center at the University of Oklahoma provided tremendous institutional assistance in the final stages of editing the manuscript. Ron Peters, Director of the Center, was extremely generous in providing support, and Gary Copeland, Associate Director, read the manuscript and shared his valuable insights. In addition, Albert Fellow Ken Cosgrove conducted extensive and thoughtful editorial work.

It is fitting, too, that I acknowledge the people I interviewed for this study, all of whom, as busy people in the Washington pressure cooker, shared their time, insights, and frank musings on themselves, their religious beliefs, and their political strategies. I know that my work has not done them justice, but I thank them all the same.

I am grateful, of course, to the University of Tennessee Press, and especially to Cynthia Maude-Gembler, a particularly aggressive and astute editor. Skillful and thorough reviews conducted by James Guth and Kathleen Beatty helped me to avoid several problems and clearly enhanced the quality of the final book.

Finally, I turn to the center of my universe, my family. My parents, solid farm folk from the heartland, have suffered a never-content searcher of a son with love and patience. Their financial help and encouragement were invaluable in enabling me to pursue a scholarly career. My wife's parents similarly assisted us in making the transition. There is one person, of course, without whose support I literally would not have made it. My wife, Barbara Norton, not only encouraged me to return to the academy, financially supported us during graduate school, proofread several drafts of this book, but along the way bore two sons, who have a way of putting all vocational quests in perspective. I can say no more but to express my undying devotion.

Representing God
in Washington

1 Religious Interests in the American System

If 1976 was the "year of the evangelical"[1] in American politics, then 1984 was surely the year of "religion and politics." In nationally televised debates presidential candidates Walter Mondale and Ronald Reagan clashed over church-state relations. The Reverend Jesse Jackson brought black evangelism to the Democratic convention, culminating a campaign based largely on a network of black congregations. New York Archbishop O'Connor sparred with Geraldine Ferraro over abortion, sparking both Mario Cuomo and Ted Kennedy to issue carefully reasoned statements on the proper relation of religious values to political obligations. Meanwhile, evangelical and fundamentalist conservatives flexed their muscles at a Republican convention that featured the Reverend Jerry Falwell and a platform heavily influenced by the New Religious Right. For intellectual elites it was significant that the pages of the *New York Times* were filled with lead stories, speech transcripts, and full-page advertisements discussing, debating, and analyzing the crosscurrents of religious political activism in America.

This study grew out of the conviction that one cannot adequately understand American politics without understanding the dynamics of religious political engagement.[2] Yet, over a decade after the election of a "born again" evangelical as president, our understanding of this religious dimension in American politics remains oddly incomplete and impressionistic.[3] True, we know something about the influence of religion on voting behavior[4] and a great deal about the courts as a battleground for religious interests confronting secular powers or each other.[5] Congressional lobbying, however, has received scant attention, and most studies of religious lobbies are dated, limited in scope, or incidental to other research foci.[6]

Moreover, where scholars have dealt with the representational issues involved in lobbying, they have tended to concentrate on a narrow band of ideological groups, about which they are often critical. Thus, critics of the liberal churches tend to discount them as out of touch with lay members,[7] while other scholars view the fundamentalist activists as intolerant and lacking public support.[8] In neither case are the actual policy impacts of the activism assessed, nor is there much attention paid to the activities of groups in between the ideological poles.[9]

What is lacking in the study of religious political engagement, I would argue, is an approach that encompasses the breadth of religious interests; and it is precisely the nature of Washington lobbying that makes it an especially fruitful field for just such a comparative analysis, for three reasons. First, in contrast to the relatively narrow band of religious groups that actively engage the courts,[10] it is in Washington that nearly every modern permutation of religious belief or interest is represented, drawn by the same imperatives that have brought hundreds of groups to the nation's capital in what Jeffrey Berry calls the "advocacy explosion."[11] Indeed, lobbying reflects well the pluralistic nature of religious activism, even if some interests are better represented than others. Second, the Washington milieu represents a common ground where groups with different regional, ethnic, theological, or ideological bases meet in close proximity. It is here that leaders develop strategies, coalitions form, issues are framed, bedfellows emerge, partisans mutually adjust, and members are mobilized.

Finally, Washington presents a common challenge to religious interests, an environment to which they must adapt to be effective. It is in the capital, perhaps more than anywhere else, that the "absolutes" of religious faith confront the hard and seductive reality of practical politics. The congressional system, with its norms, rituals, parliamentary intricacies, and multiple points of access, must be mastered if a religious group wishes to achieve some success. In interviews with congressional staff members the same theme repeatedly emerges: to be effective, religious lobbyists must learn to play the game, to think strategically, and to understand the norms of congressional politics. Differences and similarities between antagonistic groups, thus, emerge within a common environment, potentially suggesting, for example, what distinguishes Catholics from Episcopalians, Lutherans from Mennonites, or evangelicals from fundamentalists, as they translate their religious values into political action.

In short, the diversity of religious groups in Washington, their close proximity to each other, and the common political constraints they face, provide an excellent opportunity for insightful analysis and for isolating those variables that pertain to religious groups in particular from those that reflect the nature of the American political system. This treatment of religious lobbies, then, attempts to examine not only how religious interests shape American politics but how the American political system, particularly the congressional milieu, in turn, channels, constrains, and in some cases alters that religious political "witness."

Contemporary Religious Political Engagement

A Lutheran pastor, upon returning from a church-sponsored trip to Nicaragua, stuns his rural congregation by attacking American support for the Contras. The collection plates at a Presbyterian congregation fill up one Sunday, not with money, but with an offering of letters to Congress supporting more food aid to Africa. An Episcopal church houses refugees from El Salvador; a Catholic community votes to support the nuclear freeze; and a United Church of Christ congregation discusses a state bill on sanctions against South Africa. Meanwhile, an evangelical church organizes a vigil at a family-planning clinic; fundamentalist ministers march on convenience stores for selling pornography; a Catholic congregation is mobilized to support a state referendum restricting public funding of abortions; Christian parents challenge the content of school curricula; church officials testify against a proposed state lottery; TV preachers implore listeners to flood the Congress with calls and letters supporting school prayer; and pentecostal Pat Robertson, founder of the Christian Broadcast Network, announces his intention of running for president in 1988.

How do we make sense of all this? One response is to observe that religious political activism is nothing new in American politics, that these manifestations are but modern variations on a continuing theme. Indeed, from the abolitionist movement of the nineteenth century, to the crusade against alcohol, to the more recent civil rights struggle, religious-based movements and organizations have attempted to influence public policy, sometimes with dramatic results. Moreover, cultural-religious cleavages, such as the Catholic/Protestant split, have in the past defined political cleavages as well.[12]

However, there is evidence to suggest that major changes are afoot, and that religion and politics are more deeply intertwined than at any time in recent history. Indeed, what is striking about current political engagement is its tremendous breadth and ideological diversity. While the high profile efforts of the Moral Majority and Christian Voice on the Right have mobilized several million previously dormant citizens through sophisticated direct-mail technologies and access to a vast network of Christian media outlets and programs, activism on the Left is also manifest. Grassroots opposition to nuclear weapons and U.S. Central American policy, plus support for sanctions against South Africa, have been strongly infused with church lay and clergy participation. Moreover, intensity of commitment, an important political resource, is evidenced by those willing to place themselves in personal jeopardy. In the highly publicized Sanctuary movement, leaders of some two hundred liberal churches have defied American immigration policy by harboring refugees from Central America, risking prosecution and inspiring declarations of sanctuary by a number of cities, including Los Angeles, and even one state, New Mexico. More dramatically perhaps, the Witness for Peace organization has sent several thousand religious people to Nicaragua with the expressed purpose of interposing themselves between the Contras and Nicaraguan residents, in effect daring the U.S.-supported rebels to risk killing American citizens.

In addition to these indications of religious political engagement, there is also strong evidence that the number and ideological diversity of Washington-based groups has mushroomed in the past three decades. In 1950 there were sixteen major religious lobbies in Washington.[13] By 1985 there were at least eighty, and the list is growing.[14] Moreover, the religious agenda is far broader than even a decade ago. Religious groups, of course, are deeply involved (on all sides) in highly charged social issues, such as abortion and the Equal Rights Amendment, and on church-state matters, such as school prayer and aid to parochial schools. However, in any given congressional session religious leaders will also be embroiled in battles over food stamp cuts, aid to the Nicaraguan Contras, civil rights legislation, South African sanctions, foreign aid, international trade, nuclear strategy, military budgets, tax reform, social security, day care funding, environmental protection, labor legislation, farm bills—and the list goes on. The complexity of modern religious lobbying is illustrated by the Catholic Bishops, who in many ways have strategically placed themselves between the ideological poles. Their unprecedented drafting of pastoral letters on nuclear arms and the economy, both widely interpreted as "liberal" documents, has added more intricate texture to the political stance of the Catholic hierarchy, which simultaneously embraces many of the aims of the fundamentalist conservatives on social issues.

One major resource for religious activists is that religion continues to be an important force in American life and culture. Contrary to evidence of significant decline in belief in some Western
European nations, American religious belief remains relatively
intact.[15] Not only do Americans express more confidence in the
church than they do in other key institutions of society, but most,
in fact, are church members. Indeed, churches present a powerful contrast to the image of America as a "mass society" of
atomized individuals physically unconnected with each other. In
any given week over 40 percent of all Americans attend church,
and nearly 60 percent can be described as regular churchgoers.[16]
The significance of these figures is that more Americans belong
to a church or synagogue than to any other private association,
union, or group,[17] making religion the premier voluntary association in the country, a fact that will loom large in the discussion
of the implications of church activism for the American polity, to
which I now turn.

Political Science and Religious Interest Groups

The politization of churches is an important sociological feature
of religious life in America, but its political significance is not
well understood. To understand the potentially unique role of
religious groups in the American polity it is necessary to summarize our current understanding of interest groups, particularly
their often ambiguous impact on American political institutions.

One of the most fascinating aspects of interest group scholarship is the attitude of many scholars toward the "factions," as
Madison[18] termed them. While many congressional scholars apparently admire the institution of Congress ("there, but for the
grace of the voters, go I"), and while students of political parties
commonly celebrate the place of the latter in American politics, scholars of interest groups reflect a far greater ambivalence
about their own subjects.[19] E.E. Schattschneider, for example,

a scholar of both parties and interest groups, viewed with alarm the collective disaster that resulted from lobbying by narrow interests. In a classic study of tariff legislation in the 1930s,[20] he documented how each business lobbied in its narrow, short-term interest for tariff protection. The resulting legislation, as we know, constricted foreign trade and deepened the Depression. In the lexicon of politics, "lobbying" continues to be associated with these unsavory overtones. Several religious leaders interviewed for this study, for example, were quick to assert that they were not "lobbyists," because they did not represent narrow financial interests.

Concern with this lack of broad societal representation helped to spawn the public interest movement in the 1970s, as Common Cause, environmental groups, and the Nader organizations attempted to represent diffuse groups of consumers and concerned citizens.[21] These relatively modest developments, however, have not stilled critics of the fragmented "pressure system."[22] Indeed, one economist blames America's inability to deal with fundamental economic problems as a function of the veto power of the particularistic interests in the American polity, which render the Congress incapable of managing such problems as the national debt, foreign competition, and declining productivity.[23] It is a conclusion that would not surprise Schattschneider.

A second concern expressed by Schattschneider and others was the nature of the groups themselves. While mass-based political parties have an incentive to reach out and mobilize those weaker, less articulate, less wealthy, and otherwise hard-to-organize citizens, interest groups are by nature elite in membership. In the pluralist heaven the choir sings with an upper-class accent, Schattschneider reminds us, and certainly membership evidence is available to back that claim.[24] The poorer members of society do not join groups and thus are not represented in the pressure system. Moreover, even if such marginalized people are organized, they will be hampered by what Schattschneider called the mobilization of bias, the fact that within the prevailing ideology of society, certain members are deemed more worthy, deserving, or legitimate than others. This theme, echoed in the work by Bachrach and Baratz,[25] stresses that some people are so intimidated by the prevailing norms of what is acceptable political practice that their voices are effectively suffocated before they can even attempt to make their concerns known.[26]

While Schattschneider pointed to the skewed nature of a polity dominated by interest groups (and without the guidance of strong, responsible parties), it was, ironically, an economist, Mancur Olson, who determined the logic behind this perceived characteristic.[27] Olson aimed his analysis at the underlying assumptions of David Truman's theory of group formation.[28] Groups form, Truman had argued, when a major economic or social disturbance threatens to undermine the way of life of a particular group of people. Though Truman never implied that all "interests" would be represented equally, as some of his critics have claimed, his theory did imply at least that people with a grievance or shared interest would naturally form a group to articulate their concerns. Olson asked a simple question, with devastating results: What incentive is there for an individual to join a group which seeks some collective good? Very little, he concluded. Indeed, a rational economic actor, say a farmer grieved by low commodity prices or a citizen desiring pollution cleanup, is tempted to be a "free rider." Why contribute when, if the group is successful, the benefit, like God's rain, will fall on contributors and noncontributors alike? The temptation to be a free rider is greatest for the poor, who can least afford to contribute to an interest group, yet have potentially the most to gain by the group's success. Because of this, Olson argued, the interest group universe is heavily skewed in favor of those organizations that represent few potential members (automobile manufacturers), can compel membership (unions), or offer some selective benefit to members only (malpractice insurance). Thus, the political system is far less representative than supposed.[29]

Recent developments have heightened concern with the nature of the pressure system. While social, technological, and political trends have favored the proliferation of interest groups in the last two decades, political parties have declined in strength, weakened by diminishing public support and reforms that have reduced the electoral influence of party leaders.[30] This broad trend, coupled with related developments in the Congress that have dispersed power and undermined party leadership and cohesion, have enhanced the influence of interest groups, who now enjoy multiple access points to the levers of power. The rise of political action committees (PACs), technological innovations in information processing, and the decline of parties have thus created a context in which interest groups are more important in politics than at any other time, leading scholars to question anew their role in the American polity. Summarizing the changes in the American political system over the past two decades, Jeffrey Berry concludes:

> Even with the increase in citizen groups, the universe of lobbying organizations favors business, labor, and the professions, at the expense of the poor, minorities, and diffuse, hard-to-organize constituencies. . . Thus both the decline of parties and the proliferation of interest groups have worked to the advantage of those already well represented in the political process.[31]

What emerges from this brief review of interest groups in the American political system is a sobering picture of fragmented politics dominated by elite-based organizations for often narrow, particularistic interests. The advocacy explosion has done little to alter the fact that membership in interest groups is an elite activity, even if some well-heeled citizens contribute to environmental groups or Common Cause. Political parties, which at least have an incentive to mobilize the less articulate, more marginalized citizens, may now be less effective in checking the collective power of interest groups than they once were. In short, many view the increasing role of interest groups as skewing the system in favor of those already well represented.

The politization of churches and the mobilization of self-consciously religious people intersects this picture in a number of intriguing ways. Indeed, it is the very nature of the pressure system as described that makes religious groups potentially so significant an addition to the system. First, of all the potential reasons for violating economic self-interest, in light of the Olsonian dilemma, the religious motivation is one of the most compelling. The religious message, at least in its Christian form, is a suprarational, paradoxical call for transcendence over one's narrow selfish interest. Christians are called, as Jesus says, to "lose their lives" to gain the Kingdom. Thus, religious motivation potentially undercuts the Olsonian dilemma of economic rationality and the attendant "free rider" problems undermining collective action. Giving money to a church or to a direct-mail religious group is not just a form of advocacy or self-interest; rather, it is a way, albeit modest, of giving oneself, of losing one's (selfish) life to save it. Indeed, Olson's rational economic actor looks remarkably like the person on the negative side of Jesus's dictum, the one who seeks to gain life, who seeks economic self-interest, and hence, cannot gain the Kingdom.

At the operational level it appears that this message has not lost its salience. Religious scholars have documented the seemingly paradoxical fact that it is often members of less elite churches who contribute the greatest share of their incomes to their local parish,[32] a finding not surprising in light of the gospel theme that the poor often understand the message better than the well heeled. Having less to lose in this world, they have the most to gain in the Kingdom. Olson alludes to the complex nature of religious motivation when he observes:

> In philanthropic and religious lobbies the relationships
> between the purposes and interests of the individual
> member and the purposes and interests of the organiza-
> tion may be so rich and obscure that a theory of the sort
> developed here cannot provide much insight.[33]

He goes on to suggest that perhaps church lobbies offer selective benefits—such as the ultimate value of salvation—but he concludes that this application of his theory oversimplifies the complexities of religious motivation. Olson did not view this special species of lobby as a serious challenge to his theoretical analysis, however, because he expected the world of lobbying to be dominated by groups with economic interests.

The paradoxical character of religious commitment is illustrated in a penetrating study by Dean Kelley (who, as a lobbyist himself, was a prominent actor in the battle over equal access legislation described in chapter 6). In *Why Conservative Churches Are Growing*,[34] Kelley documented the decline in "liberal" church membership and the concurrent rise in "conservative" membership. He concluded that the underlying dynamic was the strictness of the church, with conservative churches more often, though not exclusively, demanding more of their members than their more easygoing liberal counterparts. The dynamic operates, he observes, because the "business of religion is meaning," and those churches that demand greater commitment of members convey that they "really mean it." Whether it is asking members to publicly commit their lives to Christ, or tithe, or engage in personal evangelizing—or, with a few radical churches, demanding as a condition of membership a social commitment to, say, a "ministry for the poor"—the religious persuasion asks people to violate their "self-interest" as defined by the economist, a call to which many are evidently willing to respond. This is not to suggest that religious interest groups can avoid completely the problems of institutional maintenance that other groups face, but it does suggest that they may occasionally call upon a level of sustained commitment that other groups cannot approach.

A second intriguing feature of religious interest groups is the breadth of their work. As I demonstrate in chapter 4, religious groups, defying easy categorization, operate simultaneously as institutions with economic interests, as ideological advocates, and as public interest lobbies attempting to gain some collective good. The religious leaders interviewed for this study do not see themselves as representing narrow interests, but instead consciously attempt to advance their competing visions of the public good. Moreover, most Jewish and Christian lobbies see their roles as explicitly representing Olson's voiceless, hard-to-organize citizens, and they argue that their lobbying on behalf of institutional self-interest is merely a means to better serve society. Indeed, both liberal church leaders and conservative New Religious Right lobbyists see themselves in populist terms as representing non-elite citizens. To be sure, they disagree profoundly about what those citizens need or want. But one could make a case that both are partially correct: that poor and working-class citizens do in fact want economic security along with a share of the pie (as liberals argue) but simultaneously feel threatened by cultural change, loose morality, and the undermining of traditional values, and want to see family life strengthened, traditional values upheld, and their religious faith taken seriously (as the conservatives argue).

Finally, and perhaps most importantly, there is the nature of the constituency itself. As noted, more Americans belong to a church or synagogue than to any other voluntary association. Indeed, not only do the majority of citizens claim religious affiliation, but, contrary to Schattschneider's contention that group membership is an upper-income phenomenon, in sheer numbers the lower classes dominate church attendance,[35] leading Paul Weber to conclude that "identifiable religious societies are important for interest group theory partially because they are by far the largest non-elite group in the nation."[36] The potential significance of this fact has escaped most interest group scholars, but with the increasing politization of churches and religious people, it emerges as an important point of scholarly departure. Because church life is an important weekly aspect of people's concrete experience, access to the political system through churches may be a significant development for American politics, the potential of which has been demonstrated dramatically by the role of the black church in the civil rights movement. There are, of course, impediments to political mobilization of church people, who, by and large, do not join a church for political expression. Still, because of the nature of the potential constituency, its breadth and the shared life of religious observance, effective religious mobilization, however limited, could conceivably enhance the articulation of diverse, non-elite interests in the American political system.

There is a related, though more controversial, argument about why religious mobilization could enhance the representativeness of the American polity. It is a variation on the mobilization-of-bias theme. Richard John Neuhaus, Lutheran theologian and political theorist, observes that a profound change has marked political discourse in the United States in the past few decades. This change, he argues, is the exclusion of religion or religiously grounded values from public life, a condition he terms the "naked public square."[37] This has not happened because people have actually become secular, stopped going to church, or lost their religious faith. Rather, it is a function of a mobilization of secular bias by elites in law, education, government, and the media who have deemed religious language inappropriate to public discourse, religious values unconnected to practical politics and public education, and religious practice a purely private affair. Though not sympathetic with some goals and tactics of the New Religious Right, Neuhaus sees its emergence as a logical response to this denial of the religious faith of most Americans. Thus, the argument goes, as long as an overly broad interpretation of church-state separation is used by elites to render religious-based values as illegitimate in public discourse or dangerous in schools, the American political system, which represents a largely religious people, cannot be said to be truly representative. Religious political mobilization could conceivably break through this "elite" secular bias and encourage the articulation of religious-based values in public debate.

In summary, religious groups are significant for American politics because they potentially represent non-elite, broad constituencies and offer the prospect of articulating previously underrepresented values and concerns of many citizens. The extent to which they do so, however, is in part a function of the relation of national leaders, who articulate lobby policy, and members "out there," who sustain the Washington offices by their contributions.

Oligarchy, Representation, and Religious Lobbies

Representation is central to modern democratic theory, but as Pitkin[38] reminds us, it is a complex and multifaceted concept. Religious groups mirror that complexity and even increase it in important ways, as the discussion in chapter 4 will show. To address the issue of representation we must ask of religious lobbyists: whom or what do they represent? To what extent can or do they articulate their constituencies' needs or wants? To what degree do they know what members want? Indeed, how effective are they at translating religious values or constituent wishes into operational political strategies in Washington? Finally, is there tension between representing religious values or traditions on the one hand and articulating member views on the other?

If we survey the literature on the relation of leaders to led in political organizations, we have reason to expect frequent disparities between national policy as enunciated by leaders and the views of constituents in the field. Indeed, much of the treatment of single-interest groups[39] has centered on the oligarchical nature of leadership, which, of course, Michels[40] took to be the universal trait of organization. Oliver Garceau, for example, in a celebrated study of the American Medical Association,[41] revealed the strong oligarchic tendency of the leadership in the AMA, a finding corroborated in later empirical studies.[42] Observers of the AMA conclude that without the lucrative selective benefits to members, such as insurance, important journals, and even access to some hospitals, the organization would be moribund politically. Yet, in spite of the fact that it does not represent the views of many doctors, the AMA continues to be a major force in medical policy.

One of the few exceptions in the literature is Seymour Martin Lipset's examination of the International Typographical Union, the ITU.[43] Lipset was disturbed by the tendency toward oligarchical control in many unions, but he found in the ITU a system of intra-group democracy—in this case the existence of formal parties that competed for power within the union—that acted as a check on the autonomous tendencies of leaders. While his study challenged the inevitability of Michels's iron law of oligarchy, Lipset was quick to caution that unusual circumstances were required to overcome the oligarchic tendency in organization.

Available evidence suggests this oligarchic tendency operates for religious groups as well. Several studies conducted in the late 1960s documented the apparent gap between national lobby policy (as articulated by church officials) and the views of members in the pews.[44] Other studies cite the gap between the clergy of theologically liberal Protestant churches and the lay members, which as an organizational dynamic contributes to divergent elite-mass relations.[45]

Yet the nature of interest group politics has changed significantly in the past two decades, as direct-mail technologies have helped leaders tap new constituencies and (we might expect) maintain closer contact with members.[46] In interviews with national religious lobbyists it is clear that the perceived need to develop and maintain links with grassroots constituencies is affecting the strategic calculations of virtually all the major actors, both older denominational-based groups, as well as newer, direct-mail organizations. Some leaders, for example, now conduct polls of members, while others claim to feel compelled to concentrate on the issues that are "hot buttons" for fundraising. Still others appear to be responding to the pressure from opponents to demonstrate that they actually do represent a constituency and not just their own views. Thus the mobilization of grassroots constituencies through direct-mail and mass media technology— linked often to churches and denominational bases—is a key to understanding the dynamics of modern religious lobbying. The imperatives of mobilization, I will argue, do serve to check the oligarchic tendency in some organizations, under some circumstances. Consequently, just as Lipset sought to discern factors that contribute to greater harmony between union leaders and members, this exploration of religious lobbies seeks in part to chart those factors, whether organizational or theological, that limit the distance between leaders and led in religious America.

Jeffrey Berry argues that the proliferation of interest groups has worked to the advantage of those already well represented in the system. This assertion appears *not* to be wholly accurate, as I will show, when religious political advocacy is included in the analysis. Religion in America, as chapter 2 demonstrates, is characterized by an activism and pluralism that enhance its importance in American cultural life, particularly in the experience of non-elites. The national religious lobbies—in their growing diversity—now roughly mirror this pluralism. When these religious groups mobilize constituencies and articulate their competing religious values, they are playing a unique representational role in the "pressure system," however imperfectly or incompletely. My thesis is that in light of their mobilization efforts and their pluralism, the national religious lobbies, collectively, enhance the representativeness of the modern American polity.

What does the study of religious political activism tell us about American representation? It tells us, I will argue, that any theory of political representation in the United States must include the religious dimension, must take into account the religious commitments of Americans, a claim which would not have surprised Tocqueville in the nineteenth century, but which today seems bold indeed.

Organization of Chapters

This introductory chapter has attempted to set the stage for what is to come. Chapter 2, titled "American Exceptionalism and Religious Political Activism," places the study in its historical context and analyzes past religious political engagement within the context of the exceptional activism and pluralism of American religious practice. It argues that since religion in the United States is particularly adaptable and dynamic, changes in religious practice or commitment will often ramify in the political system. The chapter documents the historical roots of the religious lobbies and demonstrates how the pluralism of religious cultural life is now roughly reflected in Washington political advocacy. The chapter concludes by illustrating the ideological diversity of the religious lobbies, which emerges as a key aspect of their collective role in the congressional system. Chapter 3, titled "Political Strategies, Effectiveness, and the Congressional Milieu," analyzes the attempts by religious leaders to influence public policy. It demonstrates that religious lobbies are not unlike other interest groups in their tactics, and it shows how the growing importance of constituent mobilization is increasingly shaping the strategic calculations of the major actors. It indicates that religious lobbyists can be effective advocates for their positions, but that for some there is a tension between "witnessing" to their faith and winning incremental battles. The chapter concludes by showing how the imperatives of maintaining a grassroots network fosters tactical pragmatism, particularly for the fundamentalists, which in light of their militant rhetoric is an especially intriguing finding. Chapter 4, titled "Representation and the Religious Lobbies: An Introduction," begins a two-chapter discussion that develops the central argument in this book. Against the backdrop of representation theory as formulated by Hanna Pitkin, the chapter analyzes the unusually diverse representational roles played by religious lobbies. In particular, it charts the representation of church institutions, theological values, and world constituencies. Chapter 5, titled, "Representation of Domestic Constituencies," contrasts the positions of religious lobbyists with indications of member (and broader public) sentiment. The analysis reveals that on such social issues as abortion and school prayer, fundamentalist leaders (along with some Catholic and evangelical lobbyists) do roughly articulate both member and broader public opinion, especially the sentiments of non-elites and minorities. In contrast, liberal church lobbies were found to be modestly supported in some of their economic and foreign policy positions. Evidences of variance between lobby policy and member sentiment are presented, but such oligarchic tendencies are found to be less troublesome for representative democracy in light of strategic realities. It appears, in short, that groups have been most successful in mobilizing constituencies where their activities are rooted in at least moderate member support, indicating that for the religious lobbyists, in contrast to, for example, the AMA, "oligarchic" lobbying is much less effective than "representative" lobbying. The chapter also analyzes the contrasting nature of representation provided by direct-mail groups versus the denominations, and concludes that direct constituent mobilization plays a unique representational role in the system. The chapter concludes by arguing that the collective impact of religious advocacy is to broaden the articulation of diverse and non-elite interests in the American polity. Chapter 6, titled "Religious Lobbies and Congressional Policy-Making on Church-State Relations," is a case study of an important legislative battle that engaged most of the major religious actors during the 98th Congress. As the last substantive chapter, it illustrates many of the themes woven through the rest of the study. It demonstrates that religious interest groups are capable of making an impact on national policy, both as insiders and outsiders. It outlines the power of constituency mobilization to alter the strategic calculations of lobbyists and congressional members alike, and illustrates the importance of the mass base of churches as a political resource, particularly the video access to constituents enjoyed by evangelical and fundamentalist leaders. The chapter goes on to illustrate the pluralism of the religious lobbies, tracing in particular the important divisions which demarcate fundamentalists from evangelicals, and both from anti-pietists. It illuminates the nature of the strategic realm, highlighting the impact of the congressional milieu on the partisans, particularly on some fundamentalist lobbyists who have embraced the incrementalist paradigm of the Congress. Chapter 7, titled "Representation Theory and the Religious Dimension," concludes this book by offering reflections on the meaning of religious activism for American politics and religion.

A word about the title. This study is about the dynamics of national representation by religious organizations. Yet nearly all religious lobbyists conveyed, and several emphatically stressed, that they do not profess to represent "God's will" when, say, giving testimony before a congressional committee, and in this sense the title may be misleading. Still it is clear that these lobbyists *are* animated by a set of religious values, a religious vision, or a religious interpretation of world events. Thus each, in her or his own way, attempts to represent those values in the political context. In that sense, they are indeed "Representing God in Washington."

2 American Exceptionalism and Religious Political Activism

Religious interest groups, as I observed in chapter 1, are significant for American politics because they potentially represent non-elite constituencies and because their diversity increasingly mirrors the pluralism of American religious life. Indeed, the groups examined in this study are theologically diverse, ideologically pluralistic, and politically activist. These characteristics, as I will show, are rooted in the rich historical experience of religion in America.

Since any historical review is necessarily selective and interpretive, it is important to note that the theme which anchors this analysis is that American religious experience is uniquely pluralistic and activist.[1] By "pluralistic" I mean the bewildering diversity of denominations, theologies, and organizational styles which, while dramatically manifest today, has its roots both in early colonial patterns and later frontier experience. By "activist" I do not mean exclusively political activism but also the entrepreneurial spirit that is reflected in social service agencies and religious schools, in evangelical revivals, and in the daily sprouting of new congregations. An examination of the historical interplay of these two intimately related characteristics will help to explain in part the importance of religion in American cultural and political life. My argument, quite simply, is that because American religion is both pluralistic and activist, it will continue to be, as it has been in the past, an important force in American life, politics, and representation.

The pluralism of American religion, to many scholars, lies at the heart of the exceptional American experience. Herberg put it most eloquently when he observed:

> It must be remembered that in America the variety and multiplicity of churches did not, as in Europe, come with the breakdown of a single established national church; [it] was almost the original condition and coeval with the emergence of the new society. In America religious pluralism is thus not merely a historical and political fact; it is, in the mind of the American, the primordial condition of things, an essential aspect of the American Way of Life, and therefore in itself an aspect of religious belief. Americans, in other words, believe that the plurality of religious groups is a proper and legitimate condition.[2]

Although the links between religious pluralism and the political order are complex indeed, one can at least make a strong case, as Greeley does, that political pluralism—meaning a balancing of different economic, social, racial, religious, and nationality groups—became necessary because the nation was already religiously pluralistic.[3]

This denominational pluralism of religious practice was, of course, sown in the early experience of colonization. If Puritan Massachusetts was intolerant of theological "heresy," there was always Rhode Island, early haven to Baptists and Quakers, and later to Catholics and Jews.[4] Then there were the middle colonies, which not only tolerated religious and cultural pluralism but, as Ahlstrom notes, "anticipated the experience of the future American nation."[5] Moreover, it was not only Christian pluralism that flourished on the seaboard. James Reichley notes, for example, that as early as 1654 a ship carrying Jewish refugees entered New Amsterdam. An exasperated Dutch Reformed minister observed that,

> We have here Papists, Mennonites and Lutherans . . .
> also many Puritans or Independents, and many Atheists
> and various other servants of Baal among the English
> under this government, who conceal themselves un-
> der the name of Christian; it would create still further
> confusion, if the obstinant and immovable Jews came to
> settle here.[6]

The Jews were allowed to stay.

The denominational pluralism of the colonies led to an early break with European tradition on church-state relations. Indeed, the "religiously pluralistic origins of the original colonies,"[7] as Andrew Greeley notes, made the appearance of an established church impossible. To understand the uniqueness of the American experiment, it is only necessary to observe that from the time of the Emperor Constantine in the fourth century A.D. to the founding of the colonies in the seventeenth century, European practice and doctrine was to establish religion by official state law.[8] This practice continued in some colonies even after the signing of the Constitution, which was interpreted to prohibit only the federal government, not state governments, from establishing a state religion. But the national experiment, as embodied in the Constitution, set the stage for an end to legally established religion in the states. The last to go was Puritan Massachusetts, which hung on until 1831, when citizens there voted by a wide margin to ratify disestablishment.[9]

Like most political experiments, this one was the result of diverse motives and ideas. For Enlightenment deists, such as Jefferson, disestablishment was a means to inhibit clerical interference in statecraft. But for members of minority denominations, such as the Baptists, it was essential to ensure their religious freedom.[10] As Mead observed,

> On the question of religious freedom for all, there were
> many shades of opinion in these churches, but all were
> practically unanimous on one point: each wanted free-
> dom for itself. And by this time it had become clear that

> the only way to get it for themselves was to grant it to all others.[11]

Thus the denominational pluralism of the colonies, coupled with the flowering of Enlightenment rationalism, created a new relation between church and state. It is an indication of how profoundly this experiment has shaped the American character that most Americans, whether Catholic, Protestant, or Jewish, would be shocked if told that today in Sweden Lutheran ministers are paid by the state and in West Germany the government collects a tax for churches, practices which are not at all surprising in light of European history, but which are profoundly uncharacteristic of the American experience.

The activism of American religion is rooted in the same historical circumstances that ensured its pluralism. Faced with a new land and a seemingly endless frontier, religious leaders could not rely upon centuries-old social, political, and economic institutions to buttress the church. Churches had to be activist to survive, or at least to thrive. Moreover, the social needs of the people created unique opportunities for religious activism. Andrew Greeley argues, for example, that the social disorganization and feelings of anomie that resulted from the immigration from Europe created a "belonging vacuum," a need for community, which was filled in part by churches.[12] The westward expansion intensified this need, and entrepreneurial church leaders took the initiative to expand their denominational memberships by evangelizing the frontier. Thus the frontier not only provided a haven for religious dissidents and nonconformists, but it was often a fertile ground for the religious revivals that regularly challenged complacency and orthodoxy, and created new forms of religious practice. The frontier, in short, fostered in American religious practice a dynamism and evangelical spirit.

The Great Awakening of the 1730s and 1740s is the most graphic early illustration of this tendency.[13] This momentous religious revival, which found its greatest voice in Jonathan

Edwards, challenged the orthodoxy of the Bostonian Congregational elect and was characterized by a millenarian faith in progress and a belief in the special place of America in the divine plan. Equally important, it emphasized a populist and equalitarian inclusiveness plus an evangelical worship style that appealed to the "inner spirit rather than simply the intellect."[14] The movement had won over much of the interior by eve of the Revolutionary War. As Reichley summarized it, "Rationalists might prevail in the cities and for a time at most of the colleges, but the evangelicals had captured the frontier. And the frontier was to become America."[15] There were several politically salient aspects to this revival. First, many of the revivalists of this era were committed to a theology of religious freedom,[16] a fact which helped to prepare the way for the First Amendment protection for freedom of religious practice. Second, the Great Awakening demonstrated the importance and potential of an activist church leadership reaching out to the unchurched on the frontier, setting the pattern for peripatetic ministers of the nineteenth and twentieth centuries. Finally, there is considerable evidence that the Great Awakening played a vital role in preparing the citizens of the colonies for the break with England. John Adams went so far as to claim that the Revolution was sown by the Great Awakening in the "minds and hearts of the people; a change in their religious sentiments. . . . "[17] As Reichley notes, "It was the evangelical New Lights of the interior, viewing nationhood as the essential first step in God's plan for America, who rallied the farmers, mechanics, and small-town merchants whose participation was to prove crucial in the struggle for independence."[18]

The experiment with disestablishment, spawned by the multiplicity of denominations, ensured that American religion would be volunteerist and activist—which in turn fostered even greater pluralism over time. Indeed, the founding of the new nation, coupled with the westward expansion, ushered in an era of volunteerism in the nineteenth century,[19] in which people had to take ownership of their churches.[20] Largely unsupported by the state and facing the vastness of the frontier, "volunteerist churches" in America had to adapt to survive, heightening their activism and fostering a diversity of worship styles and faith interpretations. If you did not like the local minister or held unorthodox views, you could always split and form a new congregation. And if your faith was "dangerously" unorthodox, as the Mormons' was perceived to be, you could always keep moving west for safe haven.[21] Churches blossomed and denominations sprouted like weeds as religious entrepreneurs competed with one another for the loyalty of the faithful, and religious practice demonstrated an endless ability to adapt to changing economic and social circumstances. The pluralism of American religion thus promoted its activism and vice versa.

As important as all this was and is, the deeper implications of religious activism and pluralism have yet to be fully understood or appreciated. For the first time since Constantine, churches and religious leaders, in all their diversity, were reasonably independent of the state, and thus were in a unique political position to attack perceived evils of the day. Thus it was that antislavery agitation found its most forceful articulation in the uncompromising pietist fervor of the Methodists, Baptists, and other evangelicals, who saw in the crusade against slavery, as they did in the campaign against alcohol, the potential for a moral regeneration of American society, a continuing theme in evangelical thought. Indeed, as Reichley observes, the style of the abolitionist leader William Lloyd Garrison ("I will be as harsh as truth, as uncompromising as justice")[22] was "inherited from the great revivalists," and "excited the idealist tendency of evangelical Protestants to regard life as a contest between forces of perfect good and total evil."[23] The religious movement, of course, had profound political ramifications:

> When slavery came to be viewed among large numbers of northern evangelical Protestants as incompatible with the value system of Christianity, it slashed at previous party attachments. In 1860 many northern evangelicals,

> who had identified with the Democrats as the party that
> best served their economic interests or came closest
> to representing their broadly equalitarian ideology,
> shifted to the Republican party because they thought it
> more prepared to take a stand against the moral evil of
> slavery.[24]

For many evangelical leaders of the day the Civil War was indeed a great moral struggle, sanctified by the bloody end to slavery. After the Civil War, religious activism was manifested in the rural Populist movement, as such figures as William Jennings Bryan brought an evangelical fervor and language to the struggle against moneyed interests, railroads, and the gold standard. It was also evident in the prohibition crusade against alcohol, which was spawned in large part in reaction to destructive patterns of drink in the nineteenth century.[25] The temperance movement culminated, of course, in the creation of the Anti-Saloon League, one of the most formidable interest groups in American history. Leaders of the Anti-Saloon League shrewdly capitalized upon churches as their base of political organization and were able at one time to field twenty thousand speakers, who preached in every part of the country.[26]

The most graphic illustration of evangelical activism in recent history, of course, was the civil rights movement in the 1960s. The volunteerist nature of American religion, and the activist impulse associated with it, fostered in the South a network of genuinely independent, black-controlled evangelical churches. While often other-worldly in orientation, these black churches represented a unique resource for political activism—they were owned by the blacks themselves. The black minister was not only the natural leader of the black community, but was economically independent of the white community as well. The potential for independent political activism was realized ultimately through the efforts of younger, more political ministers, such as the Reverend Martin Luther King, Jr., who, true to American tradition, fashioned a fresh religious vision to compete with the old. The point cannot be overemphasized: it is impossible to imagine a civil rights movement, as it was experienced, without the existence of the black churches—which represent so vividly the heritage of a pluralistic, activist religious environment in America.[27]

This analysis indicates that religious practice, and its unique pluralism and activism, may lie at the heart of American exceptionalism. Moreover, it suggests a complex but often positive relation between periodic religious movements and the direction of American democracy.[28]

Churches in America, in summary, are activist by nature and perhaps necessity. The volunteerist character of religious practice, born of pluralism, the frontier, and disestablishment, fosters endless change, which in turn ensures its vitality. Contemporary experience confirms this. Today in America there is a greater pluralism of faith and practice than ever before. There are, in addition to the scores of Protestant denominations, "old" fundamentalists and "new" fundamentalists, radical black evangelicals and Black Muslims, white evangelicals of tremendous cultural diversity, liberal Catholics, conservative Catholics, Hispanic Catholics, Mormons, Jews from the most orthodox to the least, devotees of Eastern religions, and even a national church for homosexuals (which, not surprisingly, maintains a Washington office). A contrast with, say, the moribund "state" church in Sweden could not be more striking. In many European countries, if you are alienated from the local congregation or the broader church, you probably drift away from religion; in America you simply start a new church. Only in America, it seems, could a church for homosexuals develop, and not just any church, but one of decidedly evangelical roots and temper ("Jesus loves me and he knows I'm gay").[29] Many Americans, in short, cling to church life even when their own lifestyles are unorthodox. And the "volunteerist" nature of American religion allows and even encourages innovative organizational and theological responses to change. Because religion is important in the cultural life of the nation, changes in religious practice, whether conservative fundamentalist revivals or the articulation of radical visions of religious commitment, will have important political ramifications, a theme which is amplified below as I introduce the national religious lobbies.

Religious Lobbies and American Exceptionalism

The entrepreneural activism of American religious practice has not always manifested itself in overt political involvement, especially at the national level. Yet the potential has existed because of the active engagement of churches in society, both through evangelism and in the operation of schools, hospitals, social service agencies, and foreign missions, which bring churches in contact with political and governmental instrumentalities. For a variety of reasons, including self-defense, elite secularization, and the nationalization of politics generally, church institutions and religious entrepreneurs increasingly perceive the need to articulate their values on the national stage. The significance of this is that the incredible pluralism of religious practice in America is now more nearly represented in Washington today than ever before.[30] The circumstances that brought these groups to Washington, therefore, illustrate the legacy of American exceptionalism—the activism and cultural pluralism of religious commitment.

Liberal Protestants
It was Methodist activism for Prohibition which established the first major religious presence in Washington, and the United Methodist Building, completed in 1923, was the "nerve center for Prohibition forces."[31] Today the building, situated strategically across the street from the Capitol, houses the "peace and justice" offices of many liberal Protestant groups and is associated with the most liberal and militantly anti-pietist political witness. While Prohibition and progressivism were commonly

linked in the nineteenth century,[32] nonetheless, the transformation of Methodists from anti-drink pietists to liberal Protestants is a testament to the dynamism of American religious practice. There were several forces that transformed the "mainline" Protestant churches. The Social Gospel movement at the turn of the century, for example, emphasized the "public" mission of the church and decried the injustices of industrial capitalism. While never a major influence at the parish level, it did influence many church leaders and ministers. More important, perhaps, was the advent of liberal theology, which not only fortified the emphasis on social ministries, but simultaneously deemphasized traditional evangelism and pietist "preoccupation" with individual moral rectitude. Theological liberalism, which swept through the seminaries in the 1920s, also widened the split in Protestantism between "modernists" and "fundamentalists," and set the stage for current antagonisms.[33] The political ramifications of this split were profound. Those Protestants who viewed themselves as fundamentalists tended to retreat into the cloisters of separate institutions, fearful of the contaminating influence of the broader culture. They became, in effect, "private" Protestants. In contrast, those leaders who embraced liberal theology, with its accommodation to science and modernity, were much more inclined to advocate engagement with public issues. By default, then, "public" Protestants tended to be theologically and politically liberal, and they were the dominant Protestant voices in the nation's capital until the late 1970s.[34]

There were two major turning points for the liberal Protestant community. The first was World War II and its aftermath. The draft mobilization, for example, confronted the small pacifist churches with a major challenge, and they responded by establishing Washington offices to protect members' conscientious objector status, among other things. Thus it was that the Quakers, in 1943, established the first actual registered religious lobby in Washington, the Friends Committee on National Legislation, which is highly respected among the liberal community to this day. Other nonpacifist churches soon followed, and by the early 1950s many individual denominations, as well as the National Council of Churches, had established offices.[35] But it was the second turning point, the advent of the activist 1960s, that galvanized the liberal religious community and set the pattern for future "political witness." The spark was the civil rights movement, which (due to the efforts of black ministers) was viewed as a profound moral issue, a matter of fundamental justice. Until that time, it might be argued, religious interest groups acted much as other self-interested lobbies. Their agendas included mostly institutional and religious freedom issues, which reflected their need to protect church interests. With their aggressive lobbying on behalf of the Civil Rights Act of 1964,[36] however, religious lobbyists moved beyond "self-interest," and argued persuasively that as religious leaders it was their moral duty to fight for "justice," an argument that serves as the underpinning for much of their work today. Moreover, the tactics employed, quite successfully, also set the pattern for future efforts. James Adams observes that a favorite strategy of the Protestant lobbies was to mobilize ministers, which proved tremendously successful, as civil rights tactician Joe Rauh of the Americans for Democratic Action recounted:

> Standing outside the Committee Room was the most beautiful sight I had ever seen—twenty Episcopal priests, fully garbed, all young beautiful WASPS. I used to think that the only two people out in front for civil rights were a Negro and a Jew—Mitchell and myself. But this was something the committee membership had never seen before. I knew then we really were in business.[37]

Washington religious leaders found themselves at the very center of a historic moment. James Hamilton, Washington representative of the National Council of Churches, for example, was one of the "big four," the inner circle of tacticians for the Leadership Conference on Civil Rights, sharing that honor with Joe Rauh of the ADA, Clarence Mitchell of the NAACP, and Andrew Biemiller of the AFL-CIO.[38] The power of the church leaders came from their ability to mobilize clerics throughout the nation, who enjoyed special credibility with senators and representatives, many of whom were not used to being lobbied by "men of the cloth." It was a heady, even intoxicating experience for the clergy involved. But, as James Adams observed, "Few political issues arose in the Sixties which as clearly involved a moral decision as did the Civil Rights Act of 1964. . . . [But] the clerical activists have not permitted moral ambiguity . . . to diminish their fervor."[39] Moreover, as James Hamilton noted, the church lobbyists and ministers, in their excitement, largely neglected to bring the laity along in their political witness.[40] They found, instead, that they could borrow on their religious credibility for political access without necessarily mobilizing large numbers of local parishioners, a habit which has come to undermine somewhat their future efficacy.

The legacy of the 1960s exercises a strong influence on the liberal Protestant lobbyists—on the Methodists, Presbyterians, Episcopalians, Lutherans, American Baptists, Mennonites, Quakers, Brethren, and leaders of the United Church of Christ and National Council of Churches. If one were to summarize how these lobbyists view their work today it would be as champions of "peace and justice," a phrase which resounds over and over as one unambiguous catchword. Their mission, quite simply is to fight for justice, especially for the poor—which means support for the welfare state and third world development—and to work for peace, which translates into frequent criticism of American military and foreign policies, nuclear arms strategies, and military spending generally. While both moral ambiguity and the lack of mobilizable constituents on some issues have limited their influence, these groups do make an impact. Whether it is testifying on the experience of church-run food banks for the hungry, or providing to sympathetic congressional committees valuable political information gathered by their foreign missions, or relating experiences of sanctuary workers in Arizona, these groups are able to draw upon the legacy of church activism as a political resource. Moreover, as I demonstrate in chapter 5, on certain issues liberal church lobbies do effectively articulate underrepresented concerns of the American public. Another important legacy of these groups, perhaps, is that in "witnessing" so politically, they have demonstrated to a variety of other religious interests the need for, and potential of, Washington religious representation, which is precisely what fundamentalist lobbyists say spurred them on.

Fundamentalists

After half a century in the cloister, fundamentalists emerged with a vengeance in the late 1970s, mobilized politically by a group of leaders committed to the moral regeneration of America. And if the rallying cry of the liberals is "peace and justice," the clarion of the New Religious Right is "traditional values," a phrase which connotes a defense of the traditional family, orthodox religion, patriotism, and Puritan morality. The political movement is significant in part because of changes in religious practice that, true to American tradition, have shaken contemporary (and, in this case, liberal) orthodoxies. Throughout the late 1960s and 1970s, as mainline Protestant churches came to be dominated by liberal theological approaches to faith and worship, and as secular politics celebrated individual "self-expression" and "liberation" in a variety of forms, it was the conservative churches that grew in membership, churches that demanded moral discipline and adherence to the "fundamentals" of Christian belief.[41] In a classic analogue to market capitalism, religious entrepreneurs of the independent evangelical and fundamentalist churches were able to meet the "spiritual" needs of many people in ways that the liberal theology of mainline denominations apparently did not; the mainline churches lost members (or customers) as a result. Throughout the 1970s new churches sprang up, meeting in homes and rented schoolbuildings,[42] offering the faithful assurances of salvation not available elsewhere. The growth of the video church (another uniquely American invention) is but the most visible manifestation of the larger phenomenon of religious revival that has taken place.[43]

While the New Religious Right includes in its ranks conservative Catholic leaders and constituents, and while it draws support from evangelical moderates on some issues, it is the fundamentalists who are at the forefront. The major groups include the Moral Majority (Liberty Federation), Christian Voice, Concerned Women for America, Pat Robertson's Freedom Council, the American Coalition for Traditional Values, and antiabortion groups such as Right to Life. The confidence and frenetic energy of the New Right leaders is rooted in their populist "discovery" that secular elites in America—in the national media, the universities, the public schools, and government—are out of touch with the religious sentiments of many Americans, including many in the "mainline" Protestant and Roman Catholic churches. Thus, in their view, the problem is not so much secularization per se, which would be much tougher to fight, but elite secularization, which is an easier political target. There is credible evidence that this assessment is in part valid.[44] The image makers of commercial television, perhaps, offer the most graphic illustration. There is little portrayal of worship or religious faith on prime-time television, for example, yet such is the reality for most Americans. Moreover, the materialistic and hedonistic values embodied in commercial advertising run counter not only to religious doctrine as fundamentalists intrepret it but to the values expressed in the vast majority of Roman Catholic, Protestant, and Jewish congregations. While it is true that most Americans do not identify with such groups as the Moral Majority,[45] there is evidence that at least on some issues (see chapter 5) the New Religious Right has tapped the diffuse, but widely shared sentiment of many citizens. Just as the evangelical crusade against slavery fractured traditional party alignments in the nineteenth century, the mobilization by religious conservatives has begun to do the same in our own era, as members of fundamentalist churches abandon past attachments to the Democratic coalition, which was perceived as representing their economic interests, to vote for Republican candidates who address their moral and social concerns.[46]

The emergence of national lobbies representing "traditional values" appears to have articulated a populist frustration with the drift of cultural change. One fascinating illustration of this is the creation of Concerned Women for America (CWA), a membership organization of mostly women begun by Beverly LeHaye of California, who with her husband, Tim, had been conducting "family life" seminars for several years before she moved to the political stage. The raison d'être of Concerned Women for America is its opposition to the "feminist agenda." And while LeHaye and the other leaders of CWA are fundamentalist in persuasion, they have apparently tapped the sentiment of many Catholic and Protestant women whose experience does not square with secular feminist arguments as they understand them. Indeed, the main recruiting tool of CWA is a small brochure with *nothing but* quotes by radical feminists attacking religion and the "patriarchial" family, a brochure which they have printed by the millions.[47] Ironically, in its call for religious women to become politically active to protect family and community, the organization echoes one aspect of earlier suffragette arguments at the turn of the century. The suffragette movement, in a sense, combined a feminist demand for political equality with a conservative rationale that women were the natural protectors of family and community from destructive economic and cultural forces. Today, these two groups of women, radical feminists and conservative Christians, view each other as mortal adversaries. For CWA members, feminists are really selfish women who care only about their own personal freedom and have abandoned their societal responsibilities, while to feminists, fundamentalist women are, at best, oppressed mothers whose false consciousness leads them to support patriarchy, and at worst, religious bigots. In terms of representation, however, the emergence of conservative articulators of women's experience has led to a more elaborately textured representation of women in Washington. The National Organization for Women, for example, opposes maternity leave policies for women on the ground that, as a special privilege, it violates equality.[48] But opponents of NOW argue that this ignores the real experience of many women who face losing their jobs if they choose to stay home with their babies. Similarly, while a raging debate has been occurring within feminist circles about how to deal with pornography and its depiction of women, for Concerned Women for America, smut is clearly antifamily and must be opposed by its lobby efforts. The complex nature of the disagreements between conservative religious women, who are angry, and feminists, who are also angry, is a matter that deserves further study. It is not obvious what conclusions such an examination might reveal.

The rise of the Christian Right has sparked significant scholarly interest, much of it drawing upon Weberian arguments about the "status anxiety" of supporters of reactionary movements.[49] As the above discussion indicates, the movement can also be analyzed as a rather straightforward and self-conscious attempt to advance values previously underrepresented in the American polity. After all, leaders of the New Religious Right argue, two decades of libertarian attacks on institutions such as the family have left society rather worse for the wear. No-fault divorce, which was supposed to "liberate" women from suffocating marriages, has apparently liberated many men from the financial burdens of supporting a family. Relaxation of obscenity laws, which were supposed to liberate us from stifling vestiges of Puritanism, seemed instead to push pornography to new depths of misogynist meanness, with themes of sadism, rape, incest, and child sex common fare. Broken marriages, collapsing moral values, abortion, drug abuse, hostility toward religious conviction—these are the fruits of secular society, so they argue. While their analysis of the source of social malaise can be debated (after all, as Daniel Bell so perceptively points out, modern capitalism is itself the great engine of libertarian change),[50] certainly the problems seem real enough, particularly to beleaguered parents wondering where it will end. Thus, not surprisingly, the most sweeping critique of secular modernity has come from those nurtured in fundamentalist churches, who see the greatest disparity between their vision of the good society and the sweep of secular history.

Roman Catholics

In a way the experience of Roman Catholics in America could not be a more revealing illustration of American exceptionalism. In the nineteenth century Roman Catholics, living in a land where the Protestant Bible routinely was read in public schools, had to adopt the entrepreneurial model for survival, developing their own school system largely unaided by the state, as well as organizing a network of Catholic Charities agencies that demonstrated their involvement in the larger society. Moreover, from the Catholic Worker movement to the establishment of the Maryknoll Order for foreign missions, the church has shown both an activism and a toleration of some degree of pluralism within.

The U.S. Catholic Church, represented by the American Bishops, has maintained a Washington presence since just after World War I, when the National Catholic Welfare Conference was established. The successor to the NCWC, the U.S. Catholic Conference, owes its origins to Vatican II, which, among other things, granted greater authority to the bishops in each country, thus setting the stage for the American Bishops' pastoral letters on nuclear arms, abortion, and the economy.

The U.S. Catholic Conference presents one of the more intricately textured lobby approaches. On economic policy and foreign military policy it has aligned itself with the "peace and justice" groups, but on social issues—the ERA, abortion, aid to parochial schools, and religious observance in the schools—it has found itself allied with those concerned with "traditional values." Staff specialization at the Washington headquarters facilitates this crosscutting effort. Those staff members who concentrate on domestic economic policy or foreign military policy work closely with the liberal community. In contrast, those who concentrate on anti-abortion lobbying have forged links with the fundamentalists and evangelicals. For Catholic intellectuals, such as Cardinal Bernardin of Chicago, this public agenda is not at all paradoxical but rather is a "seamless garment" of concern for life. This argument has been adopted by some evangelical groups, who do not agree with the fundamentalists on opposition to the welfare state or support for "freedom fighters" in Nicaragua, but do agree with them on a prolife stand on abortion.

Vatican II also profoundly affected the life in the convents, and NETWORK, the "nuns' lobby," was a direct result. Catholic religious women, always the backbone of parochial education, heard a startling message from Pope John XXIII. As Catherine Brousseau, registered lobbyist for NETWORK, described it, Vatican II, and the ferment within the convents that it spawned, conveyed that "action on behalf of justice is constituative of preaching the gospel."[51] Thus, many took off their habits, left the schools and entered the ghetto or the barrio, serving as social workers in makeshift storefronts. As Brousseau recounted it, this work led to a concern for the "structural" problems that face the poor, and a "political ministry" on behalf of "justice" for the poor resulted. The initial leaders got permission from their orders to start the Washington lobby, and they continue to get support from the diverse orders of nuns and women religious. NETWORK's concern for "peace" and its critique of American foreign policy flow in part from its association with Maryknoll nuns, whose mission work in Central America and elsewhere on behalf of "the poor" has fostered a critical attitude toward American influence abroad. Thus, NETWORK commonly finds allies among the liberal Protestant community.

Jews

The American experiment with disestablishment has served well the interests of Jews, who have flourished in the United States after centuries of persecution elsewhere. Indeed, this experience has led Jewish leaders to lobby aggressively for strict church-state separation as central to their well being. As one lobbyist put it in congressional testimony against the equal access legislation (discussed in chapter 6),

> Mr. Chairman, I am one of those persons, as Mr. Tribe described, who gets carried away by the establishment clause of the First Amendment. I get carried away in awe by what it has wrought. And what it has wrought is a nation which has more religious freedom, where the practice of religion is healthier than anywhere else in the world and I suggest that we all be proud of it and defend it.[52]

Indeed, it was to combat persecution and lingering anti-Semitism that several of the key Jewish groups were formed. The first was the American Jewish Committee, formed in 1906 (in response to a Russian pogrom) to protect Jewish rights at home and abroad, and whose members today represent the elites of the Jewish community. The next was the Anti-Defamation League of B'nai B'rith, organized in 1913 to combat anti-Semitism, followed by the American Jewish Congress, made up at the time of "less establishment" Jews and devoted to the creation of a Jewish homeland in Palestine.[53] The Washington offices of these organizations are not "technically" religious lobbies, since many Jewish members of these groups do not attend temple and indeed are highly secular. Nonetheless, it seemed reasonable to include such organizations in this study because of their focus on religious freedom and because, with the exception of the Reform Congregations, the religious aspects of Jewish experience are not represented by independent lobbies.

The Union of American Hebrew Congregations, representing Reform Jewish membership, maintains the only lobby to represent temple members. The Religious Action Center of the UAHC is located in a stately mansion on Massachusetts Avenue, which is, as its literature notes, "the only Jewish building in the

United States devoted exclusively to social justice, public advocacy, and educational endeavors."[54] The UAHC building, which houses both the American Jewish Committee and the American Jewish Congress, as well as the Leadership Conference on Civil Rights, is the center for Jewish coalitional activities. The leaders of the Religious Action Center of UAHC, unabashedly liberal and aggressively activist, stress the uniquely Jewish emphasis on the positive use of government to promote political and economic equality.[55]

But if the UAHC is the most uncompromising in its support of liberal social and economic policies, its aims are generally shared by the other major Jewish organizations. The National Jewish Community Relations Advisory Council, for example, which coordinates the public advocacy of all eleven of the major Jewish national organizations, stresses "social and economic justice" as a "resounding imperative" for Jewish values and tradition. In an argument that was echoed by Hyman Bookbinder of the American Jewish Committee, the Council concludes:

> These ethical concerns coincide with the premises that guide the Jewish community relations field's response to protecting and fostering Jewish security. The social tensions and dislocations that are bred by want and inequality have erupted too often into threats and dangers to the democratic system in general, and the Jewish community in particular. For both of these reasons, issues of social justice have been, and remain, a priority concern of the Jewish community relations field.[56]

Thus both Jewish values and self-interest have worked to create an extremely activist public presence in America. Moreover, that entrepreneurial aggressiveness has arguably broadened the representativeness of the advocacy system in Washington.

In terms of their alliances, Jewish groups often agree with the liberal Protestants on church-state relations, social issues such as the ERA and abortion, federal economic policy, and on many military and foreign policy issues as well. But they part company dramatically over Israel. For many liberal Protestants "peace" in the Middle East must involve "justice" for the Palestinians, and this posture places them in tension with Jews regarding U.S. military support for Israel. For Jewish leaders the kind of peace advocated by the liberal Protestants would, in their view, profoundly compromise justice for Jews.

Evangelicals

It is a great testament to the dynamism of American religion that the term "evangelical" has carried such diverse meanings and connotations. While most Protestants in the nineteenth century would have described themselves as evangelicals, by the 1940s the term came to characterize those who had split both from the mainline Protestant churches and from the fundamentalists. Thus leaders of the National Association of Evangelicals, created in 1943, saw themselves as representing a distinct religious minority. They rejected the liberal theology that dominated the seminaries of the mainline Protestant denominations and embraced the "fundamentals" of the faith, yet they did not share the separatist cultural movement of the fundamentalists, desiring instead to "transform" the culture rather than separate from it. As a religious minority, the evangelicals established a national lobby presence to protect religious freedom, and while their agenda is broader today, church-state issues still dominate their efforts.[57] This is also true for the General Conference of Seventh Day Adventists, the Baptist Joint Committee, the Christian Legal Society, and Americans United for Separation of Church and State—all groups that can be said to represent substantial evangelical constituencies. This focus on church-state issues has produced interesting but fluid coalitions, particularly with the rise of the New Religious Right, as the evangelical groups sometimes align themselves with Jewish and mainline Protestant lobbies, and sometimes with fundamentalist groups.

The evangelical groups are characterized by a considerable pluralism of belief and experience. The General Conference of

Seventh Day Adventists, for example, traces its origins to the millenarian revival movement in the nineteenth century, a time when people literally felt the Second Coming of Christ was imminent. While Adventists continue to stress an eschatology similar to that of fundamentalists, their leaders have interpreted the meaning of that faith in a radically different way from such groups as Moral Majority (as I demonstrate in chapter 6 on the subject of equal access). Similarly, the Baptist Joint Committee has frequently aligned itself on church-state issues with Jewish groups and others opposed to fundamentalist proposals for school prayer. The Christian Legal Society is yet another illustration of the entrepreneurial spirit in American religion. Formed in the early 1960s as a Christian support society for law students, it has active chapters in many of the major law schools and has members throughout the legal profession. While the Seventh Day Adventists and the Baptist Joint Committee have generally fought "threats" to religious freedom on the Right, the Christian Legal Society, along with the National Association of Evangelicals, increasingly perceives the threat from the Left, from secular "elites" hostile to religion who, in the view of CLS leaders, "misuse" the establishment clause to restrict religious practice and freedom, especially for evangelicals.[58]

The complex texture of evangelical lobbying is reflected in the creation of a small but intellectually interesting group: Evangelicals for Social Action. Spawned by the "young evangelicals" in the early 1970s,[59] the organization's leaders have attempted to articulate a uniquely evangelical political witness, one which, in their view, recognizes the need to address military, social, and economic issues in terms of their own understanding of biblical principles, but which does not abandon the stress on personal morality. Like the Catholic Conference, the organization combines a more conservative social agenda (including opposition to abortion) with a moderately liberal economic and foreign policy agenda. Members work with the liberal community but see themselves as distinct. Justice for the poor and peacemaking are genuinely biblical, they point out, but an affirmation of certain traditional values, a rootedness in family and community, is essential to work for justice and peace. For this group, as for the Catholic Conference, the philosophy might be summarized as "peace, justice, *and* traditional values."[60] Intriguingly, some evangelical leaders who formed ESA have now created a political action committee to channel funds to candidates who, they argue, have no institutional support if they embrace this political agenda. The organization, termed JustLife, will "support candidates who value both justice and life,"[61] in other words, those who oppose abortion but also will fight the nuclear arms race or poverty.

Black Evangelicals

The activism and pluralism of American religion is reflected, finally, in the rich, unique heritage of black evangelism. As Fowler has observed, even before the Civil War, blacks in America, both slaves and free, were "overwhelmingly involved in the routines and rituals of Christianity."[62] Moreover, black religious practice evolved along evangelical lines, stressing "the spirit," emotion, and personal redemption. Still, blacks developed their own unique expression, notably with Old Testament themes of liberation and the "promised land" which weave through the Negro spirituals—evoked most eloquently by the "new Moses," the Reverend Martin Luther King, Jr. The organizational legacy of the southern experience is that today most blacks, following southern traditions, belong to one of several independent black Baptist or Methodist congregations, most of which have Washington offices. These include the African Methodist Episcopal Church, the African Methodist Episcopal Zion Church, the Christian Methodist Church, the Progressive National Baptist Convention, the National Baptist Convention USA, and the National Baptist Convention of America. These denominations maintain a modest Washington presence, but, of course, the legacy of black evangelism is diffused throughout the black civil rights organizations in Washington as well.

The creation of the Progressive National Baptist Convention is a case in point of how religion and politics influence each other. Formed in the turmoil of the civil rights movement in 1961, the denomination owes its origins to a schism within the National Baptist Convention USA. The leadership of the parent organization resisted clergy involvement in politics and attempted to enforce that policy on the membership. The young lions, however, were not to be controlled, and the Progressive National Baptist Convention emerged.[63] Thus, black ministers who led the civil rights movement also forged in the process a new denomination more sympathetic to their aims.

Summary

Born of an exceptional historical experience, religious practice in America is highly pluralistic and activist, which is another way of saying it is vital and adaptable. The activism has not always taken political form, nor has the pluralism always been reflected in national advocacy, though both tendencies seem to be increasing. What is important about the national lobbies is that today they more nearly reflect the texture and complexity of religious belief and practice in America than ever before. Because religion is important in American life, and because the heritage of American religion is so pluralistic, religious political activism may contribute to the representation of pluralist interests in ways that no other groups do, or can. Indeed, the values articulated by the diverse lobbyists described above, because of their rich texture and crosscutting sweep, reflect roughly the broad sentiments of Americans on many issues—a theme that will be explored more fully in chapter 5.

3   Political Strategies, Effectiveness, and the Congressional Milieu

National religious leaders operate much as other lobbyists do. They propose bills and amendments, testify before congressional committees, track legislation, provide information on the effects of public policies, and bring pressure to bear by mobilizing their constituencies in congressional districts and states. Two things have changed since James Adams criticized the gap between religious lobbyists and lay members in the 1960s: 1) religious advocacy in Washington, now far more diverse, roughly mirrors the pluralism of belief and practice in America, and 2) religious leaders, like other lobbyists, increasingly perceive the need to generate constituent pressure on members of Congress. This second finding contrasts sharply with the classic, but now dated, descriptions of lobbying in political science. To begin this discussion, therefore, it is necessary to chart the changing world of Washington lobbying.

It is a curious fact of American scholarship that during the 1950s and early 1960s, when "pluralist" explanations of the U.S. polity enjoyed wide acceptance, studies of actual lobbies showed them to be relatively weak actors.[1] Lester Milbrath's *The Washington Lobbyists*, for example, presented a benign view of the activities of interest groups in Washington. Lobbying was a "communications process," a cozy affair with the lobbyist acting as a de facto extension of the congressional member's staff, a friend, an insider, useful but not pushy. Most important, Milbrath found that members discounted district pressure generated by Washington lobbyists. He concluded that "most letter and telegram campaigns have little impact on decisions of officials."[2] Indeed, because of their ineffectiveness, "letter and telegram campaigns now are less frequently used than in the recent past."[3] Bauer, Pool, and Dexter found similar results in their study of business lobbies. They found that "stimulated mail," pressure obviously generated by the Washington lobbies, was dismissed by congressional members: "We found businesses leaning over backward not to exert pressure, we found politicians discounting or utterly unaware of pressure campaigns directed against them; we found politicians inviting, rather than resisting, pressures."[4]

A number of forces converged to alter this picture, including the rise of media politics, new technologies, and changing attitudes, as well as the decentralization of Congress and the decline of political parties.[5] Increased national media coverage of Washington happenings, for example, now enables skillful interest group leaders to reach millions of citizens through orchestrated news events, filled with dramatic revelations and moral outrage, often backed with factual reports and tailored research. Computer-generated direct mail and telecommunications hookups provide interest groups with the means to expand memberships and use their lists as a political resource, timing district pressure to coincide with key legislative action.

Also crucial have been changes in Congress that have fortified the role and legitimacy of "pressure" lobbying. In the early 1970s institutional changes weakened congressional seniority, dispersed power through subcommittees, and reduced party discipline. In particular, the growth in the size of staffs for individual members enhanced their autonomy and vitiated party sanctions. At the electoral level, too, the role of party leadership diminished, and candidates found themselves forging their own electoral coalitions. Candidate-centered, rather than party-oriented, campaigns have increased the uncertainty under which members operate, while the electoral environment is increasingly characterized by split-ticket voting and unpredictable impacts of mass media. These developments have dramatically altered the conditions under which members operate and respond to lobby pressure.

The most cogent description of this new environment is as "the electoral connection," a phrase coined by David Mayhew.[6] Mayhew argued that the motives and behavior of members of Congress can best be understood as dominated by the pursuit of re-election. Having gotten where they are by forging their own electoral coalitions, often independent of party influence, and faced with the enormous uncertainties of sustaining sufficient support, career-minded representatives orient their work with the district in mind. Richard Fenno provides corroborative support for the primacy of this electoral connection in his work *Homestyle*,[7] in which he discerns a profound electoral insecurity among House members, even for those from supposedly safe seats.

The point is that most representatives do not now feel, as they apparently did thirty years ago, that they can afford to discount constituent pressure, even if it is generated by Washington groups. Indeed, the credibility of Washington lobbies, even those who play the insider game well, depends in part on their ability to demonstrate that they can get the word out to members. No longer cushioned by overwhelmingly party-based voting, congressional representatives must piece together a patchwork of constituencies, and the national lobby organizations can assist in this process if they have genuine district connections.

While district mobilization is increasingly perceived as essential "backstopping" by national lobbyists, this should not be interpreted to mean that more traditional means of influence are not still important. The ability to provide useful facts on the potential impacts of legislation, the mastery of the details and norms of the legislative process, the forging of coalitions, and the drafting of actual language, are still the stock in trade of the lobby craft.[8] Indeed, members continue to view national lobbyists as extensions of their own staffs, much as they did in Milbrath's day.[9] What has changed, it appears, is the acceptance, even the expectation, that national lobbies will mobilize their constituencies, and for very good reason. The congressional member wants assurance that should he or she support a group, its members and sympathizers in the home district will be fully apprised of that fact and will respond accordingly on election day. "The electoral connection is understood," as one religious lobbyist put it, "you don't have to beat them over the head with it."[10]

To determine the strategic environment that religious lobbies face, I asked both the lobbyists and congressional staff members what they felt made an effective lobby. While answers varied, most agreed that a combination of Washington expertise and constituency support constitutes effective lobbying, while only one person out of the forty-five individuals interviewed discounted the value of constituent mobilization.[11] As Rabbi Saperstein of the Union of American Hebrew Congregations summarized it, "You can be a good lobby if you have either a strong grassroots network or a good person as the lobbyist, but the best lobbies have both."[12] A legislative director for a Republican senator put the emphasis on the quality of information, but also stressed the constituency connection, "Lobby success is based on 1) the clarity of the message, 2) the attractiveness of the message—is it internally cohesive? and 3) is it said with a groundswell of support?"[13] The perceived cohesiveness of a lobby's constituency was also viewed as an important political resource. One congressional aide directly linked constituency cohesiveness to the effectiveness of fundamentalists on school prayer, Episcopalians on abortion rights, and the United Church of Christ on Central America issues. Observing that lack of cohesiveness is often a problem for the "mainline" denominations, he contrasted them with the Jewish lobbies: "They are remarkably effective, especially on Israel, civil liberties, and church-state relations. They have clearly defined objectives, and near unanimous support from congregations."[14] Even the most venerable Washington "insiders" stressed the importance of constituent support. Hyman Bookbinder of the American Jewish Committee and Ed Snyder of the Friends Committee on National Legislation have lobbied in Washington since the early 1950s. The *New York Times* called Bookbinder one of the most respected of the Washington lobbyists,[15] and Senator Hatfield's legislative director said that, of all the lobbyists, "The best is Ed Snyder. He is trusted, dispassionate. The Senator will call him."[16] While Snyder and Bookbinder clearly enjoy classic "insider" access, and neither minimized the importance of being perceived as reasonable and dependable, both stressed that constituent mobilization is essential to their work. As Bookbinder put it, "Without backstopping in the field, our work comes close to zero."[17] Snyder echoed this, "You have *got* to have people in the field."[18] As the analysis below will show, even leaders of "mainline" denominations, who in the past borrowed on their religious authority for access, are now developing mailing lists of mobilizable constituents, who, they hope, will enhance their influence in Washington.

To understand religious political activism in America, one must look beyond the spectacular and public—whether the militant rhetoric of the fundamentalist Right or the "leftist" pronouncements of the National Council of Churches—to the more mundane and tactical level. Lobbying, as I will show, is the ideal place in which to study this strategic realm. With this in mind, I now turn to the specific strategies employed by religious lobbyists. The objective here is to let the religious leaders speak for themselves about how they translate moral and religious values into operational political strategies, and to what effect.

Lobbyists are often categorized as either "insiders" or "outsiders" on the basis of the tactics they employ. Outsiders, it is often said, resort to outside pressure tactics because they do not have the access that insiders enjoy. Insiders, as Milbrath argued, do not resort to pressure, because that would jeopardize their cozy relationships with congressional members. While this characterization is not wholly inaccurate, what emerged from my interviews was the fact that most lobbyists attempt to employ both types of tactics simultaneously. Thus, the two categories set forth below are designed to avoid the implication that they are mutually exclusive. The two broad strategies are: 1) those tactics designed to bring home district pressure on members of Congress, including mass mobilization, elite mobilization, direct electoral mobilization, and the staging of media events, and 2) those classic insider strategies designed to create a relationship of trust and dependency between lobbyists and members of Congress.

Home District Pressure

Mass Constituency Mobilization
By mass constituency mobilization I denote those strategies aimed at generating a groundswell of constituent support and designed to indicate to each member of Congress that there are hundreds or thousands of voters in her or his district who care passionately about a particular issue. While the New Religious Right has been the most successful in employing this strategy, liberal religious groups have employed it (with varying degrees of success) for several decades.[19] The pacifist Friends Committee on National Legislation, one of the oldest religious lobbies in Washington, has maintained constituent lists for forty years. NETWORK, "the nuns' lobby," which was organized to mobilize activist religious women around the country, celebrated it fifteenth anniversary in 1986, and IMPACT and Bread for the World both preceded the creation of the Moral Majority by several years. Taking advantage of an environment conducive to "pressure" lobbying, these "liberal" lobbies sought influence and access through their ability to generate grassroots pressure on members of Congress. Although fundamentalist conservative groups did not coalesce until the late 1970s, they soon eclipsed

the liberal groups in the ability to generate constituent responses by sheer volume. In part this phenomenon is due to the marriage of convenience between right-wing direct-mail entrepreneurs, such as Richard Vigeurie and Paul Weyrich, and fundamentalist leaders.[20] It is also due to the technological sophistication of the fundamentalist organizations, a sophistication borrowed from their video ministries. Finally, it stems from dynamic changes in religious practice in America, which, as I argued in chapter 2, ramify in the political system.

The most formidable of the fundamentalist groups, of course, is the Moral Majority, now the Liberty Federation.[21] While the Moral Majority maintains the largest direct-mail list, it is its advanced technology that serves as its bread and butter. Extensive use of phone banks, computer-generated phone messages dialed to targeted constituencies, and telecommunications experiments (such as a conference call between 150,000 pastors and President Reagan during his 1984 campaign) are orchestrated from its Lynchburg, Virginia, headquarters. The organization can make up to 100,000 phone calls per week, with tape messages targeted by issue orientation or religious orientation of the member. These tapes, "Call your Senator now," are even customized on the basis of preacher loyalty: some are Falwell tapes, some are Swaggart tapes, some are Robertson tapes.[22] Direct-mail mobilization, of course, is a vital part of this organization's technological sophistication. At the time of my interview the organization claimed to have several million names in its computer banks, though Jerry Falwell reported in the spring of 1986 that (only) one million members had responded to the appeal to join the Liberty Federation.[23] The membership is broken down into congressional districts, issue concerns, and religious background, to enable the organization to focus its mailings, thus reducing cost. Tracking these lists also enables the leaders to discern which issues are "hot buttons" for fundraising purposes.

The other New Right groups similarly are able to merge technological sophistication with large memberships. Christian Voice claims 350,000 members, including 40,000 pastors,[24] while Concerned Women for America claims a membership approaching half a million, which, if accurate, would make it larger than the National Organization of Women, the National Women's Political Caucus, and the League of Women Voters combined.[25] These groups also have access to the Christian media, which multiplies their mobilization efforts. As Gary Jarmin of Christian Voice summarized it, "The real revolution is Christian media. . . . We educate TV ministers, feed them information, legislative alerts to read in sermons."[26] In addition to the well-known TV evangelists, such as Pat Robertson, Jim Bakker, James Robison, and Jimmy Swaggart, the New Right groups have access to a huge network of Christian radio stations. Concerned Women for America, for example, provides a daily radio show to forty Christian stations nationwide.[27] Christian Voice, too, has the capacity to feed public service announcements to the burgeoning radio ministry, and views this as an integral part of its political strategy.[28]

Fundamentalist leaders do not attribute their success in mobilizing constituencies to technology alone. In their view it is the nature of their constituency that plays a pivotal role. As Michael Ferris of Concerned Women for America put it:

> The difference between our members and society
> at large is how important religion is to them. If you
> ask the average United Methodist or Congregational
> Church member, religion is about 15th in importance.
> But if you ask evangelicals and fundamentalists, religion
> is most important to them. Liberal Protestants compart-
> mentalize their religion. We do not; our faith in Christ
> is central.[29]

The link is thus made between the vitality of church life and political efficacy. "I don't think they [mainline churches] are effective in lives of people, and therefore translating membership to power is difficult. People don't do what church tells them, so their efforts to mobilize are ineffective."[30] A curious result of this emphasis is that New Right leaders often copy the rhetoric of the Left in speaking of their constituencies. They represent "the people," not elites and hierarchies. "Our churches are congregationally run, they [mainline Protestants] are hierarchial. We have no seminary, no hierarchial power structure, so we stay closer to the people. They are in tune with academia; we are in tune with people."[31] It is the religious dimension, New Right leaders feel, that will enable them to expand minority membership and support. Gary Jarmin, for example, was excited about the potential of black support for conservatives who speak to "family" and religious issues:

> Ministers are leaders in the black community. Many are conservative, pro-life, in favor of school prayer. . . . Our analysis is that national black leaders are bad, but local ones are good, and the national leaders are no longer relevant. Blacks see crime, drugs, pornography and teenage pregnancies, they are concerned about conservative values. E.V. Hill, a black minister in California, is one of the top ten preachers in the country. He voted for Reagan. Ten ACTV chairmen were black. If we do it and do it right by 1988, we can get 25% to 30% black support for Republican candidates.[32]

Similarly, Ferris of CWA mentioned their intention to mobilize women in the Hispanic community, who, while overwhelmingly Roman Catholic, are perceived as naturally sympathetic to traditional family values. "A Spanish outreach is going on right now. Our focus is on women who are Christians, and the Spanish ministry will be very successful."[33]

As newcomers to the political process, New Right groups experiment with different means of emphasizing the constituency connection. One of the most interesting is the "535 Program" of the Concerned Women for America. The idea is to develop a corps of women in the Washington, D.C., area who will be responsible for tracking congressional offices and who will communicate with counterparts in congressional districts around the country. The objective is to have one woman assigned to each

congressional office in Washington and a counterpart assigned
to each congressional member's home district. The job of the
Washington women is to make monthly visits, keep the congressional members up to date on the organization's concerns, and
determine the representatives' views on the issues. "It is a volunteer lobbying army. If the Capitol district liaison for Congressman Smith finds out he is waffling on school prayer, comparable
worth, or the ERA, that woman will contact the woman in his
district, who will activate prayer chains and letter-writing campaigns."[34] The organization claims to have roughly two hundred
women serving as Washington liaisons, each assigned to two or
three offices.

While the New Right groups apparently have the capacity to
mobilize literally millions of constituents on certain issues,[35] particularly school prayer, abortion, and the Equal Rights Amendment, it is less clear that they have been able to galvanize these
constituencies on other issues. While leaders claim that "non-
nuclear" space defense is a "hot button" for their members, it has
not apparently generated interest comparable to the social issues.
Moreover, the move to support the president's Central American policies, particularly aid to the Contras, has not, according
to congressional sources and published reports, even matched
the opposition to such policies by liberal church groups.[36] One
congressional staff member summarized it this way:

> The fundamentalists are mobilizing large numbers. But
> most of the fundamentalist churches cater to working
> class blue collar people. Pentecostals. Some tilt to the
> Democratic Party on income distribution issues. But
> because of the emotional fervor of personal morality
> issues, the organizations have been successful. They are
> pretty united on abortion. But it is harder to galvanize
> on other issues.[37]

The mobilization strategies of the New Right have received,
understandably, mixed reviews from other Washington actors,
both in and out of Congress. But all conceded that on certain

issues the fundamentalists are able to generate enormous grassroots response. From one unsympathetic Republican senatorial
office came this response: "They play hard ball. Compared to
the whole universe of lobbies out there, they are tough. On
school prayer they had mass rallies on the Capitol and generated
an incredible amount of phone calls and mail. They are broad-
based, organized, and mechanized. The number of people they
can generate is excellent."[38] This theme was echoed by another
senatorial aide: "Ninety percent [of religious mail] is from conservative activists. They are very fervent, they are adamant, better
organized. They don't have what they want. Before the Hatch
amendment our mail was six to one, prolife. Then the prochoice
people felt threatened and began to mobilize."[39] Their capacity
to mount pressure has earned a grudging respect for the fundamentalists among their religious adversaries. Said one director
of a mainline Protestant denomination, "They're smart. They are
employing the same tactics with more vigor, more vitality. They
have a narrow perspective. We have a thousand issues and they
have five and they go for it. They have studied us and the pulse of
the community."[40] The fundamentalists' ability to generate pressure, however, was not always viewed as having been skillfully
employed. One legislative director for a moderate Republican
senator observed that a groundswell alone is not enough, that
the "clarity and attractiveness of the message," is also critical to
lobby success:

> The New Right? They use the later Napoleon tech-
> nique. He would attack at strongholds with everything
> he had. Stupid; killed lots of people. It was the same
> thing on school prayer. They put everything into it.
> They had the numbers, but the message was not ex-
> plained in an attractive way. Equal access [in contrast]
> was easy to explain on the Hill, but prayer was seen as
> crushing religion into the faces of children.[41]

There are others who question whether mobilization alone is a
viable strategy. "Good lobbying," said one evangelical lobbyist,

"is not always based on a flood of letters. Timing is critical to passage of legislation."[42] Another evangelical lobbyist was even more dubious of the impact of the fundamentalists: "Concerned Women and Christian Voice have collected millions, stirred a lot of people up, but what have they delivered?"[43] The consensus seems to be that, while fundamentalist groups have shaped the congressional agenda in certain respects (see chapter 6 on Equal Access), their real power is nascent. This is illustrated by the analysis of one senatorial aide from a sympathetic office:

> Conservative religious groups have not mastered the Washington operation. But they have been lobbies a shorter time. It's relatively cheap to move to Washington, open up an office. But it is harder to move in the other direction, to develop a real grassroots operation. The conservatives have strength in the grassroots, which is the hardest to develop, so the Washington operations will improve. But the liberal churches will find it hard to move to the grassroots level, even though they have had Washington operations for a longer time.[44]

While the fundamentalists are most notable in this discussion, other groups are important as well. Catholic anti-abortion groups, including Right to Life (which has a large Catholic membership), have, together with the fundamentalists and evangelicals, generated enormous pressure on Congress to limit public funding for abortions and to support the human life amendment. On church-state issues the National Association of Evangelicals, with seventy-five thousand individual members and forty thousand affiliated churches, is occasionally able to generate considerable grassroots pressure. But here, too, the salience of the issue to members, and not the priorities of the Washington staff, appears to be the deciding factor. Two of the issue priorities for the NAE in 1984, for example, were support for equal access legislation and opposition to U.S. diplomatic relations with the Vatican. As one staff official admitted, "We got a good response from members on equal access, but less on the Vatican. That was not a big issue for them."[45] Jewish groups, too, have the capacity on certain issues to generate considerable pressure, particularly in congressional districts with large Jewish populations. But the impact of such mobilization is dependent upon the circumstances of the issue. On aid to Israel, where their constituencies are unified and the opposition is not well mobilized, their impact is considerable. On some church-state issues, on the other hand, the Jewish groups are not able to generate a volume of mail comparable to their fundamentalist adversaries, and "insider" strategies become more important.[46] The Jewish groups do concentrate on maintaining healthy constituent networks. The Union of American Hebrew Congregations, for example, brings two thousand members to Washington annually for seminars on politics.[47] Moreover, active chapters of the American Jewish Committee and the American Jewish Congress in a number of cities provide forums for community mobilization that most religious groups lack.[48]

For the liberal church lobbies—the "peace and justice" cluster —the picture is more mixed. Since most of these groups are financially sustained by church denominations, and not by direct member contributions, contact with large numbers of constituents is not the rule, though there are important exceptions. Thus, while the liberal lobbies take positions on scores of issues, ranging from labor legislation to the environment, it appears that only on hunger and "peace" has the liberal community, *collectively*, been able to generate respectable constituent pressure. But the operative word is "collectively." As I will attempt to show, were it up to the mainline Protestant churches alone, the impact would be considerably less than it is. Thus the very limited mobilization efforts of the mainline churches are fortified greatly by the activities of smaller "peace churches," some Catholic groups, and the work of direct-mail groups such as NETWORK and Bread for the World.

While all of the liberal church groups maintain policies on foreign and domestic "hunger issues," most of the lobbying in the past has been "insider-based," not bolstered by constituent mobilization. Officials from such organizations as Catholic World Relief, Church World Service, Lutheran World Relief, and World Vision have provided and continue to provide expert testimony on international aid and trade issues, but do not generally attempt to mobilize constituencies around those issues. The main locus for mobilization on hunger issues has been Bread for the World, a member-based organization that began recruiting through direct mail in 1974. Calling itself a "Christian Citizens' lobby," the organization, brain child of Arthur Simon, brother of Illinois Senator Paul Simon, claims members from mainline Protestant, Catholic, conservative evangelical, and Orthodox faiths. The organization conducts research on both domestic and foreign policies that influence food availability for the world's poor. It then attempts to mobilize members and churches to bring pressure on Congress. Its membership is modest, around forty-five thousand individuals, but on highly salient issues their impact is multiplied by the activities of "covenant churches," congregations that collectively vote to join BFW. One of its more interesting strategies is the offering of letters: members of covenant churches are asked to place letters to Congress, rather than money, in collection plates. In addition, the organization maintains a corps of congressional district organizers (three hundred effective ones according to the lobby's director), and has about eight thousand people on telephone trees for quick targeting of constituent pressure. While the organization's membership has remained relatively stable over the past few years, efforts are now underway within church denominations to enlist more support for the organization. Both the American Lutheran Church and the Presbyterian Church are undertaking measures to enlist more members for Bread for the World (with the ALC reportedly planning to enlist 5 percent of each local church membership). Moreover, an effort to expand membership into the black community has met with some success through cooperation with the African Methodist Episcopal Church and the Christian Methodist Episcopal Church.[49]

While the record is somewhat mixed, Bread for the World has developed a credible reputation for the ability to generate constituent pressure. Its greatest successes in mobilizing constituents have come during well-publicized hunger crises, such as the Cambodia starvation in 1979 and the recent famine in Ethiopia.[50] While observing that Bread for the World still lacks Washington sophistication, congressional aides acknowledged that it has developed a good grassroots organization. Said one aide, "I can tell you when a Bread for the World alert went out in Connecticut. They have the ability to generate."[51] This was echoed by an aide to Republican Senator Rudy Boschwitz of Minnesota, "They have good grassroots, and they work on a bipartisan basis. Rudy works closely with them."[52]

Bread for the World is important to the liberal church community, in part, because it has been more succesful in soliciting members. IMPACT, the principal effort of the mainline denominations to develop a direct-mail constituency, has a total membership of only fifteen thousand individuals. Given that IMPACT is a combined effort of the major denominations—Methodist, Presbyterian, Episcopal, Lutheran, National Council of Churches, American Baptist, United Church of Christ—its "peace and justice" network is very modest compared to the BFW lists, and minute compared to fundamentalist memberships.[53] The focused concern on hunger, in this case, seems more successful in attracting contributors than the multi-issue and more overtly ideological approach of IMPACT. [54]

The relative weakness of the mainline Protestant denominations at the constituent end is illustrated by the small sizes of their own direct-mail lists. The Presbyterian, Methodist, Lutheran, and Episcopalian offices maintain lists averaging around two thousand names, while some other denominations have little more than a thousand persons to whom they communicate regularly. While the leaders of the mainline Protestant denominations admitted the relative weakness of their constituent work, most wanted to do more. The representative of the Episcopal Church said this, "We are just moving into this work [constituent communication] because of the recognition that it is a means to increase effectiveness, and a way to educate the broader church community about our activities."[55] The Public Policy Network of the Episcopal office, as its director observed, is new, "about two years old, with some two thousand persons around the country, broken down by issue concerns. These are committed people who are expected to mobilize letter-writing campaigns on upcoming legislation. It is a new but growing network, and in the next few years it will be a real force."

While the constituent work of the "mainline" churches pales in comparison to their fundamentalist adversaries, they have successfully mobilized constituents on "peace" issues—in particular, opposition to nuclear weapons and American involvement in Central America.[56] However, it appears that this "ability to generate" is a collective effect of a very unified, broad alliance on foreign and military policy, an alliance that includes mainline Protestant denominations, as well as small, but active, peace churches, Catholic groups and clergy, plus liberal Jewish groups. Without the collective impact of this peace network, individual mainline efforts would likely seem less significant.

What is this peace network? The pacifist denominations, such as the Quakers, the Brethren, and the Mennonites are one leading force. These denominations, while relatively small in membership, maintain correspondingly large Washington offices and direct-mail lists.[57] The Mennonites, for example, mail legislative alerts to about six thousand people and, like the Quakers and Brethren, can reach member congregations quickly through well-developed communication lines. Moreover, the pacifist tradition in these churches ensures that many lay members share the objectives of their lobbies. Thus, strategies aimed at reaching beyond the mailing lists to local churches often meet with greater success than comparable efforts in other denominations. These churches also concentrate on a few issues, in contrast to the extremely broad agendas of the mainline bodies. Consequently, when such issues as the MX missile or aid to the Nicaraguan Contras come up for congressional action, mobilization efforts are relatively successful. In addition to the peace churches, there are a number of small direct-mail peace groups and magazines, often centered in a variety of "peace" communities, that mobilize the counterculture of the Christian Left.[58] Nuclear weapons and Central American issues, moreover, appear to have galvanized, as no other issues, the activist clergy in Protestant and Roman Catholic churches. During the MX debate, for example, many congressional offices received calls from clergy around the country, mobilized by various informational networks. The office of one Republican senator reported receiving over 150 calls on the day of the vote, many from ministers and bishops opposing the weapon.[59] The United States Catholic Bishops have joined the peace network by issuing their much-publicized pastoral letter on nuclear arms. The pastoral letter has activated lay Catholic antinuclear groups, enhancing their credibility and access to local parishes, and it has apparently influenced lay opinion on the issue as well.[60] Also important in "peace" mobilization is the seven-thousand-member "Catholic social justice lobby," NETWORK, which magnifies its impact through direct association with a number of Catholic religious orders and convents. One phone call from the Washington office, for example, could conceivably generate scores of letters from the "Good sisters of the Sacred Heart," opposing aid to the Contras, an issue of special interest to NETWORK. An aide to Congressman Les Aspin observed that these efforts are very effective. "The sisters write predominately on defense and foreign affairs, El Salvador and Nicaragua. Nuns are good, they bring in personal background. They also know when to write." Finally, several Protestant denominations have successfully developed small but active peace lists that overshadow their other constituent efforts.

For example, the predominant constituent work of the Presbyterian Office, Presbyterian Advocates on Central America, has two thousand members around the country, committed not only to writing themselves but to generating letter-writing campaigns in their local churches.[61] Of all the mainline Protestant denominations, the most respected on this issue is the United Church of Christ. Unlike many of the Washington offices, the UCC office appears more fully integrated into church life. For example, the UCC Washington office developed a five-week curriculum for congregations on Central America. In addition, it has developed a "Peace Network," led by 250 congressional district organizers, whose specific tasks are to recruit a person in each local UCC church to serve as the peace contact. As Gretchen Eick, the organizer of this effort, observed, in some cases the churches actually elect or appoint the person.[62] When congressional votes are imminent, the Washington office uses phone trees to reach as many of the local church contacts as possible. Eick notes that some of the district organizers show excellent initiative. In one congressional district in Iowa, for example, the organizer got contributions from several hundred church members to place a newspaper ad and was also successful in generating "good pressure on Smith, Grassley, and Harkin."[63] In addition to its district organization, the UCC maintains a direct-mail list of some eight thousand names. Moreover, the UCC, like the peace churches, and unlike most mainline counterparts, focuses its work on a few select issues to enhance its impact. Its two priorities in 1984, for example, were opposition to the MX missile and to the Nicaraguan Contras.[64]

While any one of these efforts alone would probably not amount to great constituent pressure on Congress, collectively the unified "peace network" has become a genuine force. It also confirms what I have argued elsewhere, that issue salience is critical to constituent mobilization. While the New Right groups have attempted to counter liberal opposition to Reagan-administration nuclear and foreign policy initiatives, they have not apparently generated mail and phone pressure on members of Congress comparable to the collective work of the liberal church lobbies."[65]

While the mobilization efforts of mainline churches have been relatively modest up to now, there is evidence that major changes may be underway. It is commonly observed that members of the large mainline denominations often know little of the political activities of their church lobbies. Fundamentalist critics argue that these liberal lobbies want to keep their members in the dark because their policies are so wildly out of tune with lay church members. On the "peace" issues, particularly opposition to U.S. military policies in Central America, there is evidence that lobby policy is not generally out of sync with broad lay-member sentiment (see discussion in chapter 5). It seems, consequently, that churches have grown correspondingly more bold in attempting to mobilize lay members through announcements in church bulletins, which are distributed by the thousands on Sunday morning. The American Lutheran Church (ALC), for example, took the unusual step of mailing hundreds of thousands of bulletin inserts to its churches. The one-page insert concluded with this clear statement of policy:

> Official ALC resolutions have called for an end to U.S.
> military involvement in the region, especially an end
> to support of the "contra" forces attacking Nicaragua.
> The ALC calls for negotiated settlements of the region's
> conflicts and for justice for its impoverished majority.[66]

This statement was distributed in Lutheran churches on April 6, 1986, one week before the House of Representatives was scheduled to vote on the Contra issue. Such active attempts to mobilize members may have profound ramifications, not the least of which is that members will become cognizant of the political stands of their church bodies. Consequently, if church lobbies move in this direction, using direct membership mobilization as a political resource, they may also expose weaker flanks where member sentiment is less supportive.

Elite Mobilization and Key Contacts
Distinct from these attempts to move Congress by the sheer weight of constituent mail are the more targeted lobbying strategies. One of the most interesting is what might be termed "elite mobilization," that is, attempts to bring pressure through the quality rather than the quantity of the constituent contacts. This strategy is consciously employed by a number of groups. For example, Hyman Bookbinder, Washington representative for the fifty-thousand-member American Jewish Committee, noted that its ability to mobilize comparative elites in the home districts of congressional members is a major political resource: "The AJC represents the upper levels of Jewish society. It has people who are established, credible in their communities. They know their congressmen, have a strong sense of political efficacy." [67] The U.S. Catholic Conference, similarly, employs this strategy:

> There are 30 state Catholic Conferences. We can call
> up a state conference director, they are lawyers (or have
> lawyers). They lobby at state legislative level, and they
> have access to local congressmen and senators. Each of
> us maintains a key contact network. For example, we
> might alert diocesan social development coordinator,
> or Catholic Charities director of important legislation.
> There is a Bishops Committee on Human Life Amend-
> ment. They will call up other bishops and have them
> call congressmen. [68]

Key contact networks are a related form of targeted mobilization. These lists consist of politically sophisticated members who can respond quickly to appeals from the Washington office. Rabbi Saperstein of the UAHC, for example, contrasted this strategy with the methods of New Religious Right: "The Moral Majority and Christian Voice are good on the constituent end, but not good on key contacts. Out of 535 congressmen, I can have key contacts reach 500 within hours."[69] Groups as diverse as the Mennonites, the Catholic Conference, and the Evangelicals for Social Action (ESA) consciously employ this key contact strategy. Bill Kallio, Executive Director of ESA noted, "We have an urgent action network. For example, on Central America whenever there is a missing church worker we can generate 120 congressional contacts within twenty-four hours, to put pressure on the State Department."[70] Delton Franz, Director of the Mennonite Office echoed this approach, "Our team in Managua, Nicaragua, communicates with us and we can send the message out (via hot line) to 240 key people in the U.S. We ask a return card if they took action, and we get high response."[71] A major reason for using key contact strategies is the importance of timing in lobbying. As the NETWORK lobbyist put it, "The problem with a mailing alert is that it may take five or six days to reach the West Coast, with a full two weeks turnaround . . . so we have developed a phone tree as a main strategy. We have thirty-nine state coordinators and three hundred district coordinators who activate the local phone trees. We can get about a forty-eight-hour turnaround."[72]

The focused approach appears to be a main constituent strategy for a number of the liberal groups. Given the visibility of churches in the communities across the country, lobbyists feel that key contacts can be a very effective means of gaining access. A representative of the American Baptist churches said this: "We'll call up our key contact and say, 'Can you get in touch with Baker,' or, 'Claiborne Pell is preaching at your church. Tie him up. Find out how he plans to vote.'"[73] This approach was echoed by the Brethren office, "In swing districts we send letters out to pastors and urge them to contact their legislator and back our position."[74] It often appears, however, that—unlike the situation with Jewish groups—this key contact approach among Protestants is a substitute for the lack of a mass constituency. For example, the executive director of the Baptist Joint Committee noted that his organization needs mass contacts but does not have them. As a substitute, it was implied, the organization got the word out to the leadership, to elites, "We have some targeting by committee, a batch of lists, newspapers, denominational leaders, publications. We have a monthly magazine which gets to leadership. And we are plugged into the Baptist press. . . . All aimed at stimulating concern from the districts . . . like any good lobby, get at grassroots."[75]

Direct Electoral Mobilization

Direct electoral efforts historically have been eschewed by most church lobbyists. The most aggressive use of actual congregations for electoral mobilization, of course, has been in the black church, an example which, though not necessarily linked with Washington lobbying, is noteworthy. In the 1984 election the evidence suggests that black evangelicals were far more likely to be urged to vote for Walter Mondale by their preachers than white evangelicals were urged to vote for Reagan by their preachers.[76] With the exception of the fundamentalists, however, none of the other national religious lobbies have engaged in any substantial electoral efforts. The closest some get to direct electoral involvement is the mailing of "report cards" on congressional representatives to their members, leaving them to draw their own conclusions about which candidates to back. Bread for the World has advanced slightly by sending questionnaires to candidates and providing election kits to district organizers. But of the groups included in this study, clearly the direct electoral field has been left to the fundamentalists, who have registered voters in fundamentalist churches, openly backed candidates and mobilized for them, and even established Political Action Committees (PACs) to provide campaign contributions to friends, something none of the other groups have been willing or able to do.

The umbrella under which the fundamentalist electoral efforts were organized was the American Coalition for Traditional

Values (ACTV, pronounced "active"), a broad, potent coalition of Washington lobbies and the leading evangelists. Chaired by Tim LeHaye, ACTV focused on voter registration and mobilization for key candidates. By focusing on the independent Baptist and fundamentalist churches, leaders were able to register a large number of new voters. Gary Jarmin, who ran the field staff for ACTV, described the approach: "The evangelical community is very diverse, no one leader can appeal to all . . . [so] our principal focus was to get everybody in on the coalition. . . . In ACTV we had all the key leaders of the evangelical community, [and] the major emphasis was on voter registration, a response to all the liberal groups' voter registration. . . . We registered for sure at least 1.3 million to 1.8 million and possibly as many as 2 to 2½ million voters."[77] Independent press reports and other evidence indicate that, indeed, the ACTV voter registration campaign did bring many new voters into the election. In North Carolina, for example, successful efforts to register blacks were outweighed by counter efforts to register fundamentalists, a key factor in the victory of Republican Senator Jesse Helms over Governor James Hunt. Christian Voice also enlisted Roosevelt Grier (the black former football star, Christian singer, and close associate of Robert Kennedy) to campaign for Helms.[78]

In addition to voter registration, ACTV coordinated support for sympathetic candidates, which was notably successful in North Carolina and Texas. Summarizing their efforts, Jarmin said, "We know we are responsible for eight of the fourteen Republican [House] seats gained in the 1984 elections. Three seats in Texas weren't on anybody's list, but Vandergrif, Patman, and Hightower—we did them in. We backed Barton in the primary and he won by eleven votes, then won the general election."[79] One of the principal tools employed was the distribution of Christian Voice's voter report cards, decidedly unsubtle comparisons of candidates' stands on issues. For example, the report card comparing Mondale and Reagan:

Report Card on Traditional Values[80]

Walter Mondale	*The Issues*	*Ronald Reagan*
Supports	Abortion on Demand	Opposes
Supports	Secular Humanism	Opposes
Supports	Acceptance of Homosexuality as an Alternative lifestyle	Opposes
Opposes	Voluntary School Prayer	Supports
Opposes	Tax Credits for Christian Schools	Supports
Opposes	Balanced Budget Amendment	Supports
Supports	Equal Rights Amendment	Opposes

Similar report cards were printed on senatorial and congressional races. Christian Voice, according to Jarmin, printed 2.5 million of the report cards in Texas alone, 600,000 of them in Spanish (a favorite strategy borrowed from the Left). Outside of Texas and North Carolina, New Religious Right leaders claim credit for the upset victory of Mitch McConnell over Senator Walter Huddleston in Kentucky. His victory, said Jarmin, "Surprised everyone but us. . . . Most of our evangelical members come from Democratic families. . . . We backed him, [and] he did better in some Democratic precincts than Republican precincts. He got the white Protestant vote."[81]

The electoral efforts of fundamentalist leaders on behalf of conservative Republican candidates and their success in moving the white born-again constituency into the Republican fold[82] have, paradoxically, created tension within the previously staid GOP, which, as George Will put it, "is suffering the dyspepsia of prosperity."[83] This tension, in part, is between the blue blood Republican establishment ("preppies," "three martini Episcopalians")[84] and the conservative religious populists. Said Jarmin: "The Republican party doesn't know what to do with success. It wakes up and sees a party it doesn't recognize. Evangelicals and young people—Republicans don't know how to handle."[85] In the calculations of fundamentalist leaders the Republican party needs the evangelicals and fundamentalists, and not just their numbers but their fervor and superior grassroots organizations, in order to become the new majority party. Their concern, privately expressed, is that Republican party leaders will continue to coach candidates to put distance between themselves and the Christian Right (out of fear of alienating the yuppie vote). Said one leader, off the record: "We told them to have candidates embrace the Christian agenda. But the NRCC instead told their candidates to stay away from the Christian Right. Stupid advice. The only chance the Republicans will have is if we take over the party." Thus one of the most fascinating consequences of the electoral efforts of Christian fundamentalists, as we see here, is that the Republican party is now experiencing an internal contentiousness historically characteristic of the New Deal Democratic coalition.

Media Strategies
The most indirect means of bringing pressure to bear upon members of Congress is what might be termed "dramaturgy," that is, attempts to captivate media outlets with dramatically staged events. A religious group brings to Washington a Guatemalan Indian woman, in colorful native dress, to tell her story of how she narrowly escaped after her whole family was killed by the U.S.-supported military.[86] Famous athletes testify in favor of school prayer in a packed committee room,[87] while other religious leaders, in full clerical garb, stage a press conference on the Capitol steps, stating their reasons for opposing the president's school prayer amendment. Members of the Witness for Peace organization march to the Capitol with crosses bearing the names of Nicaraguan citizens allegedly killed by the U.S.-financed Contras. These tactics are aimed, in effect, at the fourth branch of government, the press, with the hope of influencing both the Washington community and, if possible, attentive constituents around the country.

One group that does not actively lobby but does frequently employ dramaturgy, with varying degrees of success, is Sojourners Fellowship, a radical evangelical group. In the spring of 1985, for example, the group organized a "Peace Pentecost" in Washington, D.C. The idea behind the Peace Pentecost, as the organizers described it, was to dramatize their "consistent ethic of life" philosophy, which weaves together foreign policy pacifism, concern for the poor, and opposition to abortion into one "seamless garment." Organizers chose six sites for prayer demonstrations: 1) at the White House, to pray against the nuclear arms race, and for "the poor who are its principal victims"; 2) at the South African Embassy, to pray against apartheid; 3) at the Soviet Embassy, to pray against the "brutal violence in Afghanistan"; 4) at the Supreme Court, to end the death penalty and pray "for victims of crime and violence"; 5) at the Department of Health and Human Services, to pray for the unborn and for "an agenda of justice and compassion for women and children which will create alternatives to abortion"; and 6) at the State Department, to pray for an end to violence in Central America.[88] While bold in scope, this attempt was perhaps too complex for the press to handle, judging from somewhat garbled media reports of the event. It did touch a sensitive nerve among the fundamentalist branch of evangelicalism. In response to the Peace Pentecost, the Reverend Jerry Falwell charged that Jim Wallis, Sojourners' founder, was "not a real evangelical."[89]

To summarize this section, religious lobbies increasingly feel the need to generate pressure on Congress, employing diverse means to mobilize their constituents. Successful lobbying, however, involves more than constituent letters, and it is the use of "classic" insider techniques by religious lobbyists to which I now turn.

Classic Insider Strategies

Congressional aides and religious lobbyists described the insider game in a variety of ways: "the micro process," "sausage-making," "slugging it line by line in committee," "the detail work." While the objective of grassroots mobilization is to shape the congressional agenda, create a favorable environment, or predispose members of Congress to respect your power, the detailed lobby work is designed to affect precise legislative language or the outcome of particular bills. In conducting interviews with both lobbyists and with selected congressional staff members, I attempted to gain an understanding of the extent to which religious lobbyists engage in this kind of detail work and to what effect. At the outset, it is important to distinguish genuine insider lobbying from token lobbying. The Washington environment provides innumerable opportunities for religious groups to "witness," making known their positions without really engaging the legislative process in a specific way. While these approaches have their purposes, they do not constitute insider lobbying. Classic insider lobbying involves those activities designed to affect precise policy outcomes, including: drafting bill language, offering amendments, forging coalitions behind the scenes, negotiating with opponents over compromise provisions, and providing useful facts and arguments to members during legislative debates. Two major findings emerged from this analysis of religious lobbying: 1) with a few exceptions, there is an overall weakness at the detail level, and 2) despite this weakness, religious groups are episodically effective in playing the insider game.

Religious Weakness at the Micro Level
"Most church groups are poor at details of legislation; that is a practiced art."[90] This assessment was echoed again and again by congressional sources. There are a number of reasons for this weakness of the religious lobbies at the operational level. One reason is staff size. Most church lobbies have modest staffs of from three to eight full-time employees, and even the ones with larger staffs (such as Bread for the World, with forty-five employees) must devote substantial time to activities other than direct lobby-

ing. In contrast, the National Education Association, for example, has twenty-eight lobbyists in its governmental affairs program, backed by several hundred other Washington staff members.[91] For religious groups, consequently, staff time for close legislative tracking is limited, particularly in light of their broad agendas and the highly decentralized congressional system. Since a single issue could be tracking through several committees in each house, it is difficult for religious groups to maintain even a small physical presence in committee deliberations.

Another problem is focus. Ethically minded, socially concerned religious leaders are tempted to take stands on a multitude of issues. This is particularly true for the mainline Protestant denominations, which churn out new public policy resolutions on an annual basis. The book of resolutions for the United Methodist Church, for example, is printed in two volumes and covers nearly every major public policy issue on the national agenda. This creates a major problem of lobby focus. Referring to the Protestant groups housed in the United Methodist Building, one senatorial aide observed, "They're spread too thin. You can only focus on one or two areas, [but] they want us to do everything. There are so many battles, and the number of people they can call on is small—maybe thirty offices or so—so they work their friends harder. . . . Their political savvy is lacking—strategic thinking, what to fight, what not to fight."[92] Religious leaders themselves recognized this problem, even if some had no immediate solution: "We need a clear vision, and a strategic one; identify areas where we can best do the job. We need to be focused. If I can't do that, I'll leave. I've got to see at the end of a year some progress."[93] It is perhaps not surprising that those offices that have been most focused often appear to have the greatest credibility. Gretchen Eick of the United Church of Christ, for example, was lauded by a number of her colleagues as one of the most effective in the United Methodist Building. As she observed:

> You have to focus to be effective, and to manage a grass-
> roots network. We do sign letters, but we don't spend
> time on all issues. We think we can win on aid to the
> Contras, so there are lots of things we don't concentrate
> on.[94]

Another problem is that many church lobbyists are not very assertive in expanding their access on the Hill. One staff member for a liberal Democratic congressman summarized it this way:

> Many are not very assertive. Often they come in and
> just want to talk, don't have a specific plan of action.
> What you need to do is 1) get a clear definition of the
> issue, 2) show how there is something very specific for
> the congressional office to do, and 3) ask for a commit-
> ment, no, *get* a commitment. It's just like making a sale.
> Some people aren't good sellers because they never
> close the sale. Many of the religious lobbyists don't
> come around to demanding a commitment. I counsel
> these groups all the time.[95]

A senatorial aide echoed this in referring to the evangelical groups, "NAE is present, but not active. I love 'em. I push 'em. They are reactors. Christian Legal Society likes to say, 'we are the moderates.' That's fine for *Christianity Today*, but that is odd to us on the Hill. We want to know where you stand and why."[96] Perhaps the best summary of this was the advice of Rabbi David Saperstein of the Union of American Hebrew Congregations:

> Access is surprisingly easy to get. But most of the main-
> stream Protestants don't do it. They don't have chutzpa.
> They call the secretary [of the congressional office] and
> ask who deals with blank issue. I call the principal, or
> his AA [Administrative Assistant]. The Methodists,
> etc. . . . are not good on either grass roots or lobby
> smarts. . . . The product is there but the marketing is
> not good.[97]

Saperstein noted that some of these groups were getting better, but he *then* observed that this was due in part to the fact that *he* was educating them to do so. Chutzpa.

On this score, at least, the fundamentalist groups have shown some understanding of the system. Roy Jones of the Moral Majority, for example, expressed his desire to expand his access to congressional offices, including those potentially hostile to the aims of the group. "We have access to around two hundred members of Congress, and by that I mean I can call up the AA or the member by the first name. Some people believe they have access if they know a legislative assistant. I can call Ted Kennedy's office and they will eventually call us back, but I don't call that access."[98]

Another problem for some religious groups is simply their lack of experience. One of the newer groups, Bread for the World, with a relatively large total staff of forty-five, has problems in controlling overzealous staff members. Rather than working to judiciously expand their access and gain commitments from a wider circle of congressional members, the organization, according to two staff members interviewed, simply burdens its friends. "They are a young staff, overzealous. They overlobby, harass, call two or three times a week. Waste your time. Good lobbyists must be sensitive to congressional pressures."[99] Experience is an important factor, not only because it allows the lobbyist to build up a network of relationships but because it provides a well of knowledge about the norms of the system and the pressures on members. Two of the most senior religious lobbyists, Hyman Bookbinder and Ed Snyder, echoed the congressional sentiment that a good lobbyist understands the pressures on members, knows when to press but also when to leave well enough alone, especially with one's friends.

Finally, a number of congressional aides felt that religious lobbyists, or many of them, face a unique psychological impediment to mastering the details of the legislative process—that strategic thinking and compromise are often difficult for the religious person. One AA summarized this issue:

> The pastor of a large fundamentalist Baptist church said to the congressman, "I hate the word compromise." I

> envy their assurance. We see compromise as a creative
> process . . . finding a middle way. We are concerned
> with means rather than ends, we move toward con-
> sensus. Nothing is over here. And the religious mind
> doesn't think in those categories.[100]

This theme was echoed continuously by congressional staff members, who selected different groups for their comments. Referring to the fundamentalists, one aide to a liberal Republican
senator said,

> In terms of issues, the ability to dialogue or compro-
> mise, they are incapable of that. They have a hard-core
> moralistic agenda which prevents them from reach-
> ing out to more. They have changed the agenda of
> the White House and have some electoral power. But
> they can't get far around here on black and white ap-
> proaches. You have to do a lot of massaging around here
> to be effective. The black/white approach violates
> the rules of the game. Their truth leaves no middle
> ground.[101]

From another senatorial aide, an almost identical sentiment was
expressed with regard to the liberal religious lobbies: "The MX
people were ruthless, nothing gentle about them. On Central
America I agree with the liberal church people on Contra aid, but
they are unrestrained. But somehow it is wrong for religious people on the Right."[102] In referring to mainline Protestant groups
one aide used the case of Lutheran lobbying for the Civil Rights
Restoration Act as an example of this impediment to detailed
lobbying:

> Mainstream churches are strong in terms of conscious-
> ness-raising, but not nitty-gritty lobbying, i.e., how
> should it read? Congress searches for consensus policy.
> And the subtext [of legislation] is hard for them. We've
> had Lutheran groups come in and say on civil rights,
> "We want restoration." But the dispute over the bill was
> more technical: how to restore without opening up a
> can of unexpected worms. The concept of restoration is

> great, but how do you write a bill when there was not a
> consistent practice prior to Grove City?[103]

At the heart of this difficulty, it seems, is a tension for some religious leaders between "witnessing" to their religious values and making a political impact. When asked about how she evaluated her lobby effectiveness, the director of the Presbyterian office replied, "I don't try to evaluate effectiveness. I am more concerned with the biblical basis on which I stand."[104] It does seem, indeed, that for some religious leaders, especially those in the United Methodist Building, the "prophetic" purity of the lobby position is more important than the strategic reality. And it calls into question the very purpose of the religious lobbies. speaking to this debate, Gretchen Eick of the United Church of Christ, said this:

> There is a tension between religious values and political realities. We are a member of the arms control lobby. The most radical (but still credible) witness was to hold to current military spending. But some said the religious community cannot support such a conservative stand. [But] *we* are concerned about winning, not witnessing. The debate goes on all the time.[105]

The Bread for the World lobby director expressed a similar tension: "There were fears about moving to Washington from New York, that we would suffer from Potomac fever. Some of our more radical members get frustrated with incremental change, want prophetic legislation."[106]

It is this prophetic temptation that can keep the religious mind from focusing on the mundane details of the legislative process. In a lengthy and reflective interview, Alexander Netchvolodoff, Administrative Assistant to Senator John Danforth, mused:

> There are so many religious leaders now who want to talk like prophets. But they don't live like prophets. The Old Testament tradition is that prophets are scorned by their society and live at personal peril—a

> long religious tradition. But when Falwell says that the
> Department of Education is evil because God told him,
> well that's prophesy, and I don't think he is one. Or
> when freeze people say vote for the freeze because it's
> *right*, or divestiture people say the same thing about
> South Africa, that's prophesy.[107]

Insider lobbying is mundane, technical, incremental, and does
not lend itself to prophetic stands. But as Netchvolodoff noted,
focused lobbying is designed to have an impact on actual policy.
When asked who exemplified this type of lobbying, he volunteered the name of Larry Manier, lobbyist for Church World
Service and Lutheran World Relief:

> Larry Manier will monitor the complexities of trade
> legislation. He will call up and say, "There is a provi-
> sion on trade that might help African development. I
> think I can get it through if the Senator calls so and so."
> Manier is best on hunger issues; he is in to win. He is
> not acting as a prophet but as an old-fashioned lobbyist,
> concerned about religious values.[108]

While the tension between a vision of religious purity and a
desire for political efficacy characterizes most religious groups,
it seems to be particularly troubling for the so-called mainline
churches. As one liberal aide put it,

> The whole Methodist building, beyond church-state
> issues, has a credibility problem. They are out of the
> mainstream of Congress. Often their information has
> to be processed to make it moderate enough so that we
> aren't laughed at. A friend of mine calls 100 Maryland
> Avenue "The God Box."[109]

There is a curious paradox here. While many liberal Protestants
seem eager to embrace the "prophetic," they are simultaneously
perceived by others as secularized. The most sardonic of the appraisals was given by one legislative director, who asked, perhaps
wisely, not to be identified:

> The Lutheran Council, the National Council of
> Churches, the United Church of Christ, etc., have
> become the butt of jokes. They are totally secularized
> people who could give a damn about religion. They are
> shadows of a religious past, echoes without authority.
> Secular liberals would agree with everything they stand
> for, but the nagging question: why are they religious
> at all? Why bother? Does this policy flow out of a pro-
> found, transcendental sense—or as a hasty addition
> to liberal politics. I have friends, liberal Jews, they
> think of them as jokes—what is this religion? With the
> Catholics you have a real sense of debate. But in the
> mainline churches there is no sense of debate. They are
> thoughtless, predictable fools. Where is Bonhoeffer?
> Where is Niebuhr?

While it might seem that denominational affinity between lobbyists and members of Congress would provide natural access, this is not always the case. A number of the lobbyists for the mainline Protestant groups volunteered that they engage in no special lobby efforts to reach senators and representatives of the same denomination: "We do no special outreach to Presbyterians in Congress."[110] "We haven't focused on UCC congressmen."[111] In part this is due to the small number of congressional members some denominations can claim. A Lutheran lobbyist, for example, noted that out of the 535 members, only 23 were Lutherans.[112] The United Church of Christ, similarly, has only 21 members in the Congress.[113] Another reason such methods are not attempted is the nature of issue specialization. The Lutheran Lobby, for example, given its concern with southern Africa, civil rights, and church-state issues, is more strategically concerned with key committee members rather than with randomly placed Lutheran representatives and senators. Even when lobbies do concentrate on denominational members, it is not clear that they are able to capitalize on that affinity. Pluralism of opinion within most denominations and idiosyncratic district pressures on members of Congress make it difficult to expect automatically sympathetic responses; indeed, sometimes the opposite is the case. While the Methodist lobby has employed the strategy of meeting with the sixty Methodist members of Congress, for example, twelve of those members publically criticized their church's stand against nuclear deterrence in a letter sent to the Methodist Bishops.[114]

Religious affinity, however, does play a role in lobbying effectiveness. The most dramatic example concerned House Speaker Tip O'Neill, Catholic to the core, who led the effective Democratic opposition to U.S. aid to the Nicaraguan Contras, and whose views were profoundly shaped by the lobbying of activist nuns. O'Neill's frequent response to arguments that the Contras were fighting for democracy, was to retort, "That's not what the sisters tell me." This, indeed, is a form of political access money cannot buy.

Denominational affiliation, however, often is not indicative of the deeper dimensions of religious experience and thus does not predict the affinity that may exist between religious lobbyists and certain members of Congress. As Benson and Williams demonstrate so convincingly in their study, *Religion on Capitol Hill*,[115] the most politically salient religious differences among members of Congress are not denominational, but experiential. In other words, the different ways congressional members experience or express their faith have a lot to do with their political philosophy and legislative behavior. Thus, for example, Catholic legislators who view God as a "judge," may have more politically in common with "legalistic" Baptists, Methodists, or Lutherans who share that experience, than with Catholics who view God as a "liberator." Similarly, evangelical legislators who experience God as a "loving" presence have more in common with Catholics or Methodists who share that view than with evangelicals who emphasize a divine demand for personal moral rectitude. While their study is quite complex, Benson and Williams demonstrate that their categories of religious experience are strongly correlated with legislative voting on a number of issues. They conclude that:

> To know whether a member is a Catholic, a Protestant, a Jew, or even more specifically whether one is a Southern Baptist or an Episcopalian, tells us little about voting. What matters is how religion is experienced, how it works and functions within one's life. These religious dynamics, occurring quite independently of church affiliation, are the "handles" that provide insight into how and why religion and voting are connected.[116]

This discovery helps to explain the findings of Mary Hanna on the close ties between certain senators and the groups of the Religious Right.[117] These senators are denominationally diverse, and include three Catholics, three Baptists, two Mormons, two United Methodists, a Presbyterian, and a Lutheran. Yet they are united by a similar religious orientation, characterized by an emphasis on strict personal morality and national pride. My own study reveals, moreover, that even some Jewish members of Congress maintain links with fundamentalist conservatives, despite the deep suspicion Jewish lobbyists have for the New Religious Right. Senator Rudy Boschwitz, for example, has been strongly supported by anti-abortion groups in Minnesota,[118] and Ken Kramer, congressman from Colorado, received a 100 percent rating by Christian Voice.

Episodic Effectiveness on the Inside
While the foregoing discussion has documented the relative weakness of religious lobbyists at the insider game, this should not be interpreted to mean that this is true of all the groups all the time. Hyman Bookbinder, Washington representative for the American Jewish Committee, for example, is the quintessential Capitol insider. Moreover, most lobby leaders and congressional aides could point to specific circumstances in which religious organizations made an impact, however sporadic, at the micro

level. Most often, this success is due to some special interest in the particular issue. For example the Seventh Day Adventists, as sabbatarians, have a unique interest in protecting Adventist workers who cannot work on Saturday. "We helped write the EEOC [Equal Employment Opportunity Commission] guidelines in 1964 and 1972 because of this fear of our members of losing jobs because of their faith and Saturday worship. The sabbath from Friday night through Saturday, is non-negotiable for us."[119] Bookbinder of the AJC, not surprisingly, mentioned Israel as such an issue, "Support for Israel was one of our notable successes this past session."[120] A representative of the National Association of Evangelicals mentioned a couple of instances of real insider effectiveness, on a drunk driving bill and on technical amendments to the Social Security Bill:

> We made a difference on the Social Security Bill in 1983. The issue was the tax on religious institutions and their integrated auxiliaries [agencies run by churches but treated by the IRS as secular, such as nursing homes, and so forth]. Dole had no solution to the entanglement issue if it passed as proposed. Forest Montgomery [the NAE attorney] found the compromise which kept entanglement and IRS definition to a minimum."[121]

The Lutherans claimed similar influence on tax legislation with regard to charitable deductions on the short form.[122] Of the fundamentalists the clearest statement of actual success was by the lobbyist for the Concerned Women for America: "I wrote the antipornography bill. I shepherded it through. I had to compromise on citizen lawsuits and had to compromise on some penalties and on procedural matters. But kept principle intact. This left some liberal Democrats with good feeling about us."[123] Bread for the World was credited with making a genuine impact on alternations in PL 480 (the so called "Food For Peace" international aid program) and famine relief bills.[124] Finally, a number of liberal church groups were cited by House Foreign Affairs committee staff members as providing unique information on the conditions in strategic countries in Latin America, Africa, and Asia (discussed more fully in chapter 4 on representation).[125] Church-state issues provide, perhaps, the clearest examples of key insider work by religious lobbyists. As chapter 6 demonstrates, religious lobbies, including Jewish, evangelical and "mainline" actors, not only battled over detailed language of the equal access legislation but negotiated over implementation guidelines in lieu of official congressional committee reports.

The quality of information provided by lobbies is critical to their success in gaining access to congressional offices. In this regard the United States Catholic Conference appears particularly adept. While the lobby office has only three staff members, it is backed by a considerable church bureaucracy in Washington. This fact, combined with the focused agenda of the Conference, has earned it the envy of both liberal and conservative church groups. One conservative congressional aide, who said he wanted the fundamentalists to be more effective, observed that: "They should take a lesson from the Catholic Conference. For example, on fetal experimentation their staff assistant got in touch with moral theologians and medical scientists to put out a position. They had been thinking about it."[126] On the liberal side, while the Bishops joined a number of Protestant lobbies in opposing the MX missile, they were able to argue that their opposition flowed out of their "carefully delineated" position in the Peace Pastoral on nuclear arms. Moreover, none of the liberal church groups has produced a document of comparable length and complexity to the Bishops' draft pastoral letter on the U.S. economy, and it is widely used now by liberal Protestants.

Insider access is demonstrated by the ability of lobbies to get senators or representatives to sponsor amendments to legislation, either in committee or on the floor. While amendments can be designed to clarify or alter bill language, a cunning strategy called the "killer amendment" deserves special note. This strategy goes to the heart of our Madisonian system, which provides numerous veto points to those tutored in its intricacies. The killer amendment is designed to fracture a supporting coalition or to reveal hidden contradictions or problems in proposed legislation. Its objective is to delay or block. The National Association of Evangelicals, for example, employed this strategy against the president's school prayer amendment. The NAE offered amendments designed to reveal contradictions inherent in the proposal, particularly the question of who would compose the recited prayer.[127]

The fundamentalists, too, have increasingly turned to this strategy to block their adversaries, reflecting their growing legislative sophistication. For example, the proposed Equal Rights Amendment to the Constitution, which failed to be ratified by the necessary three-fourths of the state legislatures, was reintroduced in the Congress in 1984. The fundamentalist opponents of the ERA decided, rather than attack frontally, to offer killer amendments instead, amendments that would "clarify" the scope of the ERA with respect to abortion, homosexual rights, and combat duty for women. As Roy Jones of the Moral Majority described it:

> We killed it in the House. We fractured their coalition by offering amendments. Our position is that we support equal rights and will support a constitutional amendment, *provided* it is made clear that it will not guarantee a right to abortion or homosexual rights. So we proposed several amendments to that effect, and it fractured their coalition. We got prominent women leaders, especially from Concerned Women for America, to work on that one.[128]

The effectiveness of this strategy is that it brought to the surface barely articulated implications of a proposal that had previously enjoyed widespread congressional support. To many feminists and gay rights activists, the ERA is indeed viewed as a means to fortify their legal ground on abortion and homosexual rights. But the past success of the ERA in the Congress had more to do with its seemingly straightforward articulation of fairness for women, with broader implications left vague. As Jerry Brown once observed, "A little vagueness goes a long way in politics," an aphorism particularly applicable to consensus-building. The fundamentalist strategy was designed to eliminate the vagueness and thus destabilize the consensus. The Sensenbrenner Amendment to the ERA, which stipulated that the ERA would not guarantee the right to abortion, is a case in point. The United States Catholic Conference joined evangelicals and fundamentalists in supporting the Sensenbrenner Amendment and sent telegrams to every member of Congress informing them of that support, a move that enraged Geraldine Ferraro.[129] A number of Catholic and evangelical legislators, who had previously voted for the ERA, were prepared to vote for the amendment and could do so while affirming their support for the ERA concept. Faced with the prospect of a watered-down ERA, feminist strategists decided instead to withdraw it. Thus, feminists who have been able to frame the ERA issue in terms of basic equality and common sense now must confront a coalition riven by the abortion issue, among others. What is clear from this analysis is that fundamentalists, while they have yet to initiate much new legislation, have gained the sophistication needed to veto some legislation they detest.

A particularly graphic illustration of the effectiveness of the killer amendment is the fate of the Civil Rights Restoration Act. The Act was proposed in 1984 in response to a Supreme Court ruling that narrowed civil rights laws barring discrimination in institutions (notably colleges) that received federal funding. The Court, in *Grove City College v. Bell*, ruled that only the specific department receiving federal funding, rather than the whole institution, was subject to Title IX provisions barring gender discrimination. In response, the Reagan administration announced that it would give a similar narrow reading to the laws barring discrimination on the basis of age, race, or handicap. The Civil Rights Restoration Act was designed to restore coverage to the entire institution, and it enjoyed widespread initial support, actually passing the House in June 1984 by a vote of 375 to 34.[130] But fundamentalists and some evangelical groups, which lauded the *Grove City* decision, opposed the restoration bill, feeling that it might make things even worse, in their view, than pre-*Grove City* conditions. The strategy, once again, was to load down the act with complicating amendments. As Moral Majority lobbyist Roy Jones summarized it, "We believe it is too much government control. Our strategy was to make it a Christmas tree. We forced fifty-one votes on amendments, so liberals abandoned."[131] Nearly two years later the issue is still mired in amendments that complicate consensus-making. The U.S. Catholic Conference, for example, which supported the Act in 1984, proposed an amendment to remove abortion from its coverage in 1985. The amendment focused on a little-known regulation that required schools and colleges to treat all pregnancy-related conditions, including "termination of pregnancy," like any other temporary disability for the purposes of their employee medical insurance plans or student health services. As one Catholic Conference official put it, "We didn't catch it the first time around."[132] The *New York Times* reported that "the episode has severely strained the customary civil rights coalition, of which the Catholic Conference is a long-time, active member. . . . The church's new stance made the bill a lightning rod for anti-abortion sentiment, and the 1984 majority evaporated."[133] The outlook for the legislation is still uncertain as of this writing.

A final indication of insider influence is the ability of certain lobbyists to foster and lead coalitions for particular ends or to help create new groups. Hyman Bookbinder of the AJC, for example, chairs the "First Tuesday Group," which includes all the Washington representatives of the national Jewish groups. Roy Jones of the Moral Majority, similarly, termed himself the ad hoc chair of the coalition of thirty to forty conservative Christian groups. Among the many liberal coalitions one of the most notable for its effectiveness is a Central American alliance led by Gretchen Eick of the United Church of Christ. Finally, as one indication of its influence in Washington, the Friends Committee on National Legislation has helped other groups to get started. The NETWORK leaders, for example, said that FCNL helped them set up their organization. "They were, for a time, the only registered [religious] lobby in the city. So the Friends taught us Government 101. They also gave of their staff time, and allowed us to use their WATS [telephone] lines."[134]

Coalitional efforts do generally enhance the effectiveness of lobby work, and the liberal groups seem particularly adept at creating them. There are a number of issue-specific groups, most housed in the United Methodist Building, which are characterized by religious leadership and participation, among them: the Washington Office on Africa, the Washington Office on Latin America, the Coalition for a New Foreign and Military Policy, the Religious Coalition for Abortion Rights, Interfaith Action for Economic Justice (formerly Interreligious Taskforce on U.S. Food Policy), and numerous task forces of the Washington Interreligious Staff Council (WISC). Some of these groups, such as the task forces of WISC, have no independent staffs but operate through the staff contributions of church bodies. This allows the collective liberal church lobby to develop specializations along issue lines. More intriguing, perhaps, are the organizations created with substantial church support, including staff time and cash contributions, but then weaned as independent organizations. The Washington Office on Africa and the Washington Office on Latin America are two examples of this. The Washington Office on Africa, begun in 1972 with the financial backing of church denominations, now has a mailing list of some four thousand contributors. Though it still receives ongoing financial support from churches, and indeed is housed in the United Methodist Building, its staff of six appears to be relatively autonomous, with an advisory board, but no governing body. Its focus is southern Africa, and its mission is "to support liberation." Its approach is to develop close ongoing relationships with House and Senate foreign affairs subcommittee staffs and key members. For example, the Office was successful in getting congressional committees to add four South African-related provisions to the Export Administration Act.[135] While its lobbying is incremental, its philosophy is radical. The office staff sees itself as a "voice in favor of justice and liberation in South Africa" and supports liberation movements. In regard to the Sullivan principles, the group is dubious: "We dismiss arguments about 'humanizing companies'; you see Coke and Pepsi on the side of oppression."[136] In regard to the liberation movements in South Africa and Namibia: "We know that these are non-aligned movements. We are in close contact with them. We have studied their political programs, [and] the Marxist claim is a smoke screen. They stand for justice and democracy."[137] The Washington Office on Latin America, similarly, was begun by church support, though now less than half of its financial backing is from churches (the rest coming from individuals and foundations). It also operates with relative autonomy: "We try to represent people in Latin America. We don't speak for people who give us funding."[138] The staff see themselves as "a voice for the voiceless" in Latin America. Its ten employees work with key congressional committees, providing information "useful" to countering administration programs in the region. "We are information brokers," one staff member observed, "We don't have five million people like the NRA."[139] The success of this effort is indicated by the group's documentation of atrocities by the Nicaraguan Contras, which received wide press coverage around the country.

According to a recent Ph.D. dissertation on the foreign policy constituencies of House members, these two offices are viewed as particularly useful to congressional representatives and committee staffs, a finding that was corroborated in my own interviews. With respect to conditions in strategic countries, they provide information (independent of the administration or state department) that congressional members opposed to Reagan policies find valuable.[140] What is curious about this effectiveness is that, of all the groups interviewed for this study, these two operated with the least accountability to anything other than the vision of the staff. Critics of the liberal churches, such as the Institute for Religion and Democracy, argue that this is nothing new, but part of a pattern of frequent channeling of church money into radical organizations—"laundering" operations, in effect—that attenuate accountability. Whether or not this characterization is completely accurate, the flexibility of national churches to support these coalitions constitutes a frequently successful insider strategy.

Religious Political Activism and the Congressional Milieu

Often critics of religious groups, on the Right and the Left, focus on speeches, pronouncements, and resolutions to illustrate the militancy and dangerous extremism of their adversaries. The militant rhetoric of fundamentalists and the "leftist" pronouncements of liberal Protestants provide ample ammunition for such attacks. Thus People for the American Way and other secular critics of the fundamentalists have a field day quoting the militant rhetoric of this new social movement. Jerry Falwell: "One day Jesus is going to come and strike down all the Supreme Court rulings in one fell swoop." Tim LeHaye: "250,000 secular humanists control the basic institutions of America, including broadcast media, public schools, and the Methodist Church."[141] Similarly, critics of liberal church leaders find plenty of evidence that the latter are "unpatriotic apologists for Marxism" in statements such as these: "Our nation today is the very fount of violence in many places in the Third World";[142] "The present government of Vietnam should be hailed for its moderation and for its extraordinary effort to achieve reconciliation among all its people"; "A theological rebirth is evolving in Cuba that we believe can inform Christians around the world with a new intensity and depth of insight about the meaning of faith."[143]

While these statements do tell us something about their originators, they tell us little about concrete efforts to affect national policy. Even the most "prophetic" or militant groups, when they seek to influence the Congress, adapt to its norms and priorities. The congressional milieu, I would argue, exercises a powerful influence on partisans, and "movement" rhetoric inevitably seems to give way to lobby strategies aimed at change on the margins. In this section I amplify on this theme and demonstrate the ways in which the Congress, or better, the congressional milieu, influences the religious groups.

One place where congressional influence appears is in the language of the lobby craft. For those concerned that "religious fanatics" are entering politics, the evidence should be reassuring. The norms and rules of the game appear to mold the message. For example, religious lobbyists, in general, did not feel it was wise to use overtly religious language in attempting to convince legislators of their position. As James Dunn of the Baptist Joint Committee put it,

> When we interpret for our *constituency* we use biblical themes and Christian principles; but when we move across the street and start rendering to Caesar what is Caesar's, we explain in terms of social utility and not our theological rootage. We enter the political marketplace of ideas. We don't talk about sin, but about the greatest good for the greatest number—not that we don't see sin. . . .[144]

The Bread for the World lobby director echoed this theme: "We don't say vote for this because you're Christian. It's because we are Christians that we are concerned. It's in the outreach to the church that we use religious language."[145] Ed Snyder of the Friends Committee on National Legislation observed, "We don't use words that would set off people. We use words that have universal appeal. We don't tend to use religious language, yet we do speak of 'reconciliation.'"[146] While this theme was echoed by a number of lobbyists, the clearest indication of a strategic avoidance of religious language came, ironically, from the fundamentalists. Said Jones of the Moral Majority,

> We are not a religious organization, and we have some nonreligious people who support us because of our stand for a strong national defense. We don't try to use scripture or words of Christ to convince people. If we started to use scripture we would bleed ourselves to death. We want to influence government.[147]

While the Concerned Women for America distinguishes itself from the Moral Majority by self-consciously identifying itself as a Christian organization, its lobbyists, too, avoid religious themes:

> We are motivated by religious values, but don't use the Bible to persuade. We guide our truth around their mental roadblocks. We speak to congressmen in terms that give respect to their goals and attitudes. On the ERA, for example, we make a constitutional case, argue facts. If a congressman says "I'm for the ERA, I think equal pay for equal work is good"; we say "but the constitutional amendment cannot govern private action." We don't quote Ephesians 5 and 6 ("Wives, be subject to your husbands . . .").[148]

Curiously, some of the mainline Protestant lobbies have not developed such clear strategic guidelines. The lobby director for the United Methodists, for example, mused that perhaps they needed to employ *more* clearly religious language:

> It would strengthen our position if we used the language in resolutions (which is religiously oriented). Most people on the Hill are church-related. And Reagan is being influenced by people who talk God language to him in a way we are not. I don't want to be viewed as a politician. I don't want the church to be viewed as a lobbyist. The church has a broader calling.[149]

While all religious lobbies adapt themselves to the congressional milieu to a greater or lesser extent, one of the most dramatic findings to emerge from the analysis of interview data was the extent to which the fundamentalist groups have adopted pragmatic strategies aimed at lobby success, a finding that contrasts sharply with the militant and uncompromising image of them that often emerges from the pages of the elite press. In part this pragmatism is due to their dependence on key legislators to sponsor their proposals. As challengers of the status quo, fundamentalist leaders are particularly dependent on sympathetic legislators. As Gary Jarmin of Christian Voice summarized it: "In lobbying you always need a chief sponsor, and you need to adjust your priorities to theirs. You need that lead, the point man for legislation, someone who will go to the mat on it, or we don't introduce."[150] In contrast, many of the liberal Protestant lobbyists have spent the Reagan years attempting to block legislation rather than initiate it (with the possible exception of Bread for the World). Another reason for this new tactical pragmatism is the fundamentalists' dependence upon constituent support, both financial and political. As the Moral Majority lobbyist described it, that organization had to start showing some success to maintain contributions from members: "In 1981 the Moral Majority went through a difficult period. We didn't have victories, and we needed victories for our membership."[151] The leaders learned that pragmatic, incrementalist strategies were the means to ensure some victories, however partial. Jones, indeed, was unabashed about admitting the implications of such a shift: "Incremental approaches take us out of the business of being radical. We are not for radical change; we're for incremental change."[152] This sentiment is echoed by the lobbyist for Concerned Women for America, "I have difficulty on purist approach on abortion or tuition tax credits. We have to eat the elephant a bit at a time. We have to accept partial victories. And we have some tension with membership on these problems."[153] The last statement indicates that fundamentalists, too, suffer from tension over the difference between winning and witnessing to religious absolutes. Jones echoed Ferris: "Our pragmatic stance has produced tension. Prolife groups wrote Falwell calling him a murderer, because he said there should be exceptions on abortion in cases where life of the mother is in danger and in cases of rape and incest."[154] In spite of tension with some members, fundamentalist leaders think that strategic adaptation is essential to effective representation of their constituents. Fundamentalists want to win, to have an impact, and they appear willing to compromise to succeed. As one congressional aide put it, they seem more motivated because, "They don't have what they want."[155]

In the 1960s Saul Alinsky taught radical community organizers that "The price of a successful attack is a constructive alternative."[156] Fundamentalist leaders now seem to be applying that rule to their work. On abortion, for example, the lobby work is linked to other efforts:

> In a way the prolife movement closed their eyes to the real needs of unwed mothers. Since 1973 it has been seen as too negative. So the Moral Majority has moved into the issue by providing an alternative to abortion with our Save-a-Baby clinics. We work with teens, either to learn how to be a mother or to put up for adoption. We allowed the prochoice people to frame the issue so they would be perceived as caring. Framing the issue is the key to success.[157]

In a related instance, providing an alternative was again perceived as critical:

> Baby Doe was a winner for us. We were deemed as the caring sector of the debate. But if we had said, "You bunch of murderers," we would lose. Instead, we had people line up to adopt Baby Doe.[158]

Jones mentioned several cases in which it was deemed strategic for the organization to offer an alternative to a measure they were opposing. One example was the Genocide Treaty:

> A good idea, but practical implications were bad. Helms
> wanted to oppose outright. But we didn't want to com-
> promise our pro-Jew stance. So we 1) reiterated our
> support for Israel, our pro-Jew stance, 2) said there was
> a need for a genocide treaty, but not this one, and 3) of-
> fered to present an alternative, which we are currently
> drafting.[159]

This last example illustrates another way in which fundamentalist leaders show strategic inclinations. They have forged, or are
attempting to forge, alliances with a number of "strange bedfellows." The most obvious, of course, is the pro-Israel stand, which
has nudged Jewish leaders to rethink their hostile responses to
the New Religious Right. Hyman Bookbinder of the American
Jewish Committee noted a shift in his own thinking: "Things are
not so simple, we are not saying that everything Falwell favors we
reject. We are for discipline and traditional values, and maybe
pornography and abortions went too far."[160] Intriguingly, while
Bookbinder noted that there was some tension between Jewish groups and liberal Protestants over Israel, he acknowledged
the support from the fundamentalists: "We don't like Falwell's
reasons for supporting Israel, but will accept support wherever
we can."[161] Fundamentalist lobbyists seem willing to forge coalitions wherever they can, with Catholics on abortion, with Jews
on Israel, even with the National Council of Churches on IRS
legislation. The approach is strategic. In contrast, the leader
of the Methodist lobby seemed to be moving that organization
in a different direction with respect to coalitional work: "We are
now re-evaluating these coalitions, looking at stronger criteria for
coalition involvement, specifically affirmative action criteria."[162]
There is some evidence, consequently, that the assessment of
one senatorial aide may be partially correct: "The conservatives
will transform faster than the liberals. They [the fundamentalists]
like it out of the cloister, are more open to moderation than the
NCC crowd."[163]

Summary

Washington religious leaders, whether they wish to characterize what they do as lobbying or not, do engage in diverse strategies aimed at influencing congressional decision-making. Moreover, they are increasingly attempting to bring "pressure" on members of Congress through the mobilization of constituents, which, given the potentially broad base of churches, has important implications for the American polity (as I show in the following chapters). While this is especially true of the fundamentalists, it is also a growing strategy of the "mainline" Protestant leaders, who are striving to develop lists of "hot names"—denominational members who share their activist vision of Gospel imperatives. Further, the congressional milieu fosters a tactical pragmatism on the part of religious groups, some of which maintain radical long-term goals but must engage the process in incremental steps. Particularly for those groups who wish to win and not just "witness," the norms and rules of the game dictate a molding of political messages into acceptable—meaning consensus-producing—forms. Moreover, a growing reliance on grassroots mobilization seems to heighten leaders' interest in tactical pragmatism. Whether they lobby for Moral Majority and Concerned Women for America on the Right, or NETWORK, Bread for the World, and the United Church of Christ on the Left, leaders who rely on constituent mobilization for power acknowledged that they strive for tangible legislative successes to keep their networks alive. Since, as one scholar observed, "success = compromise,"[164] this organizational imperative moves groups toward an accommodation with the system they are attempting to influence. Religious lobbyists, in short, do influence public policy, but are themselves influenced by their participation in the national public square.

4 Representation and the Religious Lobbies: An Introduction

The issue of representation is central to an understanding of the role of religious organizations in the American polity. As I observed in chapter 1, a review of interest group scholarship reveals a sober picture of fragmented congressional politics dominated by elite-based organizations for often narrow, particularistic interests. Religious lobbies are significant, in light of this picture, because they potentially represent non-elite constituencies and attempt to articulate broad (albeit competing) visions of the public good. But what is the actual nature of their representation? This chapter begins an extensive two-chapter discussion of the subject by analyzing the unusually diverse representational roles that religious lobbies attempt to play. To appreciate fully the significance of this finding it is essential first to explore the concept of representation itself, so central to Western democratic thought, yet complex and often misunderstood.

The Concept of Representation

"Whom or what do you represent?" This simple question, addressed to the religious leaders interviewed for this study, elicited a rich and complex diversity of answers. Such an outcome should not be surprising in light of the pioneering work by Hanna Pitkin[1] on representation. As she observes, the study of the concept of representation produces an embarrassment of riches in interpretations of a seemingly straightforward idea. Even so, religious lobbyists not only mirror the complexity Pitkin describes but also express notions of representation that go beyond her formulations, a finding that helps to explain the scholarly lack of understanding about their activities.

In the now classic *The Concept of Representation*,[2] Hanna Pitkin uses historical, etymological, and ordinary language analysis to illuminate the Western notion of representation as a central concept of democratic theory. What she discovers is that there are multiple meanings or usages to the concept of representation. First, Pitkin describes formalistic representation, in which a person is broadly authorized, almost in a legal sense, to act in the place of another. Church leaders in some traditions receive this kind of authority to speak for the church. Roman Catholic Bishops, for example, are authorized to speak as vicars of the church. Other religious leaders, particularly in the Congregational and Baptist traditions, where local church autonomy is revered, are not so broadly authorized.

A second usage is descriptive representation, which preoccupies those concerned with the objectively describable characteristics of the representative body. This notion of representation implies that the representative should be cut from the same cloth as the people represented, or more broadly, that a representative body should be, as John Adams mused, "a portrait, in miniature of the people at large, as it should think, feel, reason, and act like them."[3] Religious lobbyists present an interesting tension here. On the one hand they dramatically illustrate descriptive representation. Rather than hire Washington law firms or professional lobbyists, national religious organizations are indeed represented by people cut from the same religious cloth as the people they represent. Most, in fact, are ministers of those denominations. The lobby director for the United Methodist Church is a Methodist minister, the Washington Director for the Mennonite Central Committee is a Mennonite, and the leader of the Union of American Hebrew Congregations is a Reform Rabbi. This is also true for the newer direct-mail organizations, which tend to draw people from particular traditions, even if they are open to anyone to join. Thus NETWORK, a "Catholic Social Justice Lobby," while open to anyone willing to contribute, draws its members largely from religious orders. Its leaders and staff in Washington, similarly, are all women, most of whom are nuns, former nuns, or members of other Catholic religious orders. Likewise, while the Reverend Jerry Falwell emphasizes that the Moral Majority (Liberty Federation) is open to anyone who agrees with its conservative philosophy—and indeed claims membership of Orthodox Jews and Rabbis—the vast majority of its members are recruited from the independent fundamentalist and Baptist churches, especially in the South, of which Falwell is one representative. Thus the "descriptive" pluralism of religious life in America is mirrored in Washington.

On the other hand, some religious lobbies, especially those representing the so called mainline churches—the Methodists, Presbyterians, Episcopalians, and sometimes Lutherans—are often criticized for being out of touch with members in the pews, not cut from the same *ideological cloth* even if they are out of the same denominational heritage. Some critics go so far as to claim that these religious leaders are "really" leftwing ideologues first and Christians (or Methodists et al.) second. It is a subject that will receive fuller treatment later. For the moment, what this illustrates is the extent to which disagreements flow from different opinions about *which* descriptive characteristics matter the most.

A third kind of representation is symbolic. Pitkin's etymological analysis reveals that our modern concept of representation emerged in part from medieval notions of priests and bishops symbolically representing the form of Christ to the people. Pitkin curiously omitted the second sense in which representation was used in the medieval religious context, which was to reverse the direction and view priests and bishops as representing the people to God or before God as intermediaries, a notion that, of course, was challenged in the Protestant Reformation. Still, the religious origins of the concept of representation, especially in its symbolic form, are intriguing. It does appear that there is a symbolic aspect to modern religious representation. For example, while one mainline religious leader was described as ineffective by a key congressional source (of the same faith), nonetheless, denomination newsletters speak of "our man in Washington." It could be, indeed, that members and ministers of a religious tradition feel pride and take comfort in the fact that their religious tradition or faith is made present in some sense in the nation's capital, that their representatives are flying the flag, showing national political leaders that "we exist," that "we matter," irrespective of specific policy impacts.

One of the most insightful contributions of Pitkin's analysis is her discussion of the ongoing controversy about the proper role of a representative. Pitkin was intrigued by the fact that the mandate-independence controversy, as she termed it, has lasted so long without any resolution. She suspected that it had something to do with some inherent paradox in the concept itself. Indeed, her "resolution" of the controversy reflects this understanding. The debate began with Edmund Burke, whose formulation of the "trustee" role of the representative is well known. A representative, Burke argued, owed his constituents his independent judgment, and he did not act in their best interest if he surrendered his judgment to their passing opinions, or worse, to their passions. Burke's analysis, however, clashed with a growing liberal ideology that viewed people as having particular, attached interests which could only be represented well by a "delegate" faithfully articulating the public mandate.

The enduring nature of the controversy led Pitkin to conclude that the problem lies in the paradoxical nature of the concept itself. She concludes:

We have said that the central core meaning of "representation" is a making present in some sense of what
is nevertheless not literally present. I believe that this
paradoxical requirement—that a thing be simultaneously present and not present—is what reappears in
the conflicting mandate-independence positions. The
mandate theorist keeps trying to tell us that nothing
will count as representation unless the absent thing is
really made present in some meaningful sense. If the
representative's actions bear no relationship to his constituents' needs, interests, wishes, or welfare, or even
conflict with these, then he is not making them present
by his actions. The independence theorist keeps trying
to tell us that nothing will count as representation if the
absent thing is literally present, acting for itself. Unless
the representative is sufficiently independent so that he
himself acts, his constituents are not represented, but
simply present in the action.[4]

Pitkin's resolution of this conceptual puzzle is to observe that,
while both components must be present, a wide range of legitimate roles is possible. The representative must be independent,
must exercise judgment, and indeed may deviate occasionally
from the prevailing opinion of members (in that sense must be a
trustee). But the representative's actions must bear some relation
to the values, needs, and opinions of members, cannot habitually
be at odds with them (in that sense must be a delegate). This
sets the outer limits, in her view, of representation. As Pitkin
observes:

The more a theorist sees representatives as superior in
wisdom and expertise to their constituents, the more
he will stress the need for independent judgment. . . .
The more, on the other hand, a theorist sees a relative
equality of capacity and wisdom between representatives and constituents, the more it will strike him as
arbitrary and unjustifiable for representatives to ignore
the opinions and wishes of the people."[5]

This delegate-trustee division emerged cogently in interviews
with the religious lobbyists. Representatives of the established

church denominations, for example, tend to view themselves as "trustees" of the faith, while leaders of the direct-mail membership organizations often see themselves as "delegates" articulating the concerns of their constituents. The implications of this split, explored more fully in chapter 5, are complex. Serving as a trustee of religious faith does not necessarily put one at odds with lay members, nor does adopting a delegate role ensure responsiveness to constituents on all issues. Yet for some church leaders the concept of trust, implying a purpose transcending temporal concerns, can indeed operate contrary to common notions of representation.

What is clear is that, for the religious lobbyists, the concept of representation, in its manifold meanings, is central to questions of organizational identity, purpose, and claims of legitimacy. For example, each Jewish group distinguished itself from the others on the basis of its perceived constituency: "The basic philosophy [of the American Jewish Committee] is representation of Jewish concerns, broadly construed."[6] "We [the American Jewish Congress] represent younger, less established Jews."[7] "This group [The Union of American Hebrew Congregations] is unique among the Jewish groups in that it represents politically the Reform Jewish congregations."[8] Similarly, for fundamentalist groups different claims of representation helped to distinguish them, both from other religious groups and from each other: "We [The Moral Majority] represent families, not young professionals, mostly blue collar, the kind of people who stuck close to Mom and Dad, and who reject situational ethics."[9] "I didn't like the non-Christian approach of the Moral Majority. They bring anybody in their camp. I left the Moral Majority because I wanted to stay with a Christian organization [Concerned Women for America]. Interest groups should stay with their natural constituency and not apologize for it or hide it."[10] "In 1977 we [Christian Voice] decided that conservative Christians needed a lobby. I would see the liberal clergy in the halls of Congress with their collars turned backward, United Methodist, Lutheran . . . they don't represent anyone. They are more representative of Marx than Methodists. . . ."[11] Leaders of the various liberal Protestant denominations more often expressed representation in terms of their roles as trustees of church bodies with unique theological traditions: "The Washington office represents the three groups of Lutheran Churches."[12] "We [the National Council of Churches] say we are a federation of thirty-one communions. We talk of how our policies are developed. We do not pretend to represent views of each of the members of each church."[13] Occasionally, however, such disclaimers give way to broader interpretations, as when the director of IMPACT, an alliance of numberous Protestant groups, challenged a White House staff member with this statement, "We represent 90 percent of Protestant America, and we don't get an invitation to the White House religious conferences."[14] Evangelicals, too, distinguished themselves on the basis of differing notions of representation: "The NAE [National Association of Evangelicals] is limited by its constituency. NAE has many historic pacifist evangelicals. Thus we can't lobby for MX missiles and the president's budget for the military. Members temper our work, while Falwell and Robertson and Swaggart are not accountable to anyone."[15] "Because it [Baptist Joint Committee] represents such a diverse constituency its focus must be narrow, on church-state issues and religious liberty questions. At least in the past these are things that our people can agree on."[16] "I say I'm accountable to the board [of the American Baptist Churches]. I ain't no fool, no one speaks for all Baptists, with local church autonomy, the priesthood of all believers."[17] Finally, for leaders of the U.S. Catholic Conference the task of defining the nature of representation, at least in one sense, is relatively easy. As one lobbyist put it, "I'm the hired gun of the Bishops."[18]

What is particularly intriguing about the religious lobbies is not that they mirror the intricacies of the concept of representation, which they do, but that in significant ways they demonstrate even greater complexity than Pitkin found for legislators. This finding is illustrated by reviewing three kinds of representation that are distinct from the representation of members or constituents: 1) representation of church institutions, 2) representation of theological or biblical values, and 3) representation of world constituencies. (Chapter 5 analyzes the representation of domestic constituencies.) The multiple roles of church lobbyists may explain, in part, why political scientists have been unable to agree on a classification of religious interest groups. Jeffrey Berry,[19] for example, included them in his discussion of public interest groups, while Andrew McFarland,[20] in contrast, explicitly excluded them in his definition of public interest lobbies.

Representation of Church Institutions

Of the thirty lobbyists interviewed for this study at least half have a direct, functional link to a church institution. Others retain important, but less direct relationships to church bodies. It is, perhaps, this institutional representation that is most straightforwardly understandable. Church denominations, as institutions, do have distinct, tangible interests (and thus fit prevailing interest groups theories). They own property, have employees, enjoy tax exemptions, and operate an array of schools, colleges, hospitals, nursing homes, large charitable agencies, and even life insurance companies. Some churches receive governmental grants to run projects of a secular (as defined by the government) nature. Religious lobbyists, as trustees of the church institutions, thus find themselves involved in the intricacies of tax legislation, social security changes, and the like. Whether it is protecting the tax-exempt status of the parsonage, or keeping government tax investigators out of church records, institutional concerns can and do take a considerable portion of lobby time. For example, one of the three principal lobbyists for the U.S. Catholic Conference spends a large portion of his time on institutional issues, and indeed has expertise in tax law.[21] The National Association of Evangelicals similarly has an experienced tax attorney on staff, who was instrumental in working out compromise language codifying social security practice with respect to church employees.[22] On institutional issues the religious lobbyists naturally assume trustee roles. One leader, for example, mentioned that "we deal with institutional issues that our members can't relate to."[23] While the maintenance of a healthy, viable church institution presumably is good for church members, institutional advocacy remains distinct in the minds of religious lobbyists, and for good reason.

The relative emphasis on institutional issues is one factor that distinguishes groups from one another. Church structures, of course, have a lot to do with determining such emphasis. For example, the leader of the Lutheran Council lobby stressed the unique importance of these issues to Lutherans: "We speak to institutional issues more than other Protestants, because we have 375 Lutheran social service agencies, schools, hospitals. . . . so we speak to those issues along with the Catholics."[24]

The institutional issues often produce some of the most interesting and uneasy coalitions. A number of liberal church groups, by no means sympathetic to the aims of the Unification Church, filed amicus briefs on behalf of Reverend Moon, in large part because U.S. government action against him (as a religious figure) threatened, in their view, to set harmful precedents. The tension created by these uneasy alliances was underscored by a lobbyist of a moderate evangelical group. The organization decided to support Bob Jones University's tax-exempt status (which was under attack for alleged racial discrimination), on the grounds that removing the exemption would result in excessive entanglement of government with a religious institution. Said the lobbyist, "I remember sitting in a room with Bob Jones supporters and thinking, 'I can't stand this,' but that is the nature of coalitions."[25]

Institutional representation can and does overlap with the other categories. For example, churches are the beneficiaries of a large percentage of the charitable giving in the country, particularly in the form of numerous small contributions. Churches as institutions thus have a major interest in the tax code, which in the past provided no opportunity for small givers (who usually take the standard deduction) to reduce their tax liability as a result of their contributions to the church. Church lobbyists across the theological and political spectrum pushed for changes that now allow nonitemizers to take a special deduction for charitable contributions. As Martin Sovik of the Lutheran Council observed, "We, the National Association of Evangelicals, and the Catholic Conference took the lead on charity deductions on the short form."[26] While such advocacy was clearly in the interest of maintaining financial support for the churches, it also had the effect of providing a direct financial benefit for members.

Similarly, representation of church institutions overlaps with the articulation of theological values. Churches operate hospitals, nursing homes, soup kitchens, and homeless shelters, and view such service as flowing from their particular theological traditions or interpretations of scriptural imperatives. And the network of these church agencies is a notable lobby resource. Since one aspect of lobbying is providing information, church lobbyists, as representatives of institutions that provide social services, enjoy a natural credibility and access. As a lobbyist for the Catholic Conference put it,

> Church people are also taken seriously where they have direct interest. We can say, "We serve four thousand people at a Catholic soup kitchen in Cleveland, this proposal will cut 20 percent of our service and clients." You get congressional response. You have actual facts.[27]

Though the New Religious Right groups, by virtue of their membership structure, do not formally represent churches or church bodies, even here there is an element of institutional representation. A large number of pastors of independent fundamentalist churches belong to the Moral Majority and Christian Voice, and supporters of the rapidly growing network of private church schools are also members of these groups. Thus institutional concerns relating to tax codes and support for parochial schools are on the agenda of the fundamentalist groups.

Representation of Theological Traditions

Religious lobbyists do indeed represent different theological traditions and interpretations of biblical values. While theological content is less stressed among Jewish groups, it is hard to imagine representing the ethnic side of Judaism apart from its historic, and ancient, religious roots. Indeed, one Jewish leader argued that the "prophetic" Hebrew tradition, with its criticism of the rich and powerful and invocation of justice for the poor, created a natural bond between Jews and liberal Protestants.[28] To say that religious lobbies represent theological values is not to say that they always use religious language when lobbying. Indeed, most avoid that for strategic reasons. But most lobbyists were frank about the particular religious tradition or set of values that animated their groups' (or their own) political activism.

Representation of religious values, however, requires a translation into operational political stands, a task requiring both theological and strategic insight. As one critic of church political activism put it, "As far as I can gather, God's views on foreign and domestic policy are not known."[29] It is this translating of religious values into political terms that creates tension with members in all organizations. This tension was best expressed by the lobbyist for the Mennonite Central Committee:

> How to apply absolute standards, values, to the technicalities of legislation. We need middle axioms, so people don't feel compromised. Middle axioms operationalize values for particular strategic situations. For example, our position is to favor a freeze on military spending. We actually prefer a cut-back, but in order to be relevant and effective we had to make freeze our strategic position.[30]

This is a universal problem for lobbyists, and often the charge is that they compromise too much (whether they represent the Left or the Right). Moreover, the operational positions may be difficult to advance in some instances. One leader of a conservative religious group was frank about the dilemma:

> I have no difficulty arguing that a strong national defense is biblical, that pacifism is wrong for the state, but to translate that into too hard [an operational] reality is difficult . . . like support for a particular weapons system. I have a hard time convincing myself that support for the MX is biblical.[31]

Representation of religious values can and does lead to tension between lobby policy and member opinion. One reason for this tension is that while members of a particular church may only dimly perceive and articulate the connections between their faith and their views on political issues, religious elites, on the other hand, especially national lobbyists, make those connections more readily. One finding that emerged from my comparison of lobby policy with member interest, not surprisingly, was that elites demonstrated a far greater ideological consistency (as that is commonly understood) than lay members in the various churches. Thus liberal church leaders are more consistently liberal (as commonly defined) than members, while fundamentalist conservative leaders are more ideologically consistent than their followers.

A key theological source of this elite polarization can be traced to the fundamentalist/modernist controversy that divided Protestantism in the 1920s. Fundamentalists stressed individual piety, clear standards of personal morality, and an understanding of the role of state laws as codifying standards of proper behavior. The Ten Commandments, in this view, should serve as the religious and moral underpinning for the legal code; state action is instrumental to the maintenance of a wholesome community. For the liberal Protestant community, on the other hand, "pietist" concern for individual morality gave way to an analysis of "systemic sin"—social injustice, oppression of the poor, and war—as the great concerns of Christians.

To paraphrase Lincoln, both groups pray to the same God, invoke the same Christ, yet arrive at diametrically opposing views on most issues. Fundamentalist leaders continue to stress individual morality, while opposing welfare state spending as debilitating to the family and contrary to individual responsibility. Fierce patriots, they support American aid to the Contras and oppose Marxism in any form around the world. "Mainline" Protestants, on the other hand, stress a quasi-pacifist liberalism in foreign affairs and a concern with minority rights, women's equality, and "equity" for the poor as domestic priorities. It is not inaccurate to characterize the ideological positions of the two poles of Protestantism as representing, respectively, the liberal wing of the Democratic party and the conservative wing of the Republican party. Yet, ironically, fundamentalists draw their support primarily from previously solid New Deal constituencies, from the "poor" churches, while the liberal Protestants represent denominations that continue to house a large percentage of those who have historically identified with the Republicans, especially among Presbyterians and Episcopalians. Thus the potential exists for tension between leaders with a clear religious ideological vision and members whose interests and opinions may represent greater ideological inconsistency.[32]

In some cases, it must be noted, there may be considerable overlap between articulating a theological tradition and representing member opinion or interest. For example, the active lobbies for the "peace Protestants"—the Mennonites, the Brethren, and the Quakers—were organized initially to protect members' exemption from the military draft, especially combat duty. As the lobbyist for the Mennonite Central Committee described it, World War II was a watershed, because it was then that the Mennonite Church reached agreement with President Roosevelt over formal designation of conscientious objector status for members.[33]

Articulating their pacifist tradition, consequently, led quite naturally to tangible lobbying to protect members from violating a
central tenet of their faith. Given the unique cultural history of
these small churches, we would not expect to find the same degree of tension between lobby policy and members' opinions as
might exist elsewhere.

At the heart of the schism between the most liberal and most
conservative religious lobbies is a profound theological disagreement about the very meaning of America itself, especially its role
in world history. To the liberal church lobbies, the United States
is becoming a modern day "Roman Empire," powerful, arrogant,
dominating the less developed world, and oppressive to its own
poor, "third world" citizens. In this view, "the value system of
the United States as it exerts power and dominance in the system
of world food production"[34] exacerbates world hunger. Moreover, the American empire props up dictators around the world,
with little regard for the needs of the indigenous peoples. As the
director of the Mennonite Central Committee summarized it,

> We apply a biblical motif on empire, that empire in-
> evitably results in enough injustice and oppression that
> people will revolt. Empires have their Herods. We
> have *our* Herods in El Salvador, Honduras, and the
> Philippines [Marcos before his fall]. We live in the do-
> main of the Caesars. We would be much closer to the
> Bible by living in El Salvador, in the domain of the
> Herods.[35]

The religious implications of this world view are profound.
"True" Christians, who happen to be citizens of the United
States, are called to live as Christians in the pre-Constantine
church, to be sojourners, even outcasts, "in but not of" the empire. They must oppose the empire's leaders and identify with
the poor and oppressed who are its victims. Themes embodied
in liberation theology, which often appear in liberal religious literature, call Christians in America to abandon the easy path, just
as Roman citizens did when they converted to the seditious new

faith two millennia ago. The compelling nature of this world view is demonstrated by the commitment of some Christians, whether as Witness for Peace travelers to Nicaragua or missionaries for Maryknoll, to place themselves in the domain of the Herods, where work for the poor makes them "routinely labeled 'subversives.'"[36] Elements of this analysis infuse the thinking in the mainline Protestant churches, the pacifist churches, and liberal Catholic groups such as NETWORK and Maryknoll.

The contrast with the fundamentalist conservative leaders could not be more dramatic. Harkening back to the Great Awakening itself, and drawing inspiration from Abraham Lincoln's vision of America as the great hope for the world, these leaders continue to view America as the "shining city on a hill," a nation with a special role in the divine plan. America is, indeed, the beacon of freedom for the world, a "righteous empire," caught in a life-and-death struggle with a genuinely evil Communist empire, the Soviet Union. The real danger is that America will fail to live up to its historic and divine mission, will falter in its protection of would-be democracies threatened by Communist subversion. If America does falter, it will be in part because of the activities of liberal church people, who, while well meaning, are viewed as naive about international power and hopelessly romantic about "liberation" struggles in the third world, which inevitably bring the long dark night of totalitarian rule. America, indeed, has a special place in the eschatology of pre-millennial faith. True Christians must be vigilant, must be willing to suffer for that vigilance, to ensure that this great nation does not decay from within or succumb from without, so that it can play its proper role in God's plan.

Certainly there are many religious lobbyists whose visions are less extreme, who view America as neither "Rome" nor "righteous empire," but the nature of this theological debate has profoundly influenced the religious community, and will shape future discussions.

The special place of the poor and oppressed in biblical history also exercises a major influence on a number of religious lobbies. Liberal church lobbyists, in particular, stress the importance of representing "the poor, the voiceless, and the oppressed" as their unique mission. Indeed, for the mainline Protestant denominations, some Catholic lobbyists, the peace Protestant groups, and radical evangelical groups (such as Sojourners Fellowship), concern for the poor is virtually raison d'être. One lobbyist for the United Church of Christ summarized this theme well: "We are not lobbying on behalf of our own institutions, but on behalf of the poor, the outcast, and the alienated in America."[37] On this basis a number of religious groups have lobbied actively against Reagan administration budget priorities, arguing that the poor will suffer if programs for them are cut. In testimony before House and Senate budget committees, religious leaders expressed this concern. Bishop Joseph Sullivan of the U.S. Catholic Conference observed, "The harsh reality of America's present economic system is that, without substantial and effective government intervention, people will go hungry, families will be homeless, mothers and children will be without basic health care."[38] Mary Jane Patterson, director of the Washington office of the Presbyterian Church USA was more directly critical: "The poor have suffered enough. The current budget priorities result in social program cuts that disproportionately affect the elderly, women and children."[39] Chuck Bergstrom of the Lutheran Council expressed "dismay" over Reagan budget priorities, and the Washington Office of the Episcopal church issued a statement that said, "Increased military spending is inseparably linked with greater impoverishment of the poor and the oppressed."[40] These Christian leaders feel that biblical imperatives demand that the church side with the poor, the underrepresented. Certainly there is much in the heritage to justify that position. Indeed, Jim Wallis, leader of the Sojourners Fellowship, in debates with religious conservatives, dramatizes this by showing what the Bible looks like when all passages referring to justice for the poor, concern for the oppressed, or the sins of the rich and powerful, are cut out.

However, to critics of liberal church lobbyists, such as the Institute for Religion and Democracy, liberal rhetorical concern for the oppressed too often leads to questionable stands on complex issues, not to mention an often uncritical embrace of patently Marxist themes in liberation theology. Moreover, for many of the mainline denominations the mandates of God often seem to demand a stance at apparent odds with members' views on issues. To liberal church officials a prophetic stance requires, in a favorite phrase, that they should "comfort the afflicted and afflict the comfortable." The problem is that the "comfortable" all too often include many of their own denominational members.

Poised both theologically and (perhaps) strategically between the two poles of Protestantism are the Catholic Bishops and the evangelicals. The increasingly assertive U.S. Catholic Bishops confound conventional notions of liberal and conservative by simultaneously opposing abortion and taking liberal positions on nuclear arms and welfare-state spending. The issuing of "liberal" pastoral letters on nuclear arms and the economy, combined with continued Bishops' support for prolife forces, has confused those used to textbook notions of political ideology. The theological underpinning for this position has received its most eloquent articulation by Cardinal Joseph Bernardin[41] of Chicago, whose metaphor of "the seamless garment" has become a fixture in the religious literature. Evangelical groups, such as the Evangelicals for Social Action and Sojourners, stress the "consistent ethic of life" invoked in Bernardin's argument, as calling "biblical" Christians simultaneously to oppose abortion, nuclear arms, and oppression of the poor.

Beyond these divisions are numerous finer religious and theological distinctions, which shape political stands and demarcate the pluralistic universe of religious lobbying. In interviews with religious leaders and in reviewing their literature, it is clear that religious values are a salient force in their activities, that traditional political distinctions of class, ethnicity, and region are not alone sufficient to explain their political stands. More important, perhaps, is the fact that these manifold religious traditions and interpretations, operationalized into political terms, can place organizational leaders at odds with members' own views on political issues.

Representation of a World Constituency

Pitkin's analysis of representation presupposes a relationship between a domestic constituency and a representative. For a number of religious lobbies, however, representation involves not only a concern for the domestic church but a consideration of the international milieu as well. Many churches are, in fact, international institutions, with relief agencies, missionaries, development programs, and members scattered across the globe. While the Roman Catholic Church is the obvious example, this is also true for Lutherans, Presbyterians, Baptists, Mennonites, Quakers, the National Association of Evangelicals, the Seventh Day Adventists, and, of course, the National Council of Churches, among others.

There are several important implications of this international focus. First, the international network serves as a lobby resource for American religious lobbyists, providing them with special information and, in certain cases, unique access to policy-makers. In certain situations churches are themselves major transnational actors. For example, African famine relief was channeled through such agencies as Catholic Relief, Lutheran World Relief, and World Vision, which, as non-state agencies, enjoyed greater access and credibility in politically delicate situations than the foreign offices of granting nations. During congressional debates about American aid to Africa, consequently, church officials of these international organizations had special information to offer and enjoyed immediate access to the decision-making process.

Several lobbyists highlighted this usefulness of their international contacts. The director of the Mennonite Central Committee observed that their lobby work is "uniquely" tied to their international development program. Not surprisingly, development projects often are located in countries deemed strategic by the United States. Said Delton Franz, "We have people in the Philippines, El Salvador, Nicaragua, and South Africa, who gain knowledge of conditions in the countries and then meet with state department and congressional representatives. Their assignments are not missionary but involve real economic development, and that kind of exposure puts you directly into human rights issues. . . . We see the impact of U.S. policies, arms imports."[42] Similarly, the Lutheran lobbyists observed that their international contacts provide valuable information which they feed to congressional committees, particularly on South Africa and Central American concerns. Martin Sovik, specialist on foreign and military policy for the Lutheran Council, observed that much of their work involves countering administration statements on South Africa and Namibia (whose population is over half Lutheran). "We can counter administration statements on Namibia. We know that SWAPO is not a Marxist-Leninist terrorist organization completely controlled by the Soviet Union, because half of it is Lutheran. We fund chaplains for SWAPO. We know administration statements are false."[43] Often effectiveness is enhanced as groups work with each other, use each other's contacts. During the rule of the Argentine junta, for example, a young Mennonite woman was kidnapped. After working with the state department to secure her release, the Mennonite Central Committee brought her to Washington to testify before the Senate Foreign Relations Committee, chaired by Frank Church. After Church attached a human rights amendment to the foreign aid bill, the Mennonites teamed up with NETWORK. Noted Franz of the Mennonite Central Committee: "We linked our lobby effort with the NETWORK sisters, in which their lobby day was focused on military aid. There were 450 nuns across the hill referring to the Mennonite woman's experience. Previously the amendment was twenty-four votes shy, after the lobby effort it passed."[44]

This international connection helps to explain in part the intense church lobbying on foreign policy matters. A recent study of foreign policy constituencies of House members revealed that religious groups are viewed by committee members as the key source of information (independent of the administration) on conditions inside strategic countries.[45] My own interviews with selected committee staff members confirmed this. Said one House Foreign Affairs staff member: "They [church groups] are useful. They send delegations down, and they provide us with information. They have religious networks that we don't have, churchgoers . . . the most active ones are the Lutherans, Catholics, Quakers. We have ongoing communication with them. . . . They are also effective because of their dispersion. Church groups from Idaho go to Nicaragua, can influence regional congressmen. Churches are one of the main actors now."[46]

While the international network is a lobby resource, it can also serve to check freewheeling policy formation. Several lobbyists mentioned that before they enunciate policy they clear it with church officials in the respective country. This is the standard procedure for the Catholic Conference. As one of its lobbyists observed: "On El Salvador the U.S. Bishops came out against military aid and said that if aid was to be provided it should be linked to human rights. This was approved by the El Salvador Church. However, on South Africa, the Episcopal Conference under Archbishop Hurley, who is against apartheid, said, 'Go slow on divestment. U.S. companies have a good record.'"[47] In some cases articulation of lobby policy, particularly criticism of a foreign government, is muted out of fear for the potential harm to the work or the lives of church counterparts abroad. Sovik of the Lutheran Council observed, "We might want to oppose human rights violations in country X, but we may find that we endanger lives of Lutherans in church X or disrupt work going on, such as famine relief, therefore we do not act on a foreign policy issue unless the Lutheran church in the country approves."[48] Church lobbyists seemed particularly sensitive to their counterparts in foreign lands. A leader for the National Association of Evangelicals noted that the eleven thousand missionaries affiliated with the organization are seriously consulted in policy formation. During the debate over the Panama Canal treaties, for example, a resolution against the treaties was proposed at the NAE convention. "The missionaries said don't pass that resolution."[49] It was defeated.

The international focus manifests itself in the ways lobbyists define their roles as representatives. One of the most intriguing findings to emerge from interviews was the extent to which church leaders consciously see their roles as representing foreign constituents—church members around the world affected by U.S. foreign and military policy. The Lutheran Council, for example, not only represents the domestic church and its members, but Lutherans in Namibia, South Africa, and elsewhere. Church developments abroad thus influence the lobby emphases of the Council. The Lutheran church in South Africa, as an illustration, has taken the unusual step of making opposition to apartheid "status confessiones," or in lay language, a requirement of membership. Thus to lobby against apartheid is particularly compelling for the Lutheran Council, as a matter of faith.

Representation of foreign constituencies thus not only informs lobby policy but infuses the work with a special urgency and poignancy. Carol Franklin of the American Baptist Churches USA underscored this in her description of the organization's opposition to U.S. aid to the Contras, "There are indigenous Baptist churches in Nicaragua. We have no desire to convert folks, build hospitals and clinics with our mission dollars, then have our tax dollars spent on killing them. That just doesn't make sense to us."[50]

Since church groups clearly are vitally interested in American foreign policy, from food aid to military policy, most have ongoing contact with the state department and congressional committees concerned with foreign affairs and human rights. But it must be obvious at this point that no mention has been made of the fundamentalist organizations. The fundamentalist organizations find themselves at a disadvantage in attempting to play the insider game on foreign policy, which the Catholics, mainline Protestant, peace Protestant, and evangelical organizations are able to do. The Moral Majority, Christian Voice, and Concerned Women for America are mass-mail membership organizations and thus are not hooked into international church networks. The Reverend Jerry Falwell's extensive travel abroad, resulting occasionally in embarrassing publicity, such as his poorly timed embrace of President Marcos in the Philippines, only serves to underscore this fact. Indeed there is little evidence of any tangible lobby effort at the committee and subcommittee level by the fundamentalist groups. Moreover, the global church networks of Washington lobbies often lend themselves well to the liberalism of many church bodies, thus heightening the liberal bent of church lobbying on foreign policy. It would appear that here, perhaps more than any where else, the liberal church groups are the more effective ones. They have access to people around the globe with information, and they are increasingly using that information to mobilize domestic constituencies.

Church lobbies are unusual, if not unique among domestic interest groups, in that they view themselves as representing constituents outside of the United States (I am not including here, of course, the lobbying done by foreign governments). The closest analogue to the representation of world constituencies, perhaps, are the ethnic lobbies concerned about eastern Europe, Ireland, and—defining Jewish groups as ethnic rather than religious—Israel. But the church groups are unique because world church membership is not primarily an ethnic phenomenon. Certainly the tie between, say, the American Lutheran Church, composed of ethnic Germans and Scandinavians, and black African Lutherans in Namibia, is not ethnic but religious. Or, as one Namibian pastor described it most poetically in a letter to a Lutheran congregation in eastern Colorado, where he had interned, "water is thicker than blood, the water of our baptism into the body of Christ."[51]

While representation of world constituencies can, and does, lead to tension with domestic laity, such tension is not automatic. Certainly religious critics of the Marcos regime in the Philippines would probably be vindicated in the eyes of their members by the astonishing events of the largely peaceful revolution ousting Marcos in February of 1986. Moreover, as the analysis in the following chapter reveals, because of their unique access to information, liberal church lobbyists have effectively articulated, as has no other domestic lobby, broad American sentiment on foreign policy questions.

Summary

The issue of representation is central to an understanding of how religious leaders view themselves, distinguish themselves from others, and approach their political tasks. Religious organizations mirror the complexities of representation, but in important ways go beyond Pitkin's formulations, enriching the concept of representation further. Most notable are the representation of theological values independent of lay opinion and the conscious attempt to articulate the needs and concerns of the poor, both at home and abroad. While the representation of church institutions, world constituencies, and theological values can and does lead to tension with lay members, it need not do so, as the following chapter demonstrates. Paradoxically, the diverse representational roles of religious lobbyists enable them, in some cases, to articulate broad but otherwise underrepresented values in the American polity.

5   Representation of Domestic Constituencies

The multiple roles of religious lobbyists—in which they simultaneously attempt to represent church institutions, theological understandings, and world constituencies—can place them in tension with domestic lay members on certain issues. Hanna Pitkin observes that while a wide range of legitimate forms of representation are possible, a true representative, at least, must not habitually be at odds with constituents. Yet there is a considerable literature that suggests that national leaders of at least the established, mainline Protestant denominations do not articulate the sentiment of lay members in the pews. As early as 1951, for example, Luke Ebersole, writing on the activities of church leaders in Washington, said this: "In many cases . . . church lobbyists promote the causes in which groups of church leaders are interested rather than the views of church members in general."[1] James Adams and Alfred Hero made similar observations in their studies of church lobbying in the 1960s.[2] Indeed, the gap between activist liberal ministers and lay members has become a fixture of the religious literature.[3]

The most recent assessment is that of James Reichley,[4] who describes the relationship between mainline church leaders and lay members as "liberal establishments, moderate laity." He cites surveys conducted of northern Presbyterians in 1976 and Lutherans in the early 1980s, which reveal a difference of opinion between national leaders and lay members regarding church involvement in politics. Lay members are generally less likely to favor church involvement in politics than either ministers or church staff (although on some concerns, such as civil rights and peace issues, lay members are reasonably supportive of church involvement).[5] Reichley notes striking ideological disagreement between national denominational leaders and lay members, which emerges in voting patterns. Exit polls, for example, document well the breadth of President Reagan's popularity with Catholics and every conceivable subgroup of Protestants in America. Episcopalians, Lutherans, Methodists, Presbyterians, and American Baptists—all registered at least 60 percent support for the president's reelection. But, as Reichley documents so accurately, lobbies for these denominations are highly critical of administration policies. Moreover, a survey of Washington religious lobbyists revealed that, of the seventeen polled, twelve said they were Democrats, five said they were independents, and none said they were Republicans. Reichley concludes, along with previous scholars, that a general picture of mainline liberalism contrasts sharply with actual lay moderation or even conservatism.[6]

What is lacking in this and other studies is a more contextual analysis. When specific issues are examined, and when lobby effectiveness is assessed, a more complex picture emerges, one in which different lobbies do effectively articulate (at different times) broad segments of American sentiment. Moreover, since successful mobilization is linked with constituent support, "representative" lobbying tends to be more effective than "oligarchic" lobbying.

It is important to look at two facets of representation: first, the extent to which these national religious organizations represent their own constituents, and second, the extent to which, by virtue of their potentially non-elite mass base, they represent diffuse, less well-represented constituencies in the American polity. As one indication of this representation, I compare lobby stands against profiles of denominational sentiment and broader American public opinion. This analysis suggests that religious lobbies, collectively, do play an important representational role in the American system, in spite of contrary evidence on some issues.

How do the lobby positions of national religious groups compare to member opinion or to the opinion of the broader American population? The 1984 American National Election Study,[7] with one of the most complete denominational breakdowns, is employed to address those questions. The issues analyzed below reflect priorities of the religious lobbies and are intended to tap sentiment in each major policy area: 1) domestic social policy, 2) foreign policy and military spending, and 3) domestic economic and welfare policy.

Domestic Social Issues

The principal success of the New Religious Right in mobilizing constituencies, as I demonstrated in chapter 3, has been on such social issues as abortion, pornography, and school prayer. And contrary to assertions that the Moral Majority "represents" only a small minority of Americans,[8] the evidence presented here suggests that on these issues the fundamentalist groups do articulate broad public sentiment. School prayer provides the most dramatic example of this. Moreover, it is also one of the clearest cases of national lobby offices at apparent odds with lay sentiment, but in this case it is the liberal Protestant lobbies (and even some evangelical groups) that hold the dubious distinction. Respondents were asked this question:

> Some people think it is all right for the public schools to start each day with a prayer. Others feel that religion does not belong in the public schools but should be taken care of by family and the church. Which do you think?

Table 1, which summarizes the results for the entire national sample, indicates support for school prayer by fully two-thirds

Table 1. Opinion on School Prayer
Percent of Respondents (N = 1581)

Schools should be allowed to start day with prayer	66
Religion does not belong in the schools	26
Depends	8

Source: 1984 American National Election Study, Center for Political Studies, University of Michigan, Ann Arbor.

Table 2. Opinion on School Prayer,
by Religious Affiliation
Percent of Respondents

Affiliation	Allow School Prayer			
	Yes	No	Depends	
Presbyterian	56	37	7	(N = 75)
Lutheran (a)	64	27	9	(N = 92)
Episcopal	61	27	12	(N = 41)
Methodist	71	22	7	(N = 175)
Baptist (b)	78	17	6	(N = 139)
Fundamentalist (c)	83	9	8	(N = 149)
Southern Baptist	85	10	5	(N = 147)
Roman Catholic	64	26	10	(N = 384)
Jewish	14	80	6	(N = 35)
Born Again	83	9	8	(N = 485)
Black (d)	83	11	5	(N = 167)

Source: 1984 American National Election Study.
(a) Excludes Missouri Synod Lutherans.
(b) Excludes Southern, Independent, and Free Will Baptists.
(c) The American National Election Study included as "neo-fundamentalists" members of Holiness, Nazarines, Pentecostal, Assemblies of God, Church of Christ, Missouri Synod Lutheran, and Independent and Free Will Baptist churches. For brevity I refer to them as Fundamentalists.
(d) This racial category is included for reasons explained in the text.

of the public. The breadth of public support for school prayer
is demonstrated further by the denominational breakdown presented in table 2. We see across-the-board support for school
prayer, with the exception of the Jewish constituency, which is
strongly opposed.

As chapter 6 demonstrates, the lobbyists for the Presbyterian,
Lutheran, Episcopal, Methodist, and Baptist denominations, as
well as the National Association of Evangelicals, lobbied in the
Congress against the president's school prayer amendment, with
the Lutheran Council taking the public lead. While church-state
issues are indeed complex, there clearly is broad public sentiment for some religious practice in the public schools, and
these mainline groups have been hostile to the school prayer
proposals. Indeed, of the religious opponents to school prayer,
only the Jewish leaders appeared to be acting with strong constituent support.[9] The entrepreneurs of the New Religious Right,
in contrast, have not only articulated the opinion of their own
fundamentalist constituencies but apparently the sentiment of a
large portion of the American public as well. Indeed, an argument can be made that fundamentalist groups forced an issue
with broad support but few institutional backers to a head in the
Congress (with some success, as the next chapter shows). Thus,
in representational terms it would seem that previously underrepresented values and concerns were brought into the political
arena by the mobilization efforts of the fundamentalist conservatives. Moreover, it is clear that, while there is broad support for
school prayer, it intensifies for the fundamentalist and evangelical
constituencies, with the Southern Baptists, the fundamentalists,
and born-again Christians registering over 80 percent support.
Intriguingly, American blacks, overwhelmingly evangelical in religious affiliation, also register over 80 percent support for school
prayer, a fact whose significance is explored later in this chapter.

The religious dimension to this issue is highlighted when we
examine the relation between respondents' views on prayer with
their views on the Bible. Table 3 indicates that religious belief,

Table 3. View of the Bible, by Opinion on School Prayer
    Percent of Respondents

	Allow Prayer	Doesn't belong	Depends	
Bible is inherent word of God	79	15	7	(N = 790)
Written by men inspired by God	57	32	11	(N = 616)
God had nothing to do with it	27	66	6	(N = 99)

Source: American National Election Study

Table 4. Opinion on Abortion
    Percentage of Respondents (N = 2171)

Never permit	13
Permit only in cases of rape and incest	30
Permit only after need is established	20
Solely the woman's choice	36

Source: American National Election Study.

especially religious orthodoxy, correlates highly with support for school prayer, and only those who reject the God-derived authority of the Bible oppose school prayer as a group.

On abortion the picture is a bit more complex. Contrary to feminist assertions that the majority of Americans support unconditional choice on abortion, the apparent sentiment supports neither of the extreme prochoice nor prolife positions. Respondents in the 1984 survey were asked their views on abortion and were given four categories among which to place themselves. Table 4 presents the results for the general sample.

While a relatively small percentage of respondents would bar all abortions, only about one-third support the unconditional pro-choice position. A majority of respondents would restrict abortion to a few specified circumstances. Other polls have shown a similar cleavage, with rape, incest, and the mother's life as the conditions under which most people would permit abortion. In light of these findings, the Moral Majority strategy—born of practical politics—opposing abortion except in the case of rape, incest, and where the mother's life is at stake, is a shrewd one, though it has not been without fundamentalist critics who sense compromise and co-optation. Criticism notwithstanding, the strategic imperative appears to have moved the Moral Majority closer to its religious constituency. Table 5 indicates that while Baptist, fundamentalist, and born-again evangelical constituencies are the most strongly opposed to abortion, and would limit it to cases of rape or incest, only about one-fifth would ban all abortions. This illustrates nicely an underlying theme of this book, that strategic imperatives often pull strongly ideological religious leaders into closer conformity with their less ideologically consistent members. The point cannot be overstressed: even among evangelicals and fundamentalists there is considerable diversity. Fully 20 percent of the Southern Baptist, fundamentalist, and born-again Evangelical respondents favor the unconditional prochoice position, revealing far less ideological consistency among members of orthodox churches than commonly expected.

When we turn to the other religious denominations we find some fascinating patterns, indicating that on certain issues there *are* salient differences among the so called mainline churches. The most liberal constituencies are Presbyterian, Episcopalian, and Jewish—the only groups in which a majority of respondents support unconditional choice on abortion and, perhaps not incidentally, the most economically elite of the religious bodies. One of the more intriguing findings is that Lutherans are considerably more conservative than the rest of the mainline groups, and indeed appear less supportive of unconditional choice on abor-

Table 5. Opinion on Abortion, by Religious Affiliation
Percent of Respondents

	Never permit	Only after rape/incest	Need only	Woman's choice	
Presbyterian	5	13	28	54	(N = 93)
Lutheran	9	39	24	28	(N = 131)
Episcopal	5	11	25	58	(N = 55)
Methodist	8	33	24	35	(N = 242)
Baptist	22	28	22	28	(N = 193)
Fundamentalist	22	41	17	20	(N = 184)
Southern Baptist	16	44	19	21	(N = 194)
Catholic	15	33	16	36	(N = 556)
Jewish	4	10	21	65	(N = 52)

Source: 1984 American National Election Study

Table 6. Opinion on Abortion, by Church Attendance
Percent of Respondents

	Never permit	Only after rape/incest	Need only	Woman's choice	
Attend weekly	25	42	14	17	(N = 530)
Almost weekly	14	37	25	23	(N = 249)
Once or twice/month	12	27	29	31	(N = 298)
Yearly or never	8	25	20	47	(N = 921)

Source: 1984 American National Election Study

tion than even Catholics. Hence on some dimensions, at least, Lutherans appear closer to evangelicals and fundamentalists than to other mainline Protestants.

The religious salience of the abortion issue is illustrated by the fact that church attendance is itself correlated with opposi-

Table 7. Church or Synagogue Attendance, by Religious Affiliation
Percent of Respondents

	"Frequent" (at least once or twice per month	"Infrequent" (once or twice a year at most)	
Presbyterian	42	58	(N = 97)
Lutheran	55	45	(N = 134)
Episcopalian	36	64	(N = 58)
Methodist	42	58	(N = 252)
Baptist	60	40	(N = 201)
Fundamentalist	64	36	(N = 191)
Southern Baptist	56	44	(N = 199)
Catholic	60	40	(N = 578)
Jewish	25	75	(N = 53)

Source: 1984 American National Election Study

tion to abortion, as table 6 indicates. In three of the four categories (never permit, permit only for rape and incest, and solely woman's choice) the relationships are linear. Faithful attenders favor the unconditional choice position least, while infrequent attenders favor it the most. Since attendance varies from denomination to denomination, this finding raises the intriguing possibility that the prochoice sentiment registered in some denominations reflects largely the views of *infrequent* church attenders. To explore this possibility it is helpful first to note varying attendance rates by denominational grouping, as illustrated in table 7 (for simplicity I collapsed the five categories into two, including under "frequent" those responses ranging from "weekly" to "once or twice per month," and including under "infrequent" those responses of "never attend" to "attend only once or twice per year").

There is an interesting pattern here. The established, mainline denominations—the Episcopal, Presbyterian, and Methodist churches—have frequent attendance of less than 50 percent. Those with over 50 percent attendance include the Catholic church, the fundamentalist and evangelical churches (the Baptists, Southern Baptists, and the fundamentalists), and, interestingly, the Lutheran churches. In every case, the groups with the highest attendance are also the groups with the greatest opposition to abortion. For example, Lutheran respondents were the most likely of the mainline churches to reflect anti-abortion sentiment, and they also have the highest attendance of the mainline groups.

This brings us to the issue of representation. When religious groups lobby on abortion, whether pro or con, are their efforts well grounded in the sentiment of those who participate actively in church or synagogue life, in other words, those who attend regularly? Table 8 answers this question in part. In each denomination frequent attenders are less supportive of the prochoice position than infrequent attenders, and only among Episcopalians are the majority of those actively attending church supportive of unconditional choice on abortion. Intriguingly, the Lutheran frequent attenders (often viewed as mainline Protestants along with Methodists, Episcopalians, and Presbyterians) and fundamentalist frequent attenders are the two groups least supportive of unconditional choice.

These findings suggest that lobby emphasis may indeed relate to the strength of member support. For example, the two organizations that are viewed as leaders in the religious community on "abortion rights" are the Episcopalian office, whose active members support unconditional prochoice, and the Union of American Hebrew Congregations (which represents Reform Judaism). The Jewish sample is too small to allow us to draw any conclusions about the UAHC relative to its active constituents, but since polls generally show Orthodox and Hasidic Jews to be more conservative than Reform Jews on social issues, it is likely that the prochoice position of the Reform lobby is also well rooted in

Table 8. Opinion on Abortion, by Attendance for Selected Denominations
Percent of Respondents

	Woman's choice	Conditional or never	
Presbyterian			
Frequent	41	59	(N = 41)
Infrequent	63	27	(N = 52)
Episcopalian			
Frequent	55	45	(N = 20)
Infrequent	60	40	(N = 35)
Lutheran			
Frequent	16	84	(N = 73)
Infrequent	43	57	(N = 58)
Methodist			
Frequent	25	75	(N = 106)
Infrequent	43	57	(N = 136)
Baptist			
Frequent	20	80	(N = 125)
Infrequent	39	62	(N = 75)
Southern Baptist			
Frequent	23	77	(N = 110)
Infrequent	31	69	(N = 85)
Fundamentalist			
Frequent	16	84	(N = 117)
Infrequent	33	67	(N = 85)
Catholic			
Frequent	26	74	(N = 334)
Infrequent	50	50	(N = 220)
Jewish			
Frequent	46	54	(N = 13)
Infrequent	72	28	(N = 39)

Source: 1984 American National Election Study

Table 9. Opinion on Abortion, by View of the Bible
Percent of Respondents (N = 1754)

	Conditional or never	Woman's choice
Bible as literal word of God	77	23
Written by men, inspired by God	55	45
God had nothing to do with it	31	69

Source: 1984 American National Election Study.

active member opinion. On the prolife side, the U.S. Catholic Conference, in its anti-abortion lobbying, appears to represent generally the sentiment of those who attend mass regularly, rather than the many lapsed Catholics who are more strongly supportive of unconditional choice. Fundamentalist and evangelical groups, which universally oppose abortion, also appear to have relatively strong backing among active church followers. For all the other groups, the majority of faithful attenders would restrict abortion to specified circumstances. Thus, those Protestant denominations that have embraced the prochoice position, such as the Methodists, American Baptists, and Presbyterians, find themselves in the curious position of articulating, at best, the sentiment of infrequent attenders more than those who continue to participate actively in church life.

It appears that the issue of abortion has a strong religious dimension to it. For example, respondents were asked about their view of the Bible, and were given categories of response ranging from viewing it as God's word (all of it) to believing that God had nothing to do with it. Table 9 shows how views about abortion change with views about the Bible.

Here we see that 69 percent of those favoring the choice position said God had nothing to do with the Bible, while 77 percent of those who said the Bible was the literal word of God would restrict abortion in most instances. The strength of this relationship brings to mind Kristen Luker's work, *Abortion and the Politics of Motherhood*,[10] in which she argues that opinions on abortion are deeply interwoven with contrasting world views. As an indication of this, Luker observes that prochoice activists tend to emphasize rationalism and planning in life, while anti-abortion activists accept a certain givenness in life as obedient to God's plan. Certainly there is evidence of deep cleavages along religious lines on abortion in terms of denominational affiliation, church attendance, and views about the Bible.

Foreign Policy

If domestic social policy constitutes the major priority and the principal success of the fundamentalist groups, foreign policy is a major focus of the liberal groups and represents their greatest effectiveness in galvanizing constituents into action. Once again, the evidence here suggests that this success is rooted in support-ive member and broader public sentiment.

Of all the foreign policy concerns, the single most predomi-nant for the religious groups in recent years has been Central America. Church groups have sponsored delegations and fact-finding tours to El Salvador and Nicaragua; missionaries have become major conduits for information on the impact of United States policies in the region; and direct-mail mobilization ef-forts have been organized by national religious groups. It is an issue of passionate concern for the mainline Protestants, the peace Protestants, the major Catholic organizations, and even some evangelical groups. What this has meant is direct and un-commonly broad-based opposition to components of President Reagan's policies in the region, particularly to U.S. aid to the Nicaraguan Contras. Religious opponents of administration poli-cies were partially successful in their lobby efforts in the fall of 1984, when Congress voted to cut off military aid to the Contras. Early in 1986 sparring between the administration and members of Congress intensified, when President Reagan proposed $100 million for the Contras, staking his political reputation on the issue by appealing on national television for public support, arguing that failure of the Congress to support the Contras would likely result in the introduction of American troops in the region to stem a "red tide" at our borders. Religious organizations, in their turn, organized demonstrations in Washington against Contra aid, initiated letter-writing campaigns, and sponsored visits to Congress by clerical leaders returning from the region with fresh reports of Contra atrocities. According to national press reports the church groups were the strongest, if not the sole, lobby against the president's aid package,[11] and a number of congressional offices reported mail on the issue running heavily against the proposal. On the other side, fundamentalist conservatives attempted to mobilize their own constituencies in support of administration initiatives, though not apparently with nearly the same impact as the opponents. On March 20, 1986, the House of Representatives, by a vote of 222 to 210, rebuked the president and his supporters by voting to deny the $100 million aid request, a notable demonstration of lobby effectiveness in light of the president's personal appeals to many wavering congressmen. Even though the president eventually won his $100 million request, the Contra connection to the Iranian arms scandal may yet doom his efforts to sustain support for the Nicaraguan resistance. The religious community, by mobilizing the main opposition to the president's Nicaragua policy, has thus played a role in the still-unfolding drama.

What is the evidence of actual sentiment on this issue? Not only have a variety of national surveys shown the American public opposed, for example, to U.S. aid to the Contras, but the president's own polling has revealed that many Americans "question the wisdom of overthrowing governments, even communist governments."[12] The American National Election Study revealed similar resistance to administration policies. It asked respondents about their opinion of U.S. involvement in Central America,

Table 10. U.S. Involvement in Central America:
Comparison of Respondents' Preferences
with Their View of Reagan's Preference
Percent of Respondents

	Want more	About same	Want less	
Respondents	25	20	55	(N = 1696)
Reagan Administration	73	11	16	(N = 1613)

Source: 1984 American National Election Study.

specifically, where they would place themselves on a seven-point scale, with "1" indicating a preference for much more involvement and "7" much less. The question is somewhat ambiguous and could measure isolationist sentiment as well as opposition to administration policies. But it does serve as a reasonable indicator of sentiment about United States Central American policies for the following reason: respondents were asked not only how *they* felt about U.S. involvement but where they would place the Reagan administration on the same seven-point scale. Table 10 presents a comparison of the views of the respondents in the national sample with their assessment of the Reagan administration's preference (to illustrate the contrast most sharply I have collapsed the seven-point scale into a three-point scale). Most respondents were able to accurately place the activist policies of the Reagan administration, with 73 percent saying the administration wanted more U.S. involvement in Central America (in light of military aid to El Salvador and Guatemala, the establishing of military bases in Honduras, and funding for the Nicaraguan Contras, it is not inaccurate to describe the Reagan posture as desiring more U.S. involvement). In contrast, nearly 55 percent of the respondents wanted less involvement, and only 25 percent wanted more. It appears that a relatively strong sentiment exists that is wary of military involvement in Central America.

As I have observed earlier, political scientists argue that diffuse citizen opinion on foreign policy is often not well represented by organized lobbies in Washington. This is what makes the activities of church lobbies so significant. It is because of their contact with religious counterparts in Central America that church leaders—particularly of the liberal Protestants, the Catholics, the peace Protestants, and some evangelicals—have gained a measure of effectiveness in opposing components of the Reagan administration's policies in the region. While the Moral Majority, Christian Voice, and other fundamentalist groups are increasingly mobilizing in support of administration policies, particularly aid to the Contras, they have not gained the access to congressional committees and members that the more liberal groups enjoy. Moreover, liberal church lobbies appear to be effective in mobilizing grassroots campaigns on foreign policy concerns through reasonably well-developed "peace networks"—mailing lists of key lay and ministerial contacts around the country, employing phone trees, and the like—most aggressively cultivated by the peace protestants (such as the Quakers, Brethren, and Mennonites), the United Church of Christ, and Catholic groups such as NETWORK and Maryknoll. Consequently, the representation provided by the more liberal church lobbies on Central America, often quite effective, has served to give greater voice to what appears to be broad American sentiment anxious about, or opposed to, Reagan administration military policies in the region.

Moreover, it appears that on this issue national mainline lobbies are not generally very far out of step with their constituents. Table 11 presents a breakdown by religious denomination of responses to the Central American question. What is notable about these findings is the lack of much difference between the denominations. Resistance to increased involvement is across the board, and the modest differences fail to show any pattern. The greatest support for increased involvement comes from the Southern Baptists, but even among this group nearly half (49 percent)

Table 11. Opinion on U.S. Involvement in Central
America, by Religious Affiliation
Percent of Respondents

	Want more	Same	Want less	
Presybterian	23	26	51	(N = 80)
Lutheran	23	19	58	(N = 104)
Episcopal	30	11	59	(N = 47)
Methodist	29	21	50	(N = 175)
Baptist	29	21	49	(N = 133)
Fundamentalist	19	18	63	(N = 134)
Southern Baptist	36	15	49	(N = 131)
Roman Catholic	22	21	56	(N = 447)
Jewish	9	36	56	(N = 45)
Born Again	29	20	51	(N = 387)
Sample	20	25	55	(N = 1541)

Source: 1984 American National Election Study.

favor less involvement. Interestingly, the least apparent support
for activist policies in the region comes from the fundamentalist
group, 63 percent of whom said they wanted less involvement,
bearing out a point I noted earlier, that there are limits to where
Religious Right leaders can take their potential followers.

Several tentative conclusions can be drawn from these findings. First, the intense lobbying by the liberal church groups,
including the U.S. Catholic Conference, against military involvement in Central America is not wholly inconsistent with member
opinion on that issue. Second, this lobbying has the additional
characteristic of apparently articulating rather broad sentiment
among the public at large, including some unexpected fundamentalist constituents. Finally, these findings provide at least
some evidence that on this issue, leaders of the Religious Right,

when they lobby for aid to the Contras and other activist military policies, may not be in tune with much of the evangelical and even fundamentalist constituency.

While other measures are needed to determine the extent to which actual *contributors* to the Moral Majority or the Christian Voice differ with their leaders on these issues, there are indications that this might be the case to some extent. In newsletters to subscribers, for example, Moral Majority leader Jerry Falwell claims that his highly visible "Fight against Communism" in Central America and South Africa has hurt fundraising efforts, meaning the organization has received less in contributions from past supporters on their mailing lists. Thus, it appears that in moving into the foreign policy arena fundamentalist leaders are going to find less unanimity among their potential constituency than on other issues.

When the arena shifts from Central America to relations with the Soviet Union, however, the American public appears somewhat more hawkish. Respondents were asked whether the United States should try to cooperate more with the Soviet Union or instead should get much tougher. Differences between denominations were not dramatic, indicating that religion is not as salient on this issue as on some domestic social issues. Table 12 presents a denominational breakdown on this issue (with the seven-point scale collapsed into three categories).

Of the denominational groupings the Baptists, Southern Baptists and fundamentalists favor a tougher policy toward the Soviet Union by a slim majority, while the Jewish, Presbyterian, and Episcopal respondents lean toward more cooperation. The rest of the groups are roughly split between more cooperation and getting tougher. These findings suggest that fundamentalist lobbies, fiercely anti-Soviet, generally do reflect the sentiment of their religious constituency. Similarly, the "liberal internationalism" of the Jewish, Presbyterian, and Episcopalian lobbies is not wholly out of sync with member sentiment, though a similar posture by the Lutheran and Methodist lobbyists may indeed be

Table 12. Opinion on U.S. Posture toward Soviet Union
Percent of Respondents

	Cooperate		Get tougher	
	1	2	3	
Presybterian	43	22	35	(N = 83)
Lutheran	34	29	37	(N = 115)
Episcopal	40	25	35	(N = 52)
Methodist	29	28	43	(N = 209)
Baptist	28	20	52	(N = 152)
Fundamentalist	29	20	51	(N = 144)
Southern Baptist	27	22	51	(N = 154)
Catholic	37	20	43	(N = 487)
Jewish	49	14	37	(N = 49)
Sample	34	22	44	(N = 1706)

Source: 1984 American National Election Study

at variance with member views. These conclusions must not be overstated, since considerable diversity of opinion exists within all groups, including Jews who tend to be polarized in their attitudes toward the Soviet Union (reflecting both the liberalism of Jews and the growing concern with treatment of Jews in Russia). Because of the lack of consensus within the broad religious categories, those lobbies that represent actual contributors may be on safer ground than those representing church denominations.

On defense spending, an issue of special concern to the peace Protestants—the Mennonites, Brethren, and Friends—but also on the agenda of most other groups, religious cleavages appear modest at best, as table 13 shows. Indeed, with the exception of the Jewish group, which alone favored reduced defense spending, the broad consensus favored about the same level of military expenditures. While Baptists, Southern Baptists, and fundamentalists were somewhat more supportive of defense spending than

Table 13. Opinion on Defense Spending,
by Religious Affiliation
Percent of Respondents

	Want more	About same	Want less	
Presbyterian	19	58	23	(N = 83)
Lutheran	25	50	25	(N = 114)
Episcopal	22	44	34	(N = 55)
Methodist	30	52	18	(N = 213)
Baptist	38	43	18	(N = 156)
Fundamentalist	36	50	14	(N = 155)
Southern Baptist	39	48	13	(N = 161)
Catholic	24	50	26	(N = 483)
Jewish	17	29	55	(N = 42)
Sample	28	49	23	(N = 1721)

Source: American National Election Study

the rest, neither liberal mainline lobbies, which consistently criticize military budgets, nor conservative fundamentalist lobbies, which support increased military spending, appear to reflect a consensus of the American public or their own constituencies, broadly defined. It is quite possible, however, that actual contributors to fundamentalist direct-mail organizations, such as the Moral Majority and Christian Voice, do favor increased military spending, just as actual contributors to NETWORK, IMPACT, and Bread for the World probably favor a decrease in spending (see later discussion of direct-mail groups).

The dearth of survey data on small "peace" churches (whose members are virtually uncounted in national samples of 2,500 respondents) prohibits us from making definitive judgments about their lobbies' representation in Washington. However, given the pacifist theological tradition of the radical Protestant Reformation, from which the Brethren, the Mennonites, and the Friends trace their roots, it is reasonable to assume that antimilitary lobbying by Washington offices reflects relatively broad sentiment. Moreover, the strategic acceptance of a freeze on military spending, as described by the Mennonite lobbyist, appears shrewd in light of national sentiment.

The strength of Jewish opposition to defense spending raises some interesting representational issues. A top lobby priority for Jewish leaders in Washington is increased military aid to Israel, a cause which may hinge on sustaining overall U.S. defense spending. Thus, it may not be strategically wise for them to advocate decreases in military spending, which members favor, because that would jeopardize their fight for aid to Israel, which members also favor. This is a case requiring a classic trustee posture— where leaders, on the basis of the environment in which they operate, must make decisions that involve strategic tradeoffs.

These three issues provide some indication of the texture of American public opinion on foreign policy questions. Other issues, particularly U.S. policy toward South Africa and nuclear weapons policy, would probably indicate that liberal lobbies are not as far out of step with their members (and even the general public) as often alleged, given media polls showing widespread support for the nuclear freeze and extensive coverage of South African strife. Moreover, we might expect to see similar lack of consensus here among the potential constituents of fundamentalist groups for highly conservative foreign policy positions.

Domestic Spending and Economic Policy

Religious lobbyists, particularly the liberal ones, have lobbied aggressively to support federal domestic spending for welfare programs and environmental quality. On many of these issues there appears not to be much, if any, religious cleavage. For example, on spending for environmental quality, an issue with

**Table 14. Opinion on Federal Spending for Food
Stamps, by Religious Affiliation**
Percent of Respondents

	Spend more	About same	Spend less	
Presbyterian	21	40	39	(N = 82)
Lutheran	10	43	47	(N = 109)
Episcopal	8	53	39	(N = 53)
Methodist	10	52	37	(N = 202)
Baptist	38	35	27	(N = 162)
Fundamentalist	30	45	25	(N = 150)
Southern Baptist	28	36	36	(N = 160)
Catholic	20	49	31	(N = 459)
Jewish	25	63	12	(N = 40)
Blacks (a)	59	31	10	(N = 193)
Sample	21	46	33	

Source: American National Election Study
(a) This racial category is included for a later discussion

wide (motherhood and apple pie) appeal, religious differences
are nonexistent. Fully 92 percent of all respondents in the 1984
ANES sample wanted the national government to continue at least
current levels of funding for environmental quality (with 36 percent wanting to spend more), and no religious denomination
deviated significantly from that preference. Hence, liberal religious lobbies, such as NETWORK, the United Church of Christ,
and most of the mainline groups, appear to have relatively solid
backing in their pro-environment lobbying—which they term
"stewardship of creation"—particularly in their attempts to beat
back administration-proposed budget cuts for environmental protection.

More controversial than environmental protection is welfare

state spending, and one of its most visible components is the 18-billion-dollar food stamp program, whose maintenance is a priority of the liberal lobbies, especially Bread for the World. Opinion on food stamp spending is a bellwether of broader attitudes on the welfare state, and as table 14 indicates, some denominational differences do appear. Two-thirds of the sample would spend the same or more on food stamps, indicating respectable public support for the welfare state at a time when voters were reelecting Ronald Reagan, welfare state critic, by a landslide. Some interesting patterns emerge from the denominational breakdown. For example, Lutherans were the most conservative denomination, with nearly half of the respondents favoring cuts in food stamp spending, a finding not so surprising to those familiar with American Lutherans' rural, Germanic-Scandinavian resistance to the idea of food without labor. The strongest support for increases in food stamp spending came from the Baptists, 38 percent of whom wanted higher spending, and the fundamentalists, slightly less than a third of whom shared that opinion. The most polarized denomination was the Southern Baptist, a major target of the Religious Right. Here we see above average sentiment for *both* increases and decreases.

If the denominational lobbyists listed here, Lutherans excepted, were to view themselves as "delegates" only, faithfully representing opinion of members, the most tenable position would be support for existing levels of food stamp spending, neither cuts nor increases. Still, there is considerable diversity of sentiment within these groups. Thus, a direct-mail group, such as Bread for the World, which specializes in hunger issues, may be able to articulate reasonably homogeneous contributor sentiment more accurately than lobbies for pluralistic denominational groups. This may also be true for the direct-mail groups on the fundamentalist Right, whose leaders attack the welfare state, at least in rhetoric if not in actual lobbying. However, in light of the reasonably strong support for food stamp spending among the Baptists, fundamentalists, and Southern Baptists, one might expect less unanimity even among contributors to the New Right groups, contributors who respond predominantly to the conservative social agenda of the national fundamentalist leaders.

What are the implications for representation? In the present political environment the collective impact of religious lobbying is to support current levels of funding for food stamps, as well as other welfare state measures. In part this is because the liberal groups have been on the defensive during the Reagan era, fighting for restoration of cuts proposed by the administration. In part, too, this is due to the fact that, despite rhetoric, the fundamentalist lobbies have not concentrated their efforts in support of the administration's budget priorities, choosing for good reasons to capitalize on member backing for their battles on abortion and school prayer.

At the individual lobby level the most instructive case is provided by the Lutheran Council, which represents the Lutheran churches from which the national survey sample was drawn.[13] In a way the relation between this national lobby and its constituency could not be a more poignant illustration of the tension between representing members and applying religious faith to political action. In resolutions passed at national conventions, the Lutheran churches that contribute to the Lutheran lobby in Washington have affirmed the "biblical imperative" of providing for the poor in America through sustained welfare state spending. Yet many Lutheran parishioners apparently would not support at least a key component of that spending. As noted in chapter 4, church leaders often view themselves as trustees of the faith, not mere agents of the opinions of church members. What is troubling about this case, and others like it, is not that the church deviates from the opinion of its members (for faith is not a matter of pluralities), but that most members are uninformed about their church's political stands and the theological basis for them. This is perhaps the most serious flaw in denominational lobbying.

It is helpful here to summarize the major findings of this analysis of opinion in the religious groups. First, cases of divergence between member views and lobby policies are issue-specific and emerge sporadically for virtually all of the groups. This happens, in part, because of the pluralism of sentiment within each of the religious groups, in contrast to the more ideologically consistent national leadership. Thus the Lutheran Council, for example, apparently diverges from its lay members on school prayer and food stamp spending, but articulates their sentiment well on aid to the Contras and environmental spending. The Moral Majority, in contrast, appears to represent well the views of fundamentalists and evangelicals on school prayer and abortion, but not as clearly on aid to the Contras and opposition to the welfare state. Second, both the emphases of religious lobbies and their effectiveness in mobilizing constituents are related to the degree of member support. Thus, while several mainline Protestant churches support abortion rights for women, it is the Episcopal church, with its strong lay support for unconditional choice, that leads the lobby effort. Similarly, while the fundamentalist groups attempt to lobby on a variety of issues, their greatest emphasis, and their greatest success in mobilizing their constituents, has been on the social issues where member backing is strongest. Third, the collective impact of religious lobbying seems to represent— reasonably well—broader public sentiment. This is a function of lobby emphases and effectiveness. Thus, while the ideological diversity at the mass level leads almost inevitably to "unrepresentative" lobbying by elite leaders, at least in the delegate sense, lack of grassroots support dilutes the impact of this "oligarchic" tendency. Effective lobbying often appears rooted in either member support or broader public sentiment. Knowing this, some leaders at least are drawn strategically to concentrate on issues where the climate is ripe, and the collective impact of these decisions among the pluralistic religious lobbies is to articulate otherwise underrepresented sentiment.

The Texture of Religious Opinion

By now it must be clear that even while religious cleavages exist on a number of issues, ideological consistency (as commonly understood)[14] does not prevail within each of the denominational groups, with the possible exception of the Jewish constituency, which appeared fairly liberal on all issues reviewed here (though more detailed studies of Jews reveal significant differences between Orthodox and Hasidic Jews and the rest). This ideological texture is illustrated in a study conducted by Kathleen Beatty and Oliver Walter,[15] which compared survey profiles of different religious groups, particularly smaller denominations, through the use of aggregated data compiled over a number of years.[16] What they found, among other things, was that theological conservatives are not necessarily conservative (especially on economic issues), nor theological liberals necessarily liberal. Indeed, some groups appeared to be simultaneously very liberal on some issues and very conservative on others. The fundamentalist Pentecostals and Jehovah's Witnesses, for example, are two of the three most conservative religious groups surveyed on abortion, sex education in the public schools, and women's role in society. However, they were simultaneously two of the three most liberal on welfare spending, with Pentecostals among the most liberal on whether government should promote equality of wealth. Jews, not surprisingly, were among the three most liberal groups on all three social issues, sharing the liberal cluster with the Episcopalians, Congregationalists, and members of the United Church of Christ. Yet many mainline Protestants apparently are more conservative on economic issues, with the Presbyterians among the most conservative on government efforts to promote equality of wealth, and Lutherans and members of the United Church of Christ among the most conservative on welfare spending.

These findings are indeed complex and in part appear to reflect idiosyncratic differences between contrasting religious traditions. Jews and Jehovah's Witnesses, for example, are the closest two groups on defense spending (both taking very liberal stances against it), while they represent the extreme poles of opinion on abortion. Seventh Day Adventists, likewise, are fairly liberal on welfare and health care spending, but very conservative on pornography. Mormons and Episcopalians are the closest two groups on opinion about crime and punishment (very conservative) but are among the farthest apart on pornography. One lesson that can be drawn, consequently, is that the relative ideological consistency at the elite level, as reflected by the lobbies in Washington, will inevitably clash with member opinion on some issues. This is particularly true of lobbies for large, diverse denominations. Consequently, direct-mail groups, groups that attempt to develop more elaborately textured lobby positions, smaller, more homogeneous denominations, and groups that employ genuinely democratic decision-making procedures to produce policy consensus, will be rooted most consistently in lay opinion.

Another factor in the seemingly idiosyncratic findings of Beatty and Walter is a class cleavage operating in church affiliation. In the NORC surveys, for example, the "churches of the dispossessed," the Pentecostals, Jehovah's Witnesses, and other fundamentalist sects—with a disproportionate lower-class and working-class membership—evince a profound social conservatism combined with a modest economic liberalism. This same pattern held for the fundamentalist category in the American National Election Study, as it did for the more affluent, but still not generally elite, Baptists and Southern Baptists. In contrast, the elite Episcopalians and Presbyterians are comparatively conservative on economic issues and liberal on social concerns. The implications for representation, as well as for future alignments in the American polity, are quite profound. I have observed that both liberal and conservative church lobbies often view their work in populist terms, as representing the voiceless, the dispossessed, the underrepresented, and the poor. Liberal lobbies, whether Catholic or Protestant, find their greatest success when they report on the homeless shelters, soup kitchens, and the work of their social service agencies with the poor and those of modest means. Conservative fundamentalists argue, in contrast, that they represent humble, working-class church people, non-elites whose conservative cultural values have been ignored by establishment ("Country Club Episcopalian") elites. There is evidence to suggest that *both* efforts represent, in some sense, the needs, values, or opinions of working-class, low-income, and minority citizens. But fundamentalist conservatives believe that they now have the means to gain the broad support of most theological conservatives, in spite of the latter's previous class-based support for liberal, New Deal Democrats, because cultural issues—prayer, abortion, pornography, sex education in the schools, secularism of elites—are increasingly salient to people threatened by rapid and, in their view, unhealthy social change. Whether or not these religious conservatives, with their embrace of free-market capitalism and supply-side economics, can represent the economic aspirations of the disinherited (many of whom are evangelical blacks and Hispanic Catholics, who combine a strong economic liberalism with a pronounced cultural conservatism), is more doubtful. But they sense in the growing concern over the effects of welfare dependency on family structures, especially in the black community, an opportunity to work economic issues into the fabric of cultural conservatism.

There is considerable evidence to suggest that on social and cultural issues the majority of blacks and possibly Hispanics in some sense *are* represented almost solely by the conservative evangelical and fundamentalist religious lobbyists. While blacks are more liberal than whites on defense, foreign policy, and economic policy (with nearly 59 percent favoring increased spending on food stamps), they appear more conservative than whites on social issues. Over half (51 percent) of all blacks in the 1984 survey would restrict abortions to cases of rape and incest, compared to 42 percent of all whites, and an overwhelming 83 percent of blacks favor school prayer, compared to 64 percent of whites.

These findings are not surprising in light of indicators of black religious commitment. Over half of all blacks say they are born again, compared to 34 percent of all whites; and 70 percent are frequent church attenders, compared to 52 percent of all whites. Moreover, black religious understanding, in certain respects, is highly orthodox. For example, 70 percent of all blacks said the Bible (all of it) is the word of God, compared to 46 percent of all whites. Indeed, out of the 201 blacks who responded to the Bible question, only 7 said that it was not either God's word or written by men inspired by God. These same patterns may exist for the Hispanic population, though here the orthodoxy is to Roman Catholicism instead of Protestant evangelicalism. A national survey of Hispanics found pronounced religious orthodoxy and social conservatism among respondents. Most notably, Hispanic Catholics were found to be more adamantly opposed to abortion than either white Catholics or the general population.[17]

This brings to a close my analysis of the links between religious advocacy and the contours of public sentiment. Clearly, there is a tremendous ideological diversity and richness of texture in the mass religious public, a diversity that is increasingly mirrored in Washington. The growing pluralism of lobby groups insures that, to an extent, they check each other, exploiting each other's weaknesses. A significant source of this pluralism has been the emergence of religiously based, direct-mail membership organizations, which play their own unique representational role, as the following discussion shows.

Representation and the Direct-Mail Groups

James Q. Wilson argues that the behavior of organizational leaders is best explained in terms of their efforts to maintain their organizations and their status in them.[18] What concerns me here is the extent to which different maintenance requirements might produce different elite-mass relations. We are confronted with two distinct organizational types: the church denomination, in which lobbying is incidental to other activities, and the direct-mail organization, in which members join for specific political expression. The significance of this newer organizational type is that it seems to be on the cutting edge of change. All religious leaders are increasingly perceiving the importance of maintaining direct contact with grassroots constituencies. Thus, understanding how the imperatives of maintaining a direct-mail constituency shape policy and influence elite-mass relations may help to predict, to a certain extent, the way in which all religious groups will evolve.

In the first type of organization, the church denomination, the lobbyists are hired by and report to church offices. Funding for the Washington operation comes indirectly from members. A small portion of collection plate contributions from lay members automatically goes to the church headquarters in New York or St. Paul, and a small portion of that then is allocated to sustain the Washington staff.[19] Thus, organizational maintenance, at least financially, is not a major concern of lobbyists for these groups.

Membership organizations are sustained, in contrast, by direct member contributions, and organizational maintenance, consequently, looms much larger in the calculations of leaders.[20] This is particularly true for the newer direct-mail organizations, such as Bread for the World, IMPACT, NETWORK, Evangelicals for Social Action, the Moral Majority, Christian Voice, and Concerned Women for America. This organizational variation most closely fits the "entrepreneurial" model outlined by interest group scholar Robert Salisbury.[21] Salisbury argued that many of the new groups in Washington were started by entrepreneurs with a particular ideological bent, who created organizations and then mined the burgeoning computerized mailing lists for contributors. The New Right groups fit this model. In each case there was an entrepreneur, Jerry Falwell of the Majority, Gary Jarmin of the Christian Voice, and Beverley LeHaye of Concerned Women for America, who mobilized sympathetic constituents through the mail. But this model also fits moderate and liberal groups as well, such as Bread for the World, which preceded the creation of the fundamentalist organizations.

What links these diverse groups, and distinguishes them from the denominational organizations, is the ease of exit. Albert Hirschman, in his classic *Exit, Voice, and Loyalty,*[22] argued that the potential for exit by organizational members constrains leaders and, consequently, potentially checks their oligarchic tendency. But some organizations are easier to leave than others. Some Lutherans, Methodists, Presbyterians, Roman Catholics, Episcopalians, and Baptists, for example, may not agree with the lobby positions of their leaders, if they are aware of those stands at all; but it is unlikely they will leave their local church, to which they may have strong emotional and friendship ties, for that reason. For the membership organizations, on other hand, especially the newer direct-mail types, exit is as easy as not sending in the annual contribution. This in part explains the perpetual motion of fundraising by entrepreneurs of the New Religious Right. They must continually mine the lists to keep the organizations afloat, and in their view this acts to insure their responsiveness to their constituency. While this is certainly true to an extent, Salisbury argues that interest group entrepreneurs retain considerable latitude in interpreting constituent needs and responding to them. Moreover, as long as they meet some minimal requirements of service to member concerns, he argues, they have the freedom to address issues of special concern to them personally (but to which members are more indifferent).

A more compelling reason why we might expect different elite-mass relations between the membership groups and the contrasting denominational organizations has to do with the nature of their base of power. The assumption underlying this analysis is that those direct-mail organizations that rely on membership mobilization as their primary base of political power operate under markedly different institutional and financial constraints than do those church denominations whose political influence is derived primarily from information, expertise, or church authority. The reason for this is simple: for direct-mail organizations fundraising and lobbying go hand in hand. The lobby's influence is dependent upon members actually taking action to write congressional representatives, and fundraising appeals are successful to the extent that contributors view the organization as representing their concerns. Consequently, both because of the ease of exit and the nature of the power base, we would expect to see less tension between lobby policy and members' views in the subscription-based organizations than in church denominations. Thus, the picture of representation I have drawn, using denominational breakdowns, probably exaggerates the extent to which leaders are out of step with members. Moreover, the fact that church denominations are increasingly moving to develop direct-mail links to lobby supporters indicates that the direct-mail groups are in fact leading the way in a broad trend toward direct constituency relations, a development which, as the following analysis indicates, could act as a restraint on the autonomous actions of denominational lobbyists.

While it is difficult to obtain clear indicators of the sentiment of members of direct-mail groups, several observations can be made about the nature of elite-mass relations in the direct-mail groups. First, it is clear that actual contributors to the membership groups receive direct information, filtered and interpreted to be sure, on the activities of their leaders. The legislative alerts and monthly newsletters emanating from organizations such as Bread for the World, NETWORK, IMPACT, Evangelicals for Social Action, Moral Majority, Christian Voice, Concerned Women for America, American Jewish Committee, American Jewish Congress, and the National Association of Evangelicals contain highly specific information on legislative issues before the Congress, the positions of the organizations on those issues, and strategic advice on targeting appeals to key committees and members. Not only is a tremendous amount of "civics education" occurring, but members do gain a relatively clear sense of what their leaders are up to. Lobbyists for all of the direct-mail groups conveyed in interviews that they receive extensive mail, both supportive and critical, on their activities. Moreover, the fact that members know *whom* to write should not be minimized in importance. Lay members of a church denomination, in contrast, even if they were to learn of their church's lobby stand on an issue, might find it difficult to know to whom or where to mail criticism or comment. It does seem clear that members of direct-mail groups have more opportunities to follow the activities of their lobbyists than lay members of a church denomination, in which lobbying is incidental to other functions.

The information gap is probably not as great in smaller denominations with a distinct theological or political tradition—such as Mennonites, Friends, Brethren, and members of the United Church of Christ. The national offices of these groups maintain mailing lists and key contact networks in proportion to the size of their denominational membership. The Mennonite Central Committee, for example, maintains a direct contact list of approximately 8,000 persons. While a mailing list of 8,000 is small by Washington standards, in proportion to the 300,000 Mennonites it is significant. Moreover, these smaller denominations often operate like direct-mail groups, depending on grassroots mobilization in targeted congressional districts to gain political access, and thus maintaining a strong incentive to spread the word about their activities. We would expect that these lay members have greater opportunities to learn of their leaders' activities in Washington than, say, members of the mainline Protestant denominations, which, though much larger, maintain proportionately much smaller lists averaging 2,000 or so subscribers. Moreover, the smaller groups tend to focus efforts on a few issues of special concern, making it easier for members to comprehend their activities. Lay members of larger denominations, in light of the propensity of these church bodies to pass resolutions on literally scores of issues, are no doubt less aware of their leaders' activities on a number of issues.

The U.S. Catholic Conference is similar in certain respects to the mainline Protestant denominations. Most Catholics have no direct link to the Washington staff and probably do not know of many of the stands taken by their lobby. But the Conference is distinct in that it operates with a much more focused agenda. Moreover, the highly publicized statements of the U.S. Catholic Bishops on abortion, nuclear arms, and the economy have probably resulted in a greater level of lay awareness than exists within the large Protestant denominations. Certainly it would be surprising if many Catholics were not aware that their church was politically active in Washington in a general sense on abortion, aid to parochial schools, and even perhaps on nuclear weapons issues. It is less likely, however, that Catholics are aware of many specifics of the stances taken, such as opposition to the MX missile and work against the employer-sanctions provision of the Simpson-Mazzoli Immigration Reform bill. So an information gap likely exists here as well.

To take the two poles of Protestantism—conservative evangelical or fundamentalist versus mainline liberal—one is presented with a sharp contrast in degree of access to information. In part because evangelical and fundamentalist theology eschews hierarchy and lends itself to proliferation of independent churches, and in part due to past reluctance of fundamentalist bodies to engage in politics, conservative Christians are represented primarily by direct-mail groups, from the National Association of Evangelicals (which has a denominational membership as well, but maintains a relatively large list of individual members) to the big fundamentalist three—the Moral Majority, Christian Voice, and the Concerned Women for America. These groups collectively reach several million constituents directly, and probably several million more through affiliation with the broadcasting network of Christian radio stations and television programs. It would seem, thus, that these Protestants have a clearer sense of what their spokespersons are up to than members of the mainline denominations. Leaders of these direct-mail groups argue that this acts to insure their responsiveness to their constituency, in contrast to their mainline adversaries.

Clearly contributors to both liberal and conservative direct-mail organizations are more aware of their leaders' activities, as a group, than lay members of church denominations. Moreover, leaders of direct-mail groups are more dependent upon the response of their members to gain political access than are their denominational counterparts. Church denominations may trade on their credibility as representatives of church bodies or on their access to useful information. The direct-mail groups, on the other hand, depend almost solely on grassroots mobilization, and the electoral threat it implies, as their means of gaining access to the levers of power. Lobby leaders for the (liberal) Bread for the World[23] and the (conservative) Christian Voice[24] echoed an identical theme: that they find out quickly what issues are "hot buttons" for their members, resulting in significant letter generation to members of Congress. To ignore these hot buttons, they implied, is to risk both reduced financial and political support.

The task of maintaining a direct-contact constituency inevitably shapes policy. This is illustrated by a contrast between two liberal lobbies, Bread for the World and the National Council of Churches. James Hamilton of the NCC noted that his organization stresses underlying "structural" analyses of systems that, it is alleged, oppress the poor, women, minorities, and third world people.[25] Stephen Coats, lobby director for Bread for the World, in contrast, observed that his organization's members relate to more straightforward, concrete policy initiatives. This, he noted, is what distinguishes his organization from the NCC: "The National Council of Churches criticizes Bread for the World for not dealing with 'structural, systemic' problems . . . we're not structural enough for the NCC."[26] Coats linked this tension directly to the imperatives of maintaining a grassroots network: that is, lobbying on issues of keen interest to members (the "hot buttons"), avoiding divisive ideological issues, and working to gain at least partial, incremental victories to reward members for their efforts.

It is not surprising, in light of evidence presented here, that the "peace networks" of the Protestant denominations are the most well developed of all their direct contact efforts. As we saw in the discussion of foreign policy, there clearly is a constituency concerned enough to respond to appeals against nuclear weapons, Central American military involvement, and the like, and the churches are now the key mobilizers of that constituency.

The Moral Majority may present a special case in this analysis. It is so large, and its energetic leader maintains such strong influence over policy, that it may not fit categories easily. Falwell has moved beyond his initial base of support, concern for traditional values and cultural conservatism—on which he clearly was able to mobilize tremendous support—to broader issues, particularly foreign policy. It seems that the effort to recast the Moral Majority into the Liberty Federation was undertaken not so much in response to a constituency as in an attempt to create a new one. Whether this will succeed remains to be seen. Certainly there is evidence that he will meet resistance among some fundamentalists. From the standpoint of representation, however, the positive aspect to this reorganization is its honesty. Contributors knew generally what they were getting by donating to the old Moral Majority. Now that Falwell, ever the entrepreneur, has moved into the foreign policy arena, apparently straining his original base of support, a recast organization has emerged. Contributors, once again, should know what they are getting by sending their checks to the newly formed Liberty Federation.

The imperatives of grassroots mobilization, which dominate the direct-mail groups, and which are increasingly coming to influence the denominational groups as well, signal an important trend in the interest group system. This is, it must be emphasized, not solely a development of the Religious Right. Indeed, the pioneering direct-mail membership group is the Friends Committee on National Legislation, over forty years old, which has helped other liberal groups get started. IMPACT, the grass-roots coalitional effort of liberal Protestants and Jews, preceded the creation of the Moral Majority by nearly a decade. Moreover, all of the denominational groups are attempting to expand their direct mobilizable constituencies, because they perceive such expansion to be an essential component of their other lobby strategies. While it is true that, outside perhaps of the Jewish groups, the groups of the Religious Right have been the most sophisticated and successful in mobilizing their constituents, the trend is for all groups to move in that direction. Thus the constraints on autonomous policy-making, irrespective of member sentiment, will be felt increasingly by groups that in the past enjoyed the luxury of a more insulated lobby environment.

Summary: Representation and the Broader Picture

But perhaps it is a mistake to approach political representation too directly from the various individual-representation analogies—agent and trustee. Perhaps that approach, like descriptive or symbolic representation, leads us to expect or demand features in the representative relationship which are not there and need not be there. Perhaps when we conventionally speak of political representation, representative government, and the like, we do not mean or require that the representative stand in the kind of one-to-one, person-to-person relationship to his constituency or to each constituent in which a private representative stands to his principal. Perhaps when we call a governmental body or system "representative," we are saying something broader and more general about the way in which it operates as an institutionalized arrangement. And perhaps even the representing done by an individual legislator must be

> seen in such a context, as embodied in a whole political
> system.[27]
>   —Hanna Pitkin

> Even with the increase in citizen groups, the universe
> of lobbying organizations favors business, labor, and the
> professions, at the expense of the poor, minorities, and
> diffuse, hard to organize constituencies . . . thus both
> the decline of parties and the proliferation of interest
> groups have worked to the advantage of those already
> well represented in the political process.[28]
>   —Jeffrey Berry

What does the study of religious political mobilization and lobbying tell us about the representativeness of the American polity? As Pitkin reminds us, the ultimate measure of representativeness is not whether *some* group leaders stray from their constituents on *some* issues, for that seems inevitable in modern, complex government. Rather, the issue is their interactive and collective impact on the system as a whole: Representation is primarily a public, institutional arrangement involving many people and groups and operating in the complex ways of large-scale social arrangements. What makes it representation is not any single action by any one participant but the overall structure and functioning of the system, the patterns emerging from the multiple activities of many people.[29]

While difficult to measure precisely, the evidence in this study suggests that the interactive, collective activities of religious lobbyists play an important role in enhancing the representativeness of the American polity. This is not to suggest that Jeffrey Berry's description of the pressure system is incorrect, for it is substantially correct for most lobbies in Washington. What I would argue, rather, is that when we include religious organizations in our analysis, the system indeed appears more representative. Thus, Berry's assertion that the advocacy explosion has worked to the advantage of those already well represented, at the expense of the poor, minorities, and diffuse, hard-to-organize constituencies, is not wholly accurate. This latter conclusion, drawn in effect from the entirety of this study, is illustrated by a brief look at three dimensions of representation: issues, values, and people.

Religious lobbyists are diverse—ideologically, theologically, and organizationally—and they have represented sentiment on a variety of issues of broad public concern. For example, broad, but diffuse foreign policy opinion would not be articulated as clearly without the activities of liberal religious lobbyists who, because of their links with members around the world, enjoy special access in the Congress. Also, because liberal religious lobbyists represent churches whose ministry includes the operation of charitable agencies, they have been able to represent, in some sense, the needs of poor people who are the beneficiaries of their work. Moreover, issues such as world and domestic hunger, international trade and aid policies, and so forth, have gained greater attention of legislators because there is a mobilizable grassroots constituency out there concerned with something other than its own direct economic benefit. Conservative groups, too, have articulated broad public concerns, such as opposition to the increasingly violent pornography industry, which were spurned or simply ignored by other religious and secular lobbies. Clearly, issues of concern to many people are being given partial voice by religiously motivated lobbies in Washington.

Values, as distinct from issues, imply deeply interwoven concerns, or, to put it phenomenologically, life worlds. It is here more than anywhere else that the activities of evangelicals and fundamentalists have served to articulate previously underrepresented concerns. The American people are overwhelmingly and, to many in the academy, peculiarly religious. Moreover, religious practice seems to be stronger among the lower and working classes than the upper classes, and, as we have seen, blacks appear more religiously inclined than whites as a group. Beyond this, most Americans are rather orthodox in their religious beliefs, and this orthodoxy intensifies with less elite constituencies. In demanding school prayer (and in mobilizing massively for it), fundamentalists not only articulated general public opinion on an issue but were expressing as well a frustration felt by many over what seemed to be hostility to their faith in public schools, and a lack of a recognition of their life experience on television, in the elite press, and in the academy. While it is certainly accurate to say that public opinion surveys consistently show that the majority of Americans favor some form of prayer in the public schools, it is also probably accurate to say that what is also being expressed is a set of values. It seems incomprehensible to most Americans, and indeed would have seemed incomprehensible to most American elites a hundred years ago, that, for example, the Ten Commandments cannot be posted in a public school, or that books on Christianity would be excluded from public libraries (and even historical accounts of religion largely expunged from secondary texts),[30] or that voluntary Bible reading by students in school would be viewed with alarm. It took, it seems, very angry fundamentalists and slightly less angry evangelicals to articulate before the Congress a set of values that a large number of Americans shared. Moreover, it appears, ironically, that only the conservative Christian groups have articulated *this* aspect of black American sentiment. While blacks favor school prayer and other public observance of religious experience far more than whites, this sentiment has been ignored by liberal groups and often by many black leaders.

Related to religious orthodoxy and its lack of elite representation is the issue of cultural conservatism, which, we might say, took a beating in the 1960s and 1970s, decades of sexual liberation, rising divorce rates, teenage pregnancies, drug abuse, violent pornography, and liberal abortion laws. Here, too, religious traditionalists, both Catholic and Protestant, seem to have articulated broad anxiety about these stresses on the family, children, and society, while secular elites—both of the conservative, free market variety and of the liberal, social welfare variety—were preoccupied with other matters. The mass base of the churches enabled religious conservatives to represent the values of cultural conservatism shared in varying degrees by many

Americans. From a reading of interest groups scholars, it is not surprising that an elite-based interest group system underrepresents values of non-elite constituencies. What is significant is that when churches are the interest groups, they have access to non-elite mass constituencies and, by virtue of theology or grassroots contacts, incentives to be responsive.

Quite distinct from the issues and values articulated by religious lobbyists are the people they bring into the system. Since churches are the premier volunteer organization in the nation, and indeed, in light of evidence presented by critics of the "pressure system" that most Americans do not in fact belong to an interest group, the collective mobilization efforts of religious leaders—Jewish, liberal Protestant, peace Protestant, Catholic, evangelical, and fundamentalist—seem particularly important. And while this may be particularly true of the Protestant conservatives, it appears to be the case for the other groups as well. Bread for the World, for example, conducted a survey of its own members, and found that for a majority of them BFW membership was their first entrance into the political system, outside of voting. Finding points of access is not easy for many, and as more church bodies respond to the imperatives of grassroots mobilization, it would not be unlikely that previously dormant citizens, whether liberal, conservative, or of more complex ideology, may find channels for political participation through church-related structures. In this sense, more Americans would be following the pattern set over two decades ago by the black church, which continues to serve as the main avenue for black political participation.

What is particularly intriguing about the efforts of evangelical and especially fundamentalist leaders is that they have mobilized a constituency that historically eschewed politics. There is evidence to suggest that many previously marginalized citizens are being integrated more fully into the American polity by the efforts of the Christian conservative leaders. With participation comes political education and, importantly, an awareness of the written and unwritten rules of the game. What emerges in the millions of pieces of mail generated by the religious groups is, in effect, a massive civics lesson in American politics. Even while the rhetoric remains militant, angry, and filled with dire warnings of doom (which after all are the standard stuff of all direct-mail solicitations, as any reader of advocacy mail can attest), there is another, more practical and strategic dimension. Members are told how to write their congressional representative ("be respectful, make your case clearly, put it in your own words, ask for his or her support, don't threaten," etc.). They are educated in the intricacies of the congressional process and are told that compromise and incremental strategies win the day in the long run. Subtly, but profoundly, they are told that the system can work for them, but that they may not be able to win all they want, for that is the nature of liberal pluralist democracy, the "American Way."

In this sense, then, those who fear most the country cousins— those barefoot fundamentalist populists, with their "paranoia," their evangelical fervor, their emotional militancy—should welcome their entrance into the mainstream of American politics and society. For the congressional milieu, in particular, exercises a profound influence on those who attempt to shape public policy. It is what radicals in the 1960s called co-optation and what some fundamentalists, such as the Reverend Bob Jones, fear will happen as orthodox Christians become more overtly political. Constituencies mobilized by national leaders do have an influence on the Congress, but the congressional milieu also has its influence on their leaders, as we see in the analysis of church-state issues in the next chapter.

While this chapter has illustrated the instances in which religious leaders appear to stray from the views of their lay constituents—whether to represent God's will, world constituencies, or their own opinions—the oligarchic tendency, as I have shown, is checked by the nature of grassroots mobilization. The ability to mobilize support in the field, in congressional districts, is increasingly perceived as essential to good lobbying. This theme was stressed by congressional staff members as well as lobbyists. As Dave Connolly of the U.S. Catholic Conference summarized it: "Tell your students this, that lobbying is about grassroots. I've seen so many times when the big money boys are all there, and the congressman comes in with a letter from a constituent, and that prevails. You need to represent constituents."[31] To some extent the efforts of liberal lobbyists to develop grassroots networks is a response to criticism that they do not represent their lay members. But it also appears to be a response to the congressional environment itself.

Political effectiveness, in the end, determines whether or not "oligarchic" leadership presents an insuperable obstacle to representation. As I have argued, not only do religious lobbyists reflect a tremendous phenomenological pluralism but it appears that they are most effective when their positions reflect strong member (and often broader public) sentiment. It is not surprising, in this light, that the "peace networks" of the liberal church denominations are their most highly developed direct contact systems. Clearly there is a constituency that will respond to foreign and military issues. In contrast, the lack of effective liberal religious mobilization on other issues reflects a dearth of lay interest or support. While evidence of church leaders out of step with lay members will abound, given the propensity of some churches to adopt resolutions on scores of issues, this oligarchic tendency looks less worrisome, in terms of representation theory, when actual lobby effectiveness is factored into the analysis. For the religious groups, in general, "representative" lobbying appears far more effective than "oligarchic" lobbying.

Representation, as Pitkin observes, involves a "making present" in some sense of what is nevertheless literally not present. Religious lobbyists present a fascinating case for the study of representation. They make present before the Congress diverse interests, values, institutions, and people, including otherwise underrepresented citizens and foreign constituents. "We are," as

William O. Douglas once observed, "a religious people." One cannot understand American politics, in my view, without understanding the religious dimension. What emerges from this analysis of representation and the religious lobbies is the conclusion that, in light of the nature of modern American political institutions, the system is indeed more representative *because* "we" are religious.

6 Religious Lobbies and Congressional Policy-Making on Church-State Relations

Battles over the definition of church-state relations in America, historically the domain of the courts, have moved in recent years to the Congress, particularly with the national mobilization efforts of fundamentalist and evangelical Christians, who seek to reverse, in their view, the "secularizing" impact of Supreme Court decisions in the past two decades. Since a relatively small band of religious and civil libertarian groups actively engage the courts—in contrast to the wide spectrum of groups that lobby the Congress—the policy-making process has shifted from what Sorauf termed the "minoritarian politics"[1] of the courts to the majoritarian or consensus-seeking politics of the Congress.

What has been the impact of this shift? How has the Congress accommodated its growingly assertive religious constituencies? Have the lobby efforts of religious groups produced tangible policy outcomes? This chapter will analyze the impact of religious lobbying on congressional attempts to define national policy with respect to religious observance in the schools, an issue that has dominated the legislative church-state agenda. The specific focus is the Equal Access Act of 1984, PL 98-377, which is both an important piece of legislative policy-making on church-state relations and an illuminating example of the interplay of diverse religious interests in the congressional milieu. The legislation is significant in part because, in contrast to various school prayer proposals, it produced a consensus for passage. It is also instructive because it engaged a broad spectrum of lobbyists representing Jewish, mainline Protestant, Roman Catholic, and Christian evangelical and fundamentalist constituencies. What I found is that religious lobbyists were indeed influential, but that this impact was a result of a complex and interactive set of circumstances that converged to produce a consensus. These circumstances included: 1) the massive mobilization efforts of fundamentalists on behalf of the president's unsuccessful school prayer amendment, 2) the fracturing of the anti-pietist religious alliance of school prayer opponents, and 3) the emergence of a network of moderate evangelical lobbyists and members of Congress, who drafted the bill, forged the coalition, and negotiated with opponents over clarifying language after passage. These findings corroborate the central thesis of this study: that religious lobbies, collectively, play an important representational role in articulating widely held values before the Congress.

Equal Access—Background and Legislative History

The Equal Access Act, Title VIII of Public Law 98-377, signed into law by President Reagan on August 11, 1984, is a remarkably short and straightforward piece of legislation, consuming less than two pages of public record. Its impact on the practice of school district officials across the country, however, could be considerable. The Act stipulates that it is illegal for a school district that grants the use of school facilities to voluntary extracurricular student groups before or after school to deny the same use to student-initiated groups on the basis of "religious, political, philosophical, or other content of the speech at such meetings." While the final language of the Act included political and philosophical speech, added as a concession to critics, the intent of the legislation was clear from the start. As the House Committee report summarized it:

The Equal Access Act seeks to clarify federal policy
with respect to a question that has been troubling
school administrators for some time: how to protect students' rights to free speech, if the speech is religious in
nature, without violating the Establishment clause of
the First Amendment.[2]

The Courts and Student Religion

As the above would indicate, the legislation is an outgrowth
of the increasingly complex and often confused tangle of court
interpretations—or school district interpretations of court interpretations—on the proper place of religious expression by students in public schools. To the principal architects of the equal
access concept, such as the Baptist Joint Committee and the
Christian Legal Society, the problem is not so much Supreme
Court decisions as it is the ignorance of school officials, acting
out of fear that any religious activity, however voluntary or student initiated, could be challenged in the courts, necessitating
payment of costly legal fees. This situation, in the view of proponents, is exacerbated by the inconsistency in some lower federal
court decisions. Notably onerous, in their view, was *Brandon v.
Board of Education of Guilderland Central Schools*,[3] in which
the Court of Appeals affirmed the action of a principal who denied a request by a group of students to meet before school
in a classroom for discussion and prayer. Particularly incendi-
ary to evangelicals was the language used by the court, which
declared that such practices were "too dangerous to permit," a
phrase that has come to symbolize, for them, the hostility of some
elites toward religion, as well as an increasingly "warped" interpretation of the establishment clause. While later court cases
seemed to reverse *Brandon*, confusion has continued. For example, the Supreme Court decided in *Widmar v. Vincent*[4] that
colleges could not discriminate on the basis of religion in providing space to noncurriculum-related student groups, but left the
question of secondary schools in doubt. The Christian Legal Society, which brought the *Widmar* case before the courts, moved

into the legislative arena because it felt that definitive clarification would not come from the courts. The House committee agreed and quoted the CLS in its committee report:

> The common thread running through virtually all of these incidents reported to CLS is that student-initiated and student-run meetings with religious content have been forbidden the right to meet even though other groups of students are permitted to meet for a host of other extracurricular topics. In all but a few instances school administrators would gladly allow meetings with religious content but fear litigation from groups who contend that religious expression has no place on our public school campuses.[5]

Congressional testimony and press reports during the debate were replete with "horror stories" of questionable actions by school officials. A grade-school girl distributes valentines with tiny crosses on them, only to have them confiscated by the principal. Students are told not to read their Bibles together in the cafeteria during lunch. The chilling effect on religious freedom of overbroad interpretations of the establishment clause, one lobbyist argued, must be redressed by the Congress. To back that claim, Patrick Monaghan, general counsel for the Catholic League for Religious and Civil Rights, in testimony before a House subcommittee, recounted this story:

> A young girl, an emigrant to this country, who is legally blind, got on a schoolbus and on that schoolbus, while proceeding to school, she prayed—she prayed a rosary sitting on the bus. Her parents received a two or three-page letter from the school board's attorney telling her that if she continued to conduct herself thus, that she would be subject to suit, that she would be subject to expulsion and that the first amendment to the Constitution prohibited that.[6]

While diverse religious lobbies made their case before congressional committees, testifying poignantly of experiences of religious persecution by overzealous secular educators, it took the mobilization efforts of fundamentalist groups to spark congressional action.

School Prayer Sets the Stage

To understand the appeal of the equal access concept it is necessary to comprehend the congressional environment at the time of committee deliberations. Early in 1984 the second session of the 98th Congress found itself engulfed in the controversy over school prayer. As the Senate began debating the several proposals to "return prayer to the schools," fundamentalist Christian groups flexed their lobbying muscles and flooded the Hill with mail and phone calls. The Moral Majority, Christian Voice, and Concerned Women for America mobilized their constituencies, while the network of TV and radio evangelicals called the faithful to political action. The results were dramatic: Texas Senator Lloyd Bentsen's office received over 1,500 calls in one day, virtually all of them urging him to support the president's proposed constitutional amendment on school prayer. California Senator Pete Wilson received 2,000 calls in the last two weeks of February, compared to 5,400 in all of 1983, as religious television stations flashed his name and number on the screen.[7] New phone lines were installed, millions of pieces of mail landed on the Capitol steps, vigils where held, famous athletes came to testify, and an exasperated Senator John Danforth, Republican from Missouri and Episcopal priest, was reported to comment, "With all the calls and the mail we're receiving you would think this is the most important issue facing the country . . . but I tell people back home, 'Look, you didn't elect a pastor, you elected a Senator.'"[8]

The fundamentalist groups had two major resources in their battle: 1) the ability to reach millions of aroused constituents through direct mail and electronic media, and 2) survey evidence of broad American public support for organized prayer in the public schools, with only Jewish respondents clearly opposed.

Indeed, overwhelming support for school prayer cuts across most denominational, theological, income, and racial categories, enabling orthodox Christians to argue credibly that on this issue they articulate the sentiment of a majority of Americans, rich and poor, black and white.[9]

But fundamentalists faced major obstacles as well. As a constitutional amendment, school prayer needed support by two-thirds of the members of Congress, some of whom, while sympathetic, were chary of breaches in "the wall of separation." Moreover, effective and articulate opposition was mounted early by such secular groups as the American Civil Liberties Union and the National Education Association. Most important, perhaps, was that most of the national religious lobbies, including the Jewish, the mainline Protestant, and a number of evangelical groups, worked against the president's prayer proposal. Early in 1984 President Reagan sent a letter to religious leaders affirming his support for a constitutional amendment to restore "public prayer in our schools." Protestant and Jewish leaders responded with a letter of their own, sent to the White House and members of Congress, affirming their opposition to such an amendment. The letter was signed by four Jewish groups—the American Jewish Committee, the American Jewish Congress, B'nai B'rith, and the Union of American Hebrew Congregations—and by ten Protestant groups—the American Baptist Churches, the Baptist Joint Committee, the Church of the Brethren, the General Council of Seventh Day Adventists, the Episcopal Church, the Lutheran Council, the National Council of Churches, the Presbyterian Church, the United Church of Christ, and the United Methodist Church. Religious opponents also used the media. Led by the Reverend Charles Bergstrom of the Lutheran Council, fourteen religious leaders, all members of the clergy, staged a press conference on the Capitol steps to state their reasons for opposing the prayer amendment.[10] Thus aided, congressional opponents, led by Senator Lowell Weicker, Jr., Republican from Connecticut, were able to prevail upon forty-four senators to vote against the measure on March 20, 1984. It thus fell eleven votes short of the two-thirds needed for passage.[11]

For members of Congress, as well as for some religious opponents of school prayer, this defeat placed them in the vulnerable position of having to explain the lack of elite responsiveness to a large and newly aroused constituency. Thus the stage was set for favorable consideration of a more palatable alternative to school prayer.

The Equal Access Battle

The passage of the Equal Access Act was graced with all the intricacies of legislative sausagemaking, elaborate parliamentary maneuvering, and even human drama, as two key actors, Representative Carl Perkins, chair of the House Committee on Education and Labor, and John Baker, counsel for the Baptist Joint Committee on Public Affairs, died shortly after the legislation was signed into law. Indeed, the legislative battle is a marvelous illustration of how the Congress attempts to accommodate simultaneously groups with conflicting values and interests. The following legislative history illustrates well the recent influence of key religious constituencies on the Congress.

Several versions of the equal access concept were considered by the Congress. One version, SR 815, introduced by Oregon Republican Senator Mark Hatfield in 1983, specified only secondary schools under its coverage. A second bill, introduced by Senator Jeremiah Denton, a Republican from Alabama with ties to the Religious Right,[12] was broader in scope and included elementary schools as well, a provision that critics charged strained the nature of "voluntary, student-initiated" practice. Denton's proposal, S. 1059, was reported out of the Senate Judiciary Commmttee, chaired by Strom Thurmond, Republican from South Carolina, on February 22, 1984. No action was taken in the Senate because the school prayer debate was dominating business at that time. In the House, a proposal similar to Denton's had been introduced by Trent Lott, Republican from Mississippi, and extensive hearings on HR 2732 were held by the Subcommittee on Elementary, Secondary, and Vocational Education of the Committee on Education and Labor, both chaired at that time by Representative Carl Perkins, Democrat from Kentucky and ardent supporter of the equal access concept.

The fate of the Lott proposal in the House is instructive. While supporters and opponents mounted their arguments before the committee, it was the Baptist Joint Committee on Public Affairs, a key architect of the equal access concept, that played the decisive role. At the end of the hearings the Baptist Joint Committee submitted written testimony that affirmed its support for the equal access concept, then spelled out its objections to the Lott proposal, and concluded with this:

> After careful consideration of the bill and our reservations about it, it seems to us unlikely that HR 2732 can or will be amended in such a way that the Baptist Joint Committee on Public Affairs could support it. We can and will support an equal access bill which incorporates the provisions of S. 815, as amended, which was introduced in the Senate by Mr. Hatfield. If this subcommittee sees fit to report out an equal access bill, we urge this subcommittee to consider a House bill which corresponds to S. 815.[13]

Opposition by the Baptist Joint Committee effectively eliminated the Lott bill from consideration, and it signaled to the committee what would be acceptable. A companion proposal to Hatfield's, HR 4996, was introduced early in the next session by Don Bonker, Democrat from Washington, and was referred to Perkins's committee, where it moved swiftly to passage.

On April 5, 1984, the House Committee on Education and Labor reported out HR 5345, a clean bill incorporating amendments added to the earlier Bonker proposal, by a lopsided vote of 30-3. The bill was cosponsored by Bonker and Perkins. Only two weeks prior the Senate had rejected the school prayer amendment, setting the stage for House action on equal access. In contrast to school prayer, which was backed solely by the fundamentalists, the equal access legislation enjoyed support by a broad range of religious lobbies, including the fundamentalists (Moral Majority, Christian Voice, Concerned Women for America), the evangelicals (National Association of Evangelicals, Christian Legal Society, the Baptist Joint Committee, and the General Conference of the Seventh Day Adventists), the Catholic Conference, and several liberal Protestant bodies (including the National Council of Churches, and the national Presbyterian, Episcopal, and Quaker lobbies). In addition to this, key religious lobbies were able to mobilize tremendous grassroots support. Forest Montgomery of the NAE and Sam Ericsson of the CLS appeared on Christian radio and television programs to encourage people to contact their congressional representatives. The most effective outside pressure came from James Dobson's popular evangelical radio show, "Focus on The Family." According to one legislative aide:

> Dobson had Sam Ericsson on the show, which aired over a period of two weeks. This really got the phones ringing. Our phones rang off the hook for a two-week period, and it was more intense than school prayer, which was extended over a longer period.[14]

In spite of this formidable support, however, opposition was effectively mounted by Representative Don Edwards, Democrat from California and chair of the House Judiciary Subcommittee on Civil and Constitutional Rights. Spurred on by Jewish groups extremely concerned about the impact of the legislation on the public school environment, Edwards charged the bill was a backdoor school prayer bill and an opportunity for fringe groups to proselytize and harass school students. Aiding the opposition was the *Washington Post*, which ran no less than six editorials during the House and Senate deliberations, deriding the proposal as "Son of School Prayer."[15]

The bill also faced major parliamentary obstacles. The architects of the proposal, particularly the Baptist Joint Committee and the Christian Legal Society, felt that a closed rule, limiting debate and barring amendments, would be essential to preserve the integrity of the bill and its careful language from ill-conceived school prayer amendments, which would fracture their delicate coalition. The members of the rules committee, chaired by Claude Pepper, Democrat from Florida, however, were hostile to the proposal, and Perkins could not be guaranteed positive action by the committee. As Perkins himself put it, "It would take an act of God to get a rule."[16] Not wanting to rely completely on divine providence, Perkins pushed instead for a quick vote on the "suspension" calendar, a procedure which, while requiring a two-thirds vote, would serve as a substitute for a closed rule. The parliamentary tangle that ensued is instructive. Its lesson for religious lobbyists, especially newer ones, is that mere majority support for a bill may not be enough, given the nature of Congress and the divisiveness of church-state issues. Edwards appealed to Speaker O'Neill to delay the vote on the bill, saying, "The Democratic Party should not become involved in the already heavy politization of the issue of religion in the schools."[17] After this was granted, Edwards then rounded up signatures of eighty Democrats requesting a party caucus. This delayed the vote for a second time. Perkins finally got the measure to the floor for a vote on May 15, but Edward's delaying tactics had their intended effect of giving him time to mobilize opposition. On May 15, 1984, the vote was taken on HR 5345 and the tally, 270-151, fell 11 votes short of the two-thirds needed for passage.

This defeat appeared, for a time, to end chances for the legislation in 1984, but unexpected Senate action revived the concept. Key religious supporters worked with the American Civil Liberties Union, which had opposed the House version, to produce compromise language for a Senate equal access bill. James Dunn, Director of the Baptist Joint Committee, described the process in this way:

The final legislation was shaped by our branches, the ACLU and the Christian Legal Society. Other important actors were the National Council of Churches and the National Association of Evangelicals. We had dozens of meetings . . . and John Baker, our lawyer, chaired the meetings. We hung together. The ACLU participated on the compromise and agreed not to oppose, even though they had reservations.[18]

The compromise equal access language, which included reference only to secondary schools and specified under its protection "political and philosophical" as well as religious content (a provision recommended by Harvard law professor Lawrence Tribe, in House testimony),[19] was introduced on June 6 by Senators Mark Hatfield and Jeremiah Denton as an amendment to the popular math-science bill, S 1285, which was being considered on the floor of the Senate. Hatfield negotiated with opponents, particularly with Senator Lowell Weicker, who had threatened to filibuster against the measure, and agreed to amend the legislation to limit coverage to time before and after school and remain "silent" about activity periods.[20] This broke the log-jam, and after three weeks of debate the Senate passed the amended version of the access plan by a vote of 88-11 on June 27.

Senate passage appeared to assure success because Carl Perkins, as chair of Education and Labor, would sit on the conference committee on the math-science bill, which had already passed the House in 1983. But since the Senate bill included a judicial remedy, Representative Edwards was able to convince House Speaker O'Neill, who opposed the legislation, to deny a routine request by Perkins to go to conference. Instead, O'Neill sent the Senate bill's access provisions back to both Perkins's committee and Edwards's committee, where it would presumably die. Perkins was outraged by this and decided to bring the measure to the floor under a rarely used and obscure process known as "Calendar Wednesday," which allows committee chairs to bypass the House leadership and bring to the floor any bill that has been reported by their committees.[21] Since such a provision avoids the controls House leadership have over the flow of legislation,[22] neither Edwards nor O'Neill wanted to see it revived or popularized, and they agreed to allow the access legislation to be brought to the floor of the House under suspension of the rules.[23] Since the amended legislation was even less controversial than the earlier Bonker bill, it was passed by a wide margin of 337–77 on July 25, 1984. One week and a day after passage, Congressman Perkins died. Perkins was a particularly powerful proponent of the legislation. A New Deal Democrat and champion of much of the liberal social welfare legislation of the 1960s, Perkins had strong liberal credentials, which aided him in the battle. Yet Perkins was also a theologically conservative Baptist who believed that schools had misapplied the Supreme Court's decisions to imply that religion does not have a legitimate role in public education.[24] He was strongly motivated, able, and successful in his final legislative act.

Implementation Guidelines

Concerns about implementation surfaced quickly after passage of the legislation. As Senator Hatfield remarked, "My office (and I am sure the offices of my colleagues) have been flooded with requests for the proper interpretation of the language of the act, and some direction for local school officials."[25] Representative Bonker echoed this: "Already, my office has been contacted by numerous school officials and other interested parties concerning specific features of the act."[26] Normally, House and Senate committee reports, or agency rules drafted in accordance with legislative intent, provide whatever guidance is available for implementation of new law. But as Bonker noted, "There is no congressional report for the final version of the legislation, which was added as an amendment to the Emergency Math/Science Education Act."[27]

The need for guidelines was met, not by the Congress, but by the principal lobbyists involved, pro and con. If there ever was a clearer description of Lindblom's partisan mutual adjustment process, it would be hard to find. A working group was formed that included both the original architects and the most active opponents of the access law. Chaired by John Baker of the Baptist Joint Committee,[28] drafters of the guidelines included the following:

> American Association of School Administrators
> American Civil Liberties Union
> Americans for Democratic Action
> American Jewish Congress
> Baptist Joint Committee
> Christian Legal Society
> General Conference of Seventh Day Adventists
> National Association of Evangelicals
> National Education Association[29]

The guidelines produced by this group were read into the *Congressional Record* by Hatfield in the Senate on October 12, 1984, and Bonker in the House on October 11, 1984. While they cautioned that the guidelines did not reflect the "official" position of the U.S. Government, the message was clear: the guidelines hammered out by the partisans would substitute for congressional intent. For example, the *Equal Access Guidelines* included the names, addresses and phone numbers of group leaders who were available for advice. Moreover, the guidelines were mailed to all school districts in the country and to many of the teachers.

Representatives and senators seemed genuinely appreciative (or relieved) that the principal proponents and opponents were able to agree on clarifying definitions and implementation guidelines. Representative Goodling, who with Bonker read the guidelines into the House record, observed:

> I am pleased to place in the RECORD . . . guide-
> lines for implementing the Equal Access Act that were
> drafted jointly by leading proponents and opponents
> of the law. These groups should be commended for
> putting their differences behind them once the law

passed and working together to provide an agreed upon explanation of the act for school administrators. The text of these guidelines is entirely the product of these outside groups—not the congressional drafters of this act. We did, however, take the liberty of deleting a few misplaced statutory citations.[30]

Both Hatfield and Bonker likewise commended the groups, and Hatfield clearly felt the guidelines would aid in implementation:

I do not want to suggest that all of these groups endorse the Equal Access Act; indeed some still have serious reservations. However, all of these groups feel some direction to local officials is necessary to assure proper implementation of the legislation. No one wants any misconceptions of the legislation. Mr. President, I want to thank all the groups that have participated in the development of these guidelines, and those groups who are in general agreement with their focus, for showing the wisdom and foresight to create this useful tool for local school officials.[31]

It is instructive that neither the fundamentalist organizations nor the mainline Protestant denominations were involved in the actual writing of the document, although the National Council of Churches signed onto it afterwards. Thus the mutual adjustment process was carried on between the evangelical supporters of equal access and their Jewish, civil liberties, and education association opponents. By virtue of their lobbying approach and broad credibility, the evangelical organizations were able to meet face-to-face with those quite hostile to the legislation, and actually write a joint document to which all could accede. It is difficult to imagine leaders of the Moral Majority similarly working with the ACLU, the NEA and the American Jewish Congress. Thus, fortuitous strategic circumstances enabled evangelical organizations to represent the sentiment of the fundamentalists in a forum where the latter themselves could not. The role of personality also appears salient in this case. Interviews with lobbyists and congressional aides confirmed that John Baker of the Baptist Joint

Committee was a critical actor. Baker had worked previously with ACLU lobbyist Barry Lynn, himself a United Church of Christ minister, and enjoyed the respect of the National Association of Evangelicals. On the role of Baker, an aide to Bonker said this: "He was a great man, had credibility across the spectrum. Was a kind man, a good man. Without him I don't think it would have gone far."[32] Shortly after the end of the congressional session, John Baker died, and he was eulogized by both Senator Hatfield and Representative Bonker in the *Congressional Record*.

Much has been written by Aaron Wildavsky, his students, and others, about the problems of implementation. Often cited is the lack of incentives for representatives and senators to concern themselves with the fine points of implementation.[33] Indeed, as Murray Edelman reminds us, much legislation passed is largely symbolic, with outcomes bearing little resemblance to congressional intent.[34] What is notable about the process that produced the *Equal Access Guidelines* is that many of the antagonists agreed collectively to interpret the legislation for those most immediately affected—the school officials. This is not to imply that court challenges and other implementation struggles will not occur, for they will. Nor does it insure against the law of unintended consequences. But it does appear that the bill *will* make substantive changes in the practices of some school districts in accord with the concerns expressed by protagonists. Thus in this case the religious lobbies proved themselves valuable to the Congress, enabling it to show an unusual concern for implementation.

The Religious Constituencies:
Motives, Positions and Strategies

To understand the impact of the mobilization efforts by leaders of the New Religious Right, it is necessary to treat them, not in isolation, but as part of a system that includes other religious and secular lobbyists operating under the constraining influence of congressional norms. While the foregoing analysis has shown that religious lobbyists can be effective, the discussion that follows illustrates both how the religious lobbyists affect each other and are in turn affected by the congressional system. For purposes of organization the key actors are grouped—logically as the analysis illustrates—in the following categories: fundamentalists, evangelicals, and what I term the "anti-pietist" alliance of Jewish and liberal Protestant leaders.[35] What emerges from this analysis is the tremendous influence of the mobilization of new grassroots constituencies through mass mail and mass media technology. What I attempt to show is that all the major religious actors were influenced by this factor: the fundamentalists themselves, who largely mobilized the new constituencies and were thus motivated by the imperatives of maintaining their support; the evangelical moderates, who were caught between historical support for strict church-state separation and members influenced by the New Religious Right; the Jewish leaders, who faced new strategic challenges; and the liberal Protestants, who were forced to choose between reputational stakes and ideological predilections.

Fundamentalists

Equal access was important to fundamentalists on all fronts: ideologically, institutionally, and strategically. Ideologically, it was viewed as one of a series of attempts to redress the perceived injustice of Supreme Court decisions which had "expelled religion from the classroom." As such, it was not perceived as distinct, in any fundamental way, from the school prayer proposals. One congressional aide (who had worked previously for the Moral Majority and now serves on the staff of Senator Denton) put it this way:

> This place is a compromise puzzle palace . . . we have to move on in an incremental process . . . and we can reverse the harm of the '62 and '63 Supreme Court de-

> cisions incrementally. This is the idea: take the germ of
> injustice that lies at the heart of the school prayer de-
> bate, and ask ourselves what we can do in increments,
> half-way steps, to reverse the injustice. . . . [Equal
> Access] is a good first step.[36]

Similarly, after the initial defeat of equal access in the House, Beverly LeHaye, founder of Concerned Women for America, linked school prayer and equal access: "How much more will Christians in this nation tolerate before they take strong action against lawmakers? We have suffered two major defeats on reasonable proposals supported by a majority of Americans."[37] The Reverend Jerry Falwell echoed the same linkage when he was quoted widely as saying, "We knew we could not win on school prayer, but equal access gets us what we want."[38] Needless to say, such talk only confirmed what prayer opponents feared, that equal access was merely a back-door school prayer proposal. And it prompted equal access tactician James Dunn, Director of the Baptist Joint Committee, to remark that, "Falwell is off the wall. He is not helping."[39] It also prompted quieter efforts by the Christian Legal Society to communicate to the Moral Majority that such talk was tactically unwise.[40] This effort apparently succeeded, as fundamentalist leaders remained relatively quiet during the equal access debate.

If equal access was only another means of getting what they wanted ideologically, it served important strategic and institutional purposes for fundamentalist groups as well. As we would expect from a reading of Salisbury and Walker,[41] maintaining funding levels is of vital importance to member-based Washington groups. Groups such as the Moral Majority, Christian Voice, and Concerned Women for America, are distinct from the older denominational institutions in that they are not assured of ongoing, stable funding, and thus the connection between fundraising and lobbying is of critical importance. Leaders of these New Religious Right groups confided that they need tangible successes to sustain their organizational ties to membership. As the

Moral Majority lobbyist put it, "'83 and '84 were years we decided we had to win, had to have some victories. We were more pragmatic, used incremental approaches." As he described it, the organization could not afford to frame the issue in terms like "we have to win on school prayer," without a fallback position. Such a strategy is not good for "our members."[42] The tension between needing a victory to encourage the folks back home and pressing on school prayer, which continues to be a "hot button" for fundraising, was resolved in part by the equal access legislation.

The strategic analysis of the fundamentalist leaders was shrewd. They decided to pour all their resources into the school prayer debate and flood the Hill with mail. Then, anticipating potential defeat, they would support equal access—now sure to pass as an "out" for liberals looking for a way to show they are not hostile to religion—and reward contributing members, understandably crushed by the school prayer defeat, with a victory. In assuming smooth passage of equal access, fundamentalist lobbyists may have underestimated the strength and intensity of opposition forces. Still, their analysis was largely correct, and several congressional sources corroborated that equal access was indeed viewed as a wonderful "escape" for members who felt the need to vote against school prayer. As one top aide to a moderate midwest Republican Congressman put it, "It provided us with a dodge, a reasonable alternative. I suggested that he [the Congressman] support it. It seems to have quelled things for a while."

While the New Religious Right played well its role of agenda setting, what is intriguing about the groups mentioned is that they were virtually absent when it came to the substance of the equal access legislation—in testimony before congressional committees, during mark-up and so forth. Fundamentalist leaders played their strong suit, the outsider game, but were not disposed to do the insider work of, in the words of one committee aide, "Slugging it out line-by-line in committee." The equal access legislation was considerably changed over time, as groups such as the ACLU, the American Jewish Congress, and B'nai B'rith fought tooth and nail for amendments that would, in their view, soften the blow. The Moral Majority, Christian Voice, and Concerned Women for America, for strategic reasons, made little effort to fight these "weakening" provisions, illustrating their dependence upon evangelical moderates, who were more strategically poised to play the insider game.

Evangelicals
While for fundamentalists equal access was but one of a series of incremental steps toward major policy change, for the evangelical organizations it was the centerpiece of their legislative program. Why was it so important? It was vital because it served both powerful institutional needs and central theological precepts, and the distinctive strategic position of evangelicals as a bridge between the fundamentalists and mainline church denominations enabled them to take full advantage of that fortuitous conjunction.

To understand the institutional value of equal access, it is necessary to comprehend the tension created within evangelical ranks over the mobilization efforts of the New Religious Right, especially on church-state matters. Contrary to much public perception, a number of key national evangelical organizations did not support, and some actively opposed, the president's school prayer amendment. The reasons are generally rooted in a historical concern for separation of church and state as a means of ensuring religious freedom, especially the rights of minority religions. For the leaders of the Baptist Joint Committee (which, as the Washington representative of the Southern Baptist Convention, can be said to represent the largest evangelical constituency in the nation), the National Association of Evangelicals, and the General Conference of the Seventh Day Adventists, an institutional memory of past religious persecution makes them wary of state influence over religious practice. This led them to oppose the president's school prayer amendment, in spite of the popularity of the president with many members. This has strained relations between fundamentalists and evangelicals. As one NAE leader put it, "We get resentment every time we tell them [fundamentalists] that we cannot support the president's school prayer amendment. We felt this would allow states to write prayers. Our fundamentalist friends don't see this."[43] But more important, it has strained relations between Washington offices and lay members influenced by the campaign for prayer over the airwaves.

Leaders of evangelical organizations were forthright in discussing this tension. Gary Ross, lobby director for the Adventists, mentioned that many "members do not understand our opposition to the prayer amendment." He noted that a lot of the lobby effort is "convincing our own people. They don't understand the first amendment." The tension clearly emanates from the mobilization efforts of the fundamentalists: "We always thought the threat to religious liberty would come from the Left, and yet we had to spend four years defending against the New Religious Right—Tim LeHaye, Falwell, Robertson. We have strongly worked against them. Now, alas, some of our members are reading Schaeffer and Whitehead [leading fundamentalist writers]." Communicating the fine distinctions of church-state relations is difficult, but support for equal access enabled Adventist leaders to show that they *did* represent the concerns of members who support religious observance in the schools. Noting that the Baptist Joint Committee *had* to be for equal access for this reason, Ross admitted, "It helped me, too."[44]

The same dynamic existed for the National Association of Evangelicals. As the major representative of the independent evangelical churches, the NAE is in an important symbolic position. While NAE leaders share with fundamentalists the conviction that prayer and religious practices are salutary influences in the public schools, they felt compelled for constitutional and theological reasons to testify in hearings that the president's school prayer amendment (for organized, recited prayer) was seriously flawed. This put the NAE in the uncomfortable position of publicly aligning itself with a liberal and secular coalition, certainly not a welcome sight for members infused with anger over "humanist" and secular domination of the schools. In the highly charged atmosphere of the 1980s, equal access was thus a dramatic way for NAE leaders to show that, when the issue was properly framed, they would break from the anti-pietist coalition and join with fundamentalists to fight for "religious freedom" in the schools. But an important distinction remains between evangelicals and fundamentalists. When pressed by an exasperated legislator about how religious groups "come back every year for more" (clearly the intention of the fundamentalists), NAE attorney Forest Montgomery replied, "Well, the National Association of Evangelicals won't be back. Because this legislation [equal access] incorporates exactly what we said we're looking for in a resolution that we adopted two weeks ago. To us, this is the answer."[45]

Nowhere is the tension between membership and leadership more evident than with the Baptist Joint Committee, an increasingly uneasy alliance of the major Baptist conferences in the United States, including the Southern Baptist Convention, which has been the target of takeover efforts by fundamentalist leaders. The past president of the Southern Baptist Convention, Charles Stanley, is a founder of the Moral Majority, and he and other conservatives within the SBC have criticized the leadership of the Baptist Joint Committee as far too liberal. The Joint Committee's opposition to organized school prayer, which was endorsed by the SBC, is one indication of this. The focus of criticism is Executive Director James Dunn, an outspoken Texan who does nothing to hide his political differences with the New Religious Right: "I disagree with their priorities. They think that pornography, abortion, prayer, and arms to Taiwan are the great moral issues of the day, rather than pursuit of peace, stewardship of creation, justice for women and blacks. Those are the moral issues."[46] The tension between Dunn and elements of the SBC is reflected in comments about Dunn from fellow lobbyists and congressional aides: "Dunn is in trouble, a leader out of step with followers . . .

the Southern Baptists almost censured him, and almost passed a resolution to withdraw funds from it."[47] "The Baptist Joint Committee is always in jeopardy of losing funding. Every year John Baker and James Dunn have to protect themselves from the SBC. They are much more progressive than their southern brethren."[48] "The Baptist Joint Committee is in deep water. Dunn is in deep water. They had to be for equal access—it saved him."[49]

It is not surprising that equal access was a high priority for the BJC; indeed, that it played a pivotal role in passage of the legislation. As Dunn put it, they were looking for the proper vehicle to deal with the school prayer "mess" as early as 1981. Thus, the tensions between national leaders and members led the organization to seek a creative means of responding to member concerns in a "constitutionally sound" manner.

While organizational maintenance clearly motivated evangelical leaders, evangelical theology played its role as well. The stress on adult conversion, daily worship, and, of course, "evangelizing" places believers in frequent tension with secular institutions, especially public schools. Evangelical students, to be true to their faith, must not only evangelize, or spread the good news, but are called to live out their faith at home, work, or school. God is sovereign, and the proper response is a commitment to constant reverence. Yet this commitment, as they see it, runs headlong into the hostility or ignorance of secular school officials. Committee hearings were sprinkled with testimony from evangelical students expressing this frustration:

> We had been taught that the Constitution guaranteed freedom of speech, which was every kind of speech. We were allowed to picket and demonstrate and curse and take God's name in vain, but we couldn't get together and talk about God reverently before or after school. This frustrated us because we didn't feel like we were being treated equally.[50]

In light of this clash between evangelical theology and secular culture, equal access was, to Sam Ericsson, Director of the

Washington Office of the Christian Legal Society, literally a godsend.[51] As he summarized it, reversing the 1962 and 1963 Supreme Court decisions on organized school prayer would not have solved the problem but would merely lead to state influence over religious practice, which is both biblically and constitutionally unsound. Equal access, in contrast, was a means of assuring the freedom of students to practice their religion in a way that would be widely perceived as fair, reasonable, and constitutional. It would provide clear guidance to school officials and courts, and would solve legislatively what the CLS lawyers had not been able to solve through litigation. But most importantly, it was a political means of protecting evangelical students whose understanding of God placed them in frequent conflict with those in authority.[52]

Given the powerful merging of institutional maintenance and theology, it is not surprising that the evangelical organizations invested real resources in the equal access campaign. But those resources were successfully employed only because the evangelical organizations enjoyed certain strategic advantages which deserve elaboration. First, their traditional concern with religious liberty necessitated development of in-house expertise on constitutional law. Interviews with lobbyists and key congressional actors confirmed that lawyers from three organizations—John Baker of the Baptist Joint Committee, Forest Montgomery of the National Association of Evangelicals, and Sam Ericsson of the Christian Legal Society—were instrumental in drafting access language and in negotiating over guidelines after the bill's passage. All three had extensive experience in church-state law, had filed numerous amicus briefs, and had argued before the Supreme Court. This placed them, as Ericsson put it, in the position of offering unique legislative help: "Back in 1982 Hatfield came to us and asked if there was a way to implement legislatively the *Widmar* decision at the high school level, and please give me a memo."[53]

A second strategic advantage was the evangelicals' reputation, assiduously cultivated by some leaders, for being "thoughtful and reasonable," for using "incarnational" lobbying and gentle persuasion. Representatives of the CLS and the NAE emphasized that means are as important as ends in their theology, which, in strategic terms, translates into the dictum that one's opponent today may be an ally tomorrow, if the game is played in a Christian-like manner. Indeed, CLS attorney Ericsson seemed obsessed with moderation. "We are not a clenched fist."[54] Moreover, given their past, "but thoughtful," opposition to the president's school prayer proposal, the evangelical organizations could speak with some credibility that equal access was indeed different from school prayer, an argument central to the success of the legislation. Finally, evangelical leaders were able to frame the issue in terms sufficiently liberal to be acceptable to a broader constituency, to "get more of the marginals," as one Senate aide put it. Thus, the debate shifted from prayer as "good for kids" to one of "students rights," a cause that Nat Hentoff, civil liberties writer for the *Village Voice*,[55] and Laurence Tribe, constitutional law professor at Harvard Law School,[56] could also endorse.

Finally, and most importantly, evangelical leaders found themselves at the center of an unusual coalition of fundamentalist conservatives and liberal Protestants, who seldom talk with one another. Thus, the evangelical leaders acted as a bridge, coordinating strategies, keeping the shaky alliance together. The Baptist Joint Committee, highly respected among the liberal Protestant community, maintained links with the National Council of Churches, while the National Association of Evangelicals and the Christian Legal Society maintained close contact with the Moral Majority and other fundamentalist groups. When the Reverend Falwell made his famous remark, Ericsson of CLS intervened:

> Falwell was quoted as saying that equal access would "get us all we want." Which frightened the liberals. So, I called over to the Moral Majority office and told them to keep the lid on Falwell. He is the most teachable of the lot.[57]

This broad access extended to the Congress as well. The NAE had credibility among the most conservative senators and representatives, while the CLS could work simultaneously with Denton, Republican conservative, and Perkins, liberal Democrat. And James Dunn of the Baptist Joint Committee, as one lobbyist put it, "Can call Hatfield any time he wants. They are old friends."[58]

The Anti-Pietist Alliance

The mobilization by fundamentalists of formerly dormant constituencies—through mass mail and mass media technology—is a major new force in the congressional milieu, and it sparked countermoves by liberal church groups. The core of this anti-pietist alliance is made up of the national Jewish organizations and the mainline liberal Protestant denominations. Leaders of these groups find themselves in frequent agreement about the proper relationships of church to state and religion to politics, and they share a perception of the "pietist threat." This common bond came together, as I have already shown, on the school prayer issue.

If there is a distinction between Jewish leaders and their liberal Protestant allies, it is the relative emphasis placed on church-state issues. Several of the mainline denominations needed to be coaxed into involvement, as Senator Danforth's administrative assistant summarized it:

> The mainstream groups were not alert. It was Congress that went to religious groups and said, "Get off your butts and show there is another feeling." Danforth called Bishop Walker and said "Help us." Weicker and Mathias did the same. People like Danforth, Hatfield, Mathias, and Weicker were lobbying the mainstream churches to provide an alternative message than the one they were receiving from the New Right.[59]

Jewish groups needed no such prodding on school prayer and indeed saw themselves as leaders in the antiprayer forces. A representative for the American Jewish Congress stressed, "On school prayer issues we take the lead."[60] Rabbi Saperstein of the UAHC amplified this leadership theme, "The American Jewish Congress and *us* helped to forge the coalition behind the scenes to stop school prayer."[61]

Equal access is significant because it fractured this otherwise unified coalition. For Jewish leaders, who have consciously nurtured alliances with Protestants,[62] this development represents a serious strategic problem, particularly if it reflects, as it appears to, a growing sophistication of evangelicals and fundamentalists in framing issues in terms that at least some mainline Protestants can support.

The mobilization of pietist constituencies thus has profoundly shaped Jewish calculations. Not surprisingly, it was Jewish leaders who led the opposition to equal access, both before passage and during the drafting of guidelines. Ironically, Jewish leaders share the analysis of the fundamentalists that equal access is merely a better packaged means to the same end. But if equal access is indeed "son of school prayer," as Jewish leaders perceived it, it is a child potentially more insidious than the parent. After all, a recited prayer lasts but a few moments, but equal access could subject Jewish children to constant peer pressure and proselytizing by newly formed religious clubs. As Marc Pearl, Washington representative of the American Jewish Congress, testified:

> We believe that the bill would be the first step toward turning the public schools into beehives of religious proselytization, a dramatic shift from the current conception of the schools as places which are off limits to religious strife, places where all students are free to participate as equals in all activities, without any sense of feeling not wanted or not invited.[63]

Jewish leaders clearly saw the strategic threat of equal access, that it was indeed better packaged than the prayer amendment, and their job of opposing it would be tougher. Legislatively, their strategy was threefold: 1) kill it if possible; 2) fight for changes which would soften its impact; and 3) work on guidelines to ensure implementation favorable to their constituents. The tenacious Jewish strategy has been at least partially successful. The legislation was changed to accommodate some of their concerns, and the guidelines were drafted with the hope of giving school administrators tools to deal with disruptive organizations or hate groups. Still, given the importance of church-state relations to Jewish representatives—and indeed in light of their leadership of the anti-pietist alliance—the passage of equal access represents a major legislative defeat. In response, the American Jewish Congress announced a new fundraising campaign to hire additional constitutional attorneys, the UAHC mailed a booklet to members outlining the new law and asking members to closely monitor and report back what occurs in their schools, and Hyman Bookbinder, Washington leader of the American Jewish Committee, said his organization would consider filing amicus briefs in suits against implementation of equal access.[64] For Jewish groups, the battle is not over by any means.

For the leaders of the mainline Protestant denominations, the mobilization of new "pietist" constituencies presents a direct challenge to their authority: Who will speak for Protestant America? Given evidence of widespread support for organized school prayer among lay members of the mainline churches, leaders of these denominations have been particularly vulnerable in their outspoken opposition to school prayer proposals. Thus for some liberal religious lobbyists, support for equal access was a way to bolster their reputations in Washington. For example, James Hamilton, Director of the Washington Office of the National Council of Churches, admitted that the "Council does have the reputation on the Hill of being far out, particularly in the last four years."[65] Support for equal access, he admitted, would help improve their reputation in the Washington community. As Richard Neustadt[66] reminds us, power in Washington is in part a function of one's reputation; thus the NCC's unusual split with the liberal-secular community served powerful institutional motives. Indeed, in interviews with other lobbyists and congressional aides, it appears that the NCC's highly visible role in equal access did enhance its credibility among more moderate and conservative actors without hurting its reputation among liberals.

The key actor on equal access for the National Council of Churches was Dean Kelley, Director for Religious and Civil Liberty of the National Council of Churches. Kelley writes extensively on church-state issues and has authored an often cited and penetrating analysis of the reasons the churches he represents are declining in membership while evangelical and fundamentalist churches are growing.[67] Thus he was, no doubt, keenly aware of the stakes involved in the NCC's posture toward religion in the schools. His testimony reflects an attempt to demonstrate sensitivity to concerns expressed by evangelicals:

> The National Council of churches has been very active in opposing any form of state-sponsored religious activities in public schools. Therefore, we have a special concern to make sure that public school authorities and lower courts do not overbroadly apply the Supreme Court's decisions on that subject which might result in virtual exclusion of religious activities or references from public education as though it were somehow improper or obscene. It is important for the public school not to exclude, impair, derogate, or disparage the religious commitments, interests, or expressions of their students, but rather permit them to be carried on by the students themselves, without prejudice, discrimination, or pressure.[68]

The fact that equal access split an otherwise solid anti-pietist alliance is reflected in the testimony Kelley offered outlining the position of the NCC:

> In a way, it grieves me to be here differing with some of the allies with whom we worked to oppose the amendment of the Constitution to permit state-mandated, teacher-led prayer in public schools. But the difference,

> I think, is important because the National Council of
> Churches, by a special action in May of last year, gave
> approval to the concept of permitting students, at their
> own initiative and under their own direction, rather
> than the schools, to meet for religious purposes if they
> are permitted to meet for non-religious purposes.[69]

A number of Protestant denominations joined the NCC in supporting the access legislation, but others opposed it. Given the prevailing ideological unity of the mainline Protestant denominations in Washington (most of whom, in fact, share offices in the United Methodist Building across the street from the Capitol), it is indeed puzzling why, for example, the Episcopalians, Presbyterians, and the National Council of Churches supported equal access, while the Lutherans and Methodists opposed it. Differences in church structure or tradition could conceivably account for the contrasting positions, but the fact is that the issue emerged too quickly for most of the church bodies to develop specific policy. Thus, lobbyists and those to whom they report had to interpret equal access in light of past church pronouncements on school prayer. Consequently, idiosyncratic responses to the New Religious Right appear largely responsible for the split in the liberal Protestant community.

This is dramatically illustrated by the actions of the Lutheran Council, which emerged as the most aggressive critic of the legislation among the mainline Protestants. Indeed, in a scholarly article on equal access in the *Journal of Church and State*, it stood out:

> The Equal Access Act was not only strongly supported
> by the New Religious Right and the National Association of Evangelicals, but also by a wide range of
> mainline churches, including the national Council
> of Churches and the U.S. Catholic Conference. By
> contrast, the Act was uniformly opposed by all three
> branches of American Jewry, all Jewish civil rights organizations, and the Lutheran Council in the USA.[70]

The Governmental Affairs Office of the Lutheran Council represents three Lutheran bodies—the American Lutheran Church,
the Lutheran Church in America, and the Association of Evangelical Lutheran Churches—soon to be merged into one denomination.[71] Since the equal access concept emerged quickly,
these bodies did not have the time to develop specific policy
on the legislation. Thus, in testimony on the proposed legislation, the Reverend Charles Bergstrom, Executive Director of
the Lutheran Council, stressed concerns, some quite personal,
even as he acknowledged that he could not technically represent
Lutheran "opposition" to the bill:

> I'd like to say, in all frankness, and all directness, that
> religious clubs are the least attractive things to me in
> terms of really living in the world and making education
> more important. I would love to encourage students to
> join any other club except a religious club in a public
> school, a service club that would become inclusive and
> bring in more young people rather than gather them
> apart in their little religious, almost sometimes Phari-
> saical approach to life. . . . I do not speak—specifically
> because my church has not authorized—against this
> legislation. But I raise all kinds of concerns because of
> what I know about human nature.[72]

In written testimony Bergstrom agreed with the Jewish groups
and linked the equal access legislation with school prayer, observing that, "Given the current climate, we are afraid that this
measure, if enacted, could be perceived as a 'green light' to
groups who are seeking to make this a Christian nation." [73]

Even though Lutheran lobbyists technically only expressed
concerns about equal access and even agreed to "not oppose"
the final compromise version of the bill, in the perception of the
Washington community the Lutheran Council vociferously opposed the legislation. What accounts for this, it appears, is the
personal response of Bergstrom, as the Washington leader of the
Lutheran Council, to the rise of the New Religious Right. In

a lengthy interview Bergstrom shared his profound differences with the theology, politics, and values of the fundamentalists. He has publicly debated the Reverend Jerry Falwell. He is featured in the People for the American Way video documentary on the Religious Right. He coauthored with Rabbi Saperstein a guest editorial in the *Washington Post* warning of the dangers of the Republican party's embrace of religious fundamentalists. He evinced a profound antipathy toward the fundamentalist leaders: "The Bible is the revelation of God, they have made it into a book of rules; misused it—Falwell, Swaggart, Robertson." He finds public piety antithetical to his faith: "It is against Christ, this ostentatious [public prayer] 'see how holy we are.' I'd rather see children visit the elderly." Bergstrom acknowledges that his highly visible role has earned him a reputation: "Christian Voice called me a leader of the radical Left in their February letter. I got that tag because of school prayer opposition. I am not a liberal ACLU type that they can put down. I refuse the label." Particularly galling to Bergstrom is the use of the word evangelical. "Falwell is not an evangelical," he passionately asserted, "I am a born-again evangelical Christian who happens to be Lutheran,"[74] a theme he echoed in testimony.

It is a reflection of the dynamic character of American religion and the growing importance of the "pietist" mobilization that a battle over the label "evangelical" itself should erupt in congressional hearings. After giving his testimony before Perkins's committee, Bergstrom remained on a panel which included Forrest Montgomery of the National Association of Evangelicals. During a lively and often heated discussion, Montgomery exclaimed:

> I am dumbfounded by the hostility to religious speech that I see exhibited at this hearing. Sam Ericsson, who was here earlier, attended a school in which Bible studies were allowed. One percent attended. He's an evangelical. He's not a majority. . . . Contrary to what Judge Kaufmann said, we don't think prayer clubs are, quote, "too dangerous to permit," end quote.[75]

Chairman Perkins then interjected, "Come back, Reverend Bergstrom. You're not ostracized by any means. Come up to the
table." To which Bergstrom replied, "I think I've said it. I just
want to say I am also an evangelical and do not support the
Bill."[76] This sparked Montgomery:

> May I just say that those who constantly profess they're
> born again Christians and that they are evangelicals
> [and] feel obligated to say that, always be alert. What
> follows is absolute, untrammeled, and unqualified op-
> position to the expression of any religious thought in
> public schools, and thoughts like "Suffer the little chil-
> dren to come unto me," or "Where two or three are
> gathered in my name, I am there also," are not in their
> heads.[77]

Bergstrom ended the colloquy simply by saying, "Everybody is
getting tired. But you're the one who used the term 'evangelical'
first."[78]

What emerges here is the importance of a lobbyist's deeply
held reactions to the rise of the Religious Right, which appeared
to override, if only momentarily, his articulation of official church
policy. The high profile role played by Bergstrom has earned
him respect in certain circles. One staff aide to a liberal Democratic congressman observed approvingly: "On school prayer the
Lutherans surprised people here. Bergstrom led the religious
people against prayer. He wrote letters, had a press conference
on the steps of the Capitol. Surprised a lot of people, got them
thinking: Why would a Christian church oppose school prayer?"[79]
But if school prayer opposition enhanced Bergstrom's credibility,
opposition to equal access appears to have hurt. Several lobbyists
and staff aides concluded that Lutheran Council opposition was a
reflection of Bergstrom's personal feelings and not church policy.
Most sobering was the assessment of a Catholic lobbyist:

> The Lutherans looked foolish on equal access. They are
> threatened by evangelicals . . . I feel bad for them. I
> don't want them to look foolish. I like them—they do

a lot of good, the great social services and the international work. They are good people, they have a good product. They don't have to apologize.[80]

The mobilization efforts of the New Religious Right have confronted mainline Protestant leaders with a direct challenge to their authority as speakers for Protestant America. Different leaders have reacted differently to that challenge. Dean Kelley and his colleagues at the National Council of Churches chose to temporarily align themselves with former adversaries and bolster their reputation in Washington. For the Lutheran Council, on the other hand, a profound antipathy toward religious fundamentalists on the part of the Reverend Charles Bergstrom overrode countervailing institutional advantages that might have flowed from a more benign posture toward the legislation.

Summary

One scholar described the enactment of the Equal Access Act as "Something of a political miracle."[81] Indeed, there are those in Washington who see the hand of God in legislation that could gain the simultaneous support of Catholics, fundamentalists, evangelicals, mainline Protestants, and even secular intellectuals such as Laurence Tribe and Nat Hentoff. Three lessons emerge from this analysis: 1) that the mobilization efforts of fundamentalist leaders have had considerable influence on Congress and the religious community, 2) that the congressional milieu has, in turn, influenced the religious lobbyists, particularly the fundamentalists, and 3) that an evangelical network has emerged on Capitol Hill.

As the analysis has shown, all the major actors were influenced by the mobilization efforts of the New Religious Right, and in that sense equal access is indeed "son of school prayer." Equal access had broad appeal in part because it served powerful, but distinct, institutional needs of fundamentalist, evangelical, and

mainline Protestant supporters. For fundamentalists, whose financial well-being is dependent on continued member support,
equal access was a means to gain a tangible legislative victory and
thus reward members' efforts. For evangelical moderates, who
felt compelled to oppose the school prayer amendment, equal
access was a means of demonstrating to members their effective advocacy of "religious freedom" in the schools. For some
mainline Protestant lobbies, assured of continued financial support from denominational bodies and maintaining little ongoing
contact with members in the pews, the institutional consideration was instead a political calculus of their reputational stakes
in the Washington community. Thus, support for equal access
was a means for liberal church lobbies, often criticized for being
out of touch with members, to demonstrate an independence
from "ACLU" liberals, to bolster flagging reputations and perhaps
future effectiveness.

For opponents, too, the mobilization of millions of fundamentalists and evangelicals was a dominant consideration. For Jewish
groups it presents a major strategic challenge and has sparked efforts by leaders to intensify their own constituency mobilization.
Likewise, for such Protestant leaders as the Reverend Charles
Bergstrom the rise of the New Religious Right is so ominous that
to give in, even on a concept with wide and liberal appeal, is
to send the wrong message, to give a green light to those who
want to make this a "Christian nation." The mobilization of new
grassroots religious constituencies, of course, also shaped the
calculations of congressional members. After turning back the
school prayer amendment, moderate and liberal representatives
and senators found in equal access a less sweeping and more
liberal-sounding means of accommodating the concerns of this
new and feisty constituency. Thus this analysis illustrates how the
nature of lobbying has changed since Milbrath discounted the
efficacy of mass-mail generation as a political tool. Not only do
congressional representatives try to respond to lobby-generated

district pressures, but the calculations of other Washington insiders are also influenced by effective mobilization.

The second lesson is that religious leaders, in their attempts to shape public policy through congressional lobbying, are themselves molded by the congressional milieu, with its norms and unwritten rules. This is particularly well illustrated by the transformation that is taking place in the fundamentalist community. While fundamentalist rhetoric reflects the angry militancy of social movements, the actual lobby approach is more strategic and mundane. Equal access represents, in effect, the hinge of this transformation. For fundamentalist leaders—the "new kids on the block"—the lesson of equal access is dazzlingly clear: if you want to win you have to learn how to properly "frame" the issues. For the Moral Majority that means framing the issues in the language of rights, of classical liberalism. As the Moral Majority legislative director put it:

> For the first three years of our existence we framed the issues wrong; now we know how to do it. For example, we pushed for school prayer three years in a row, but we framed the issue in terms of how prayer in schools is good. But some people feel that prayer in school is bad. So we learned to frame the issue in terms of "students' rights," so it became a constitutional issue. We are prochoice for students having the right to pray in public schools.[82]

This statement is corroborated by other evidence of a genuine shift in emphasis at the Moral Majority. Moral Majority leaders are hammering home the message to supporters in their literature,

> People don't perceive there is a problem with students' rights violations right now, but we intend to make school prayer the Civil Rights issue of the 80's . . . voluntary school prayer must be transformed into a students-rights' issue. We must talk about the rights of

> students to choose to participate, rather than the actual
> need for prayer in our school.[83]

This embrace of the language of rights, which, the fundamentalists learned through equal access, is more appealing than the
language of moral imperatives, will extend to other issues, particularly abortion. "We can't afford to say 'God settled it, that's
it.'" Instead, as Falwell put it, "We are reframing the debate [on
abortion]. This is no longer a religious issue, but a civil rights
issue."[84]

Closely linked to this is an acceptance of incremental strategies and compromise as imperatives of successful long-run congressional lobbying. As they learned with equal access, when
the issue is properly framed they can "pick up the marginals,"
those in Congress who might not support the long-term goal but
can support the incremental step for other reasons. Intriguingly,
this strategic positioning by leaders in the Religious Right may
serve to legitimate a system from which their constituents had
previously been alienated. Indeed, that is how the lobbyist for
the Concerned Women for America put it, "Our work builds
trust in the system, if we can show that the system can work
for them."[85] Whether or not the system does indeed work for
"them" out there, leaders, in the interest of organizational maintenance, must show that it does through tangible, if incremental,
victories.

While it may be some time before the fundamentalist conservatives have the capacity or the strategic position to play the
insider game in committee deliberations, evangelical organizations have shown an ability to do so. Aiding them in this behind-
the-scenes work is the emergence of a rather well-defined, if
still modest, evangelical network on Capitol Hill, consciously
nurtured by a number of individuals and organizations. While
evangelicals share with fundamentalists an affirmation of the
"fundamentals of the faith," they remain, in their own minds,
quite distinct. And the network of these like-minded individu-

als emerged as a salient feature of the investigation of the equal access legislation. Senator Hatfield and Representative Bonker, two key sponsors of the legislation, are "evangelical brothers," as was Representative Carl Perkins, a Baptist from the Bible Belt of Eastern Kentucky. Key aides for Hatfield, Bonker, and the House Committee on Education and Labor are also evangelicals, as are, of course, lobbyists for the National Association of Evangelicals and the Christian Legal Society. The CLS best illustrates the conscious nurturing of a network of those of the faith. While the organization provides "Christian" support to law students and lawyers in chapters across the country, a clear goal is to create a "Christian" network of influential attorneys, something akin to the "old boy" network of prep school graduates. Hatfield himself is a CLS member, as is Dan Evans of Bonker's staff.

In speaking with these individuals, what is striking is the extent to which they share deeply a phenomenological "Lebenswelt,"[86] no less so than Jews and fundamentalists. The use of common language, the evidence of mutual respect, the camaraderie, even the jokes, evince a shared perception and a deep bond that crosses party and even ideological lines. These cross-party links proved especially fruitful on the equal access legislation, which passed in part because lobbyists and congressional people of different parties shared the same faith. It is the faith, indeed, not the party, that appears to be the dominant factor for some individuals. For example, when Sam Ericsson of the CLS told a Sunday School class that the Democrat-controlled House was a problem on equal access (with laughter indicating an immediate recognition that Democrats are a "problem" for evangelicals), *but then* told them that the House sponsor was "our evangelical brother Don Bonker,"[87] he was giving a powerful cue to the class that Bonker, a Democrat and a liberal environmentalist at that, was "one of us." The immediate political access evangelical lobbyists have with "one of us" in the Congress should not be minimized as a political resource for future battles.

The enactment of the Equal Access Act, in summary, is instructive for what it tells us about the religious lobbies and the political imperatives under which they operate. It substantiates my earlier assertion that to understand the impact of "New Right" religious groups, one must treat them as part of a complex system that includes other religious actors within a constraining congressional milieu. It provides a picture of the nature of modern lobbying and is a classic example of the consensus-seeking congressional process, which aims to accommodate simultaneously many conflicting values and interests. The equal access legislation succeeded not only because it was framed in liberal, "free speech" language but because it appealed to powerful institutional needs and diverse, seemingly contradictory goals. Thus it came to pass.

7 Representation Theory and the Religious Dimension

Congressional lobbying is but one manifestation of the religious politization occurring in America, yet it illuminates as no other realm the dynamics of this phenomenon, the clashing beliefs and shifting coalitions, the strategic realities and organizational imperatives, the power and constraints.

Rising out of an exceptional historical legacy, religion in America is at once highly pluralistic, dynamic, and activist. As Alexis de Tocqueville observed over a century and a half ago, churches are the prime examples of American volunteerist proclivity. Even in our supposedly secular age, belonging to a church is the key point of collective participation for most Americans in the larger society. To a great extent, thus, Americans define their cultural differences in religious terms. Because religion is important in American cultural life, religious political engagement has the potential for articulating this cultural pluralism, and increasingly is doing so.

Central to an understanding of religious political advocacy is representation, which, as Pitkin reminds us, is not merely the relation between particular leaders and followers, but is ultimately defined by the broader interaction of many people operating within the political system. When viewed collectively the religious organizations in Washington, reflecting as they do the astonishing variety of religious expression in America and articulating widely held but otherwise underrepresented opinions and values, appear to enhance the representativeness of the national "pressure system." Moreover, by mobilizing their diverse constituencies, religious lobbies provide channels for direct participation and citizen education which are invaluable for the maintenance of a democratic society.[1] Thus, the pluralism and activism of American religious practice is revealed as an important component of American political representation.

Religious groups, across the political spectrum, also bring to American representation a language of moral concern and, at their best, an articulation of competing visions of "the caring community," which are refreshingly distinct from ideas of "interest" as commonly understood. For the liberal groups this vision often involves notions of the community's moral obligation to those less fortunate. For the conservative groups it is a recognition that statecraft is soulcraft, or in other words, that the state has a role to play in creating the moral climate of a society. Thus one thing these diverse groups have in common is an explicit concern with the moral content of public policies.

As a key American political institution, the Congress that emerges from this study is a model of Madisonian wizardry, accommodating yet checking the various religious factions. The congressional environment clearly molds the activity of religious leaders and does so in a way that makes their lobby efforts more broadly palatable. Contrary to its apparent gridlock on, for example, budget matters, Congress has shown an ability, at least on equal access, to develop a consensus and craft new policy. Ironically, this raises the possibility that the same consensus-building norms that render Congress seemingly unable to control spending may equip it well to adjudicate some religious disputes in ways the adversarial system in the courts cannot match. Indeed, what seems to happen in the lobbying milieu, and less so in the courts, is a face-to-face contact where the "other" becomes less an "enemy" and more just another participant in the process, sometimes an adversary, sometimes an ally. Hyman Bookbinder of the American Jewish Committee tells the story of how he felt compelled, by wisdom he hoped, to shake hands with the Reverend Jerry Falwell at the National Prayer Breakfast, acknowledging him, at the least, where in the past he had not.[2]

The examination of religious political representation also reveals the dynamic change transforming religious life in America. The established Protestant denominations do not now appear to warrant the unqualified appellation "mainline"; indeed, the center of gravity has shifted. The growing national prominence of the Catholic church and the remarkable growth of evangelical and fundamentalist congregations represent a major cultural movement. The social conservatism of these churches, along with their growing political assertiveness and sophistication, has slashed at previous ideological and partisan alignments. Thus long-term effects on American political parties may result from the dynamics of church life in America. The Democratic party, for the moment, seems institutionally wedded to a posture that symbolically and substantively appears to reject the cultural conservatism of many Catholics, evangelicals, and fundamentalists, as well as many members of the mainline Protestant denominations. So while many of these voters may not embrace the economic or military agenda of the New Religious Right, the salience of such issues as abortion, pornography, and school prayer may move some increasingly toward the Republican party as the best representor of their traditional values. The religious factor, indeed, may contribute to the much-discussed partisan realignment in America.

The salient religious features of American political sentiment, addressed in chapter 5, deserve more penetrating analysis than I was able to give. Clearly, religious divisions are at least as important as class, ethnicity, and party in explaining the contours of American opinion, though precisely how remains largely a mystery. On certain issues, such as abortion, the religious dimension appears to be the key in explaining public attitudes, though further refinement is called for. I chose, for example, to impute anti-abortion sentiment to those who would restrict abortion under some circumstances but not necessarily ban it entirely. This is justified, I think, because feminists have framed the debate in terms of a woman's unconditional right to control her own body. Prochoice sentiment, consequently, is not adequately measured by opposition to an amendment which would ban all abortions, the statistic frequently cited by prochoice forces. But this interpretation is certainly open to question.

Another issue that deserves deeper analysis is the extent of representation of the poor by religious lobbyists. I suggest in this study that the religious community, collectively, articulates many concerns and values of low-income people. In light of the limited statistical data available, this may be stretching it. Many of the poor in our society, however, are indeed religious and attend church. Thus the potential exists for a genuine representation of these people through religious organizations. Unfortunately, this potential may remain largely unrealized. We know what the religious leaders are up to; we know vastly less, however, about the needs and values of "the poor," a diverse, often hard to define group. In part this ignorance is due to the fact that scholars who study poverty, whether in political science, history, sociology, or women's studies, often lack an appreciation of the religious or moral convictions of low-income, minority, and female citizens.

This treatment of religious lobbies, quite obviously, is a sympathetic one, and purposively so. In part I sought to compensate for what seems to be a hostile or indifferent posture toward religion by many elites in education, the media, and government. Thus, where Christian fundamentalist leaders have demonstrated a willingness to compromise and play by the rules, contrary to the received wisdom in liberal circles, I have documented it. Similarly, where liberal "mainline" lobbyists effectively articulate member sentiment, contrary to the charge that they are "generals without armies," I have noted that too. Where diverse religious lobbyists as a group seem to articulate the needs and values of non-elites, I have charted that modest impact. However, in making my arguments as boldly and clearly as possible, I have, no doubt, occasionally stretched points or imputed too much to the data. So it is appropriate here to offer more qualified reflections on the nature of religious political activism.

From the standpoint of representation theory, the most troubling case occurs within the so called mainline Protestant denominations. The dilemma, as Reichley[3] so clearly documents, is that the political agenda within these churches is dominated by liberal activists among the clergy and laity, leaving other points of view largely unrepresented.[4] One concern, then, is with a church polity, ostensibly democratic, which does not engender genuine participation in its policy-making procedures. Religious faith, however, is not a matter of pluralities, and one can argue that religious leaders, as trustees of the faith, have the right, indeed obligation, to apply their understanding of gospel imperatives in the world. A deeper problem, however, is that little effort is made to inform parishioners of their church's stands on issues. Strategically, this representational weakness may translate into political marginalization, because effectiveness increasingly requires tangible links with mobilizable constituencies.

It is important to stress, however, that this is not universally the case in the liberal churches. This study demonstrates, in contrast to earlier works, that for some of the liberal denominations, such as the United Church of Christ or the Mennonite Central Committee, political activity is indeed reasonably well integrated into church life.

One reason for the gap between national lobby efforts and lay sentiment is that some leaders take a self-consciously "prophetic" stand, chastising the rich and powerful, and challenging the complacency of their age. But, as one senatorial aide[5] observed, few religious leaders wish to live as prophets; indeed, one hears much of "justice for the poor" over aperitifs at the cocktail hour. It is this temptation to engage in "cheap prophecy" that Sojourners founder Jim Wallis so passionately criticizes.[6] Ironically, for some liberal leaders the taking of a prophetic stand also edges them toward an attitude of contempt for the pietistic religion of the poor who are ostensibly the objects of their concern.

Once again, however, I found that on some issues the liberal denominations do represent broad member sentiment. As international organizations, churches play an important role in foreign policy debates, often articulating deep public concern about U.S. military ventures. True, some church leaders seem at times naive about the Soviet Union and far too willing to embrace dictators of the Left even as they attack dictators on the Right.[7] In their critique of secrecy and military adventures, however, religious leaders are a modest counterweight to the *hubris* of an overweening security establishment. Moreover, because of their contacts within strategic countries, liberal religious leaders have successfully exposed the sanitized language of foreign policy, reminding us that "putting pressure on the Sandinistas" involves the very real killing of Nicaraguan peasants.

In terms of my analysis of the willingness of leaders of the New Religious Right to "play by the rules" of compromise and incrementalism, critics might respond thus: tactics are one thing, long-term goals are quite another. Goals, indeed, may be extreme and, for a minority of the fundamentalist community, antithetical to pluralist democracy; but the point is that fundamentalist leaders must operate within the constraints of a political system that puts a premium on checks and balances. Moreover, fundamentalists must overcome an elite bias against pietistic religion, and one way to do that is to reassure everyone that they are reasonable people, as Pat Robertson surely will do as he mounts a presidential campaign. To a certain degree, I would suggest, the message becomes the goal, and a tactical posture of reasonableness translates into an accommodation with the system.

This is not to say that the fundamentalists have not made an impact, for they have. Themes central to their message have been adopted in the liberal community. Both Mario Cuomo and Gary Hart, for example, speak often of "families" and of the "family of America." Pornography is no longer solely the concern of the blue noses. Moreover, religious conservatives seem to have tapped a deep vein of public anxiety about secular change. Fundamentalists and evangelicals argue persuasively that, contrary to the notion that they are attempting to "impose" their values on the rest of society, secular values have been imposed, not only on them and their children but on most religious Americans. And they are right. The purveyors of popular culture—commercial television, films, rock video, advertising—are organs of awesome secular indoctrination; but more than this, their messages, often violent, seductive, and avaricious, run counter to common moral sense. In an astonishing reversal of past wisdom, sex education is now taught in the public schools (divorced from messy moral questions, of course), but not religious history, ethics, or moral codes. A rich heritage is shielded from our children; religion is now taboo. Yes, paranoia may exist within the fundamentalist camp, and leaders occasionally pick issues (such as military aid to Taiwan) that seem remote from the concerns of their own followers. But the impact of fundamentalist mobilization in raising concerns about cultural and moral change has been to enhance, not detract from, the genuine pluralism of American political representation.

This raises the ultimate question about religious political activism: why now? What has compelled religious people across the theological and political spectrum to make the leap toward political engagement? Is there any common thread in the diverse manifestations of religious activism—from the far Left to the far Right? The answer lies, in part, in a shared perception that there are elite secular forces, fundamentally antithetical to the religious message, that must be challenged. For religious conservatives, of course, those forces are exemplified in the abortion culture, secular schools, and lax morality. For religious liberals and radicals, on the other hand, those forces are the God-denying materialism and militarism of their world. For them the nuclear arms race, a threat to creation itself, is the ultimate idolatry, the symbol of secular *hubris*, the prime example of our lack of faith. A profound alienation from perceived secular forces, then, may lie at the heart of the growing political engagement by religious people, who are called, after all, to be in but not of this world.

Radical critics will argue that I have succumbed in this study to the pluralist paradigm, that my analysis belies an underlying acceptance of pluralist assumptions about the nature of the American polity. I am probably guilty of that charge. On the other hand, I never attempted to argue, nor have I any way of definitively knowing, that the American system is fundamentally responsive to the needs and values of non-elite Americans; in certain respects it surely is not. What I do argue is that religious activism broadens the representativeness of the pressure system, forces elites to address otherwise unarticulated needs and values, and thus is a generally healthy development.

However, even if the general outlines of this work are accurate, as I believe they are, there may be an absolute limit to the representational role of churches in power politics. Churches, after all, are not primarily political institutions, and members do not join for such representation. To the extent that political activism undermines the religious function, it will ultimately undermine its own efficacy. Indeed, it is the existential dilemma of life itself, the search for meaning amidst the mystery of tragedy and death, which animates most believers. While political witness does not necessarily have to compromise religion's meaning-giving function, in certain forms it can and will, particularly if it crowds out messages that give spiritual comfort and guidance to individual believers. Bulletin inserts are one thing; a sermon is quite another. Individual parishioners, suffering from the death of a spouse or facing troubles at work, may not find comfort in the pastor's reflections on Nicaragua. To the extent that lay members develop a habit of discounting the minister's appeals, future representational opportunities may be lost.

There is a related reason why there may be limits to the political role of churches, particularly in American society. As Fowler so perceptively points out, churches, at their best, perform a stabilizing function in our liberal society, providing members with a sense of community and serving as a refuge from the relentless individualism that is the liberal heritage in America.[8] A preoccupation with politics in the churches could undermine the sense of community by introducing the win-lose dynamics of political struggle. It is one thing to appeal to parishioners to donate money to local food banks or to their church's charitable agencies, activities that flow naturally from the Judeo-Christian heritage and give members a sense of solidarity with the poor. Overt political advocacy, however, is quite another dimension, and it could compromise the vital role churches play in American society.

This concern, of course, brings to mind Tocqueville's classic argument about the role of religion in the maintenance of democracy in America. Religion, he observed, should be considered the first of the American political institutions, but not because it intervenes directly in government. Quite the contrary; religion is most powerful, he argued, in its indirect, cultural influence, providing the moral restraint essential in a democratic society, educating people in their obligations to each other, and directing the attention of citizens occasionally away from the self-interest, materialism, and hedonism which spring up in a society which celebrates individual freedom. If churches and ministers become too closely attached to a particular party or political faction, however, they risk being discredited by historical events, and thus may jeopardize their part in the moral socialization of American citizens.[9]

Yet while the political role of activist religious people may be thus delimited, the broader significance of religion in American representation will remain. Representative government, in classic theory, was viewed as a relation of accountability between elected representatives and citizens, a relation that has been expanded in modern scholarship to include a concern with the ongoing pressures on those representatives. In other words, is the pressure system, in some sense, representative of the citizenry? If not, what can make it more so? The conclusion that emerges from this study is that any theory of representation in America must take into account the religious dimension. To ignore the religious as either archaic, contrary to separation of church and state, or somehow dangerous to the republic, is in effect to ignore the real-life experiences, values, and interests of most American citizens, male and female, black and white, rich and poor. Whether the religious sentiments of Americans are represented by political parties, elected representatives, or by religious lobbies, they must be in some sense articulated if the system is to be evaluated as truly representative.

Appendix

Methodology

The research approach employed in this book is somewhat unusual for the study of religion and politics in that: 1) I actually spoke with key tacticians of the groups, and 2) I did not restrict myself to one ideological or theological set of lobbies but instead used the Washington milieu as a way to compare and contrast the diverse manifestations of religious activism in America. In-depth interviews with Washington representatives of national religious organizations were conducted in December of 1984 and March of 1985. In choosing the organizations for study I sought to take advantage of the tremendous diversity of groups in Washington. Thus, I interviewed leaders of thirty major organizations representing a cross-section of Roman Catholic, Jewish, "mainline" Protestant, "peace" Protestant, evangelical, and fundamentalist constituencies. This enabled me to analyze the collective and interactive nature of religious advocacy. I was also able to include diverse organizational types, from established denominations to newer direct-mail organizations. For purposes of comparison, these groups span the ideological and organizational spectrum. Some have huge grassroots networks, while others have more modest membership bases. Still others represent institutional hierarchies.

Because I sought to analyze the operational realm—where

religious values are translated into concrete political strategies—
my intent was to interview the person in each organization most
responsible for direct congressional lobbying. Most commonly I
interviewed the director of the organization itself, the director
of the Washington office, or the director of legislative liaison,
but in five cases I settled for an interview with a staff member
who worked for the lobby director, who was unavailable at the
time. In only one case was I refused an interview, that being
Right to Life (I was told that they had too many requests for
interviews). The interviews were lengthy, averaging over an hour
in duration, with several lasting up to two hours. Three of the
interviews were over the phone and were relatively short. In
addition to conducting interviews, I attended an all-day meeting
of the board of IMPACT, a liberal interdenominational coalition,
and was able to observe and speak with a number of religious
leaders there. I also attended church at Sojourners Fellowship
and conducted short interviews with several of its leaders.

In-depth interviews were chosen over other methods of in-
quiry, such as mail surveys, because the intent was to derive not
only "objective" empirical information about lobby policy, issue
priorities, and formal decision-making procedures, but to solicit
subjective appraisals by the lobbyists themselves. Thus my purpose, in part, was to view their world from within. What theological values do religious lobbyists see themselves articulating? How
do they translate these values into political strategies? How do
they view their strategic situations? What do they see as organizational constraints or member interests? How do they perceive
other religious actors? Finally, and perhaps most importantly,
whom or what do they represent? To obtain such information I
patterned the interviews after the approach commonly employed
by Richard Fenno[1] in his study of congressional members, which
in current parlance might be termed a roughly phenomenological
mode. I use the term "phenomenological" to imply an empirical
approach that values the meanings actors attach to their actions,
which is how Fenno describes his approach. I see nothing incom-

patible with simultaneously employing observable data on the actions of religious lobbyists (such as recorded testimony) along with the meanings they attach to those actions in light of world views, or more precisely "life worlds."[2]

The interviews covered comparable topics but were "semi-structured" in the sense that I employed open-ended questions and encouraged far-ranging discussion. Every attempt was made to develop a deep rapport with the persons being interviewed, to identify with their perceived situation, and to see the world, to the extent possible, through their eyes. While the extent to which this can be achieved in an interview (even a lengthy one) is limited, in my judgment it *was* achieved to some degree with all individuals, and to a considerable extent with some. What intrigued me was that success here appeared to be a function of personality and not of political ideology or religious faith. All interviews were amicable and highly informative. Indeed, the central challenge of this study was disciplining and focusing the rich data obtained from the interviews.

The information gained from these interviews was supplemented in this study by lobby documents, such as newsletters and issue papers, to develop a composite picture for each organization of lobby policy and its formation. In addition, I interviewed a number of congressional staff members and reviewed *Congressional Record* testimony and press reports to flesh out the picture further. Hence, both reported actions of these lobbyists, as well as the meanings they attach to those actions, are considered relevant data for this study.

Two of the broad foci of this study are lobby policy, on the one hand, and member interest, on the other. As one aspect of the analysis of representation, lobby policy (as indicated through interview statements, lobby documents, *Congressional Record* testimony, and perceptions of the groups' policies held by congressional staff members and other group leaders) is compared to indicators of member interest to gain an understanding of when, and perhaps why, lobby policy does or does not reflect broad sentiment of church members. The term "indicator" must be stressed, because we can never say with certainty what the "interests" of Lutherans or Catholics or evangelicals are, but we can, and as scholars must, make epistemic leaps from our indicators chosen (we hope for good reasons) to our conclusions drawn.

A major methodological challenge was deriving good indicators of member opinion, which is itself an indication of the state of the study of religion and politics in America. While we do have a growing reservoir of information about the American public through sophisticated public-opinion polling, survey designers often have not been sufficiently aware of the important religious distinctions that exist in the pluralistic U.S. environment. It was not too long ago that surveys placed respondents only in the categories Protestant/Catholic/Jew, and indeed the large media exit polls (ABC-*Washington Post*, CBS-*N.Y. Times*) continue routinely to do so, adding only a fourth category, "born-again Christian." The most sophisticated of the surveys (such as the General Social Survey of the National Opinion Research Center and the American National Election Study of the Center for Political Studies at Michigan) now attempt to plumb the diversity of religious practice through follow-up questions that place respondents in appropriate categories and explore specific religious experiences and commitments. But a recurring problem with these surveys is that only small cells exist for a number of denominations that are politically active, such as the Mennonites, Quakers, and Seventh Day Adventists. Moreover, evangelicals and fundamentalists are not easily identifiable by denominational groupings; attempts to identify them lack precision, to say the least. In spite of these drawbacks, the 1984 American National Election Study proved to be a fruitful source of information. In a broader sense, however, the methodological challenges illustrate the complexity of studying the ever changing links between religion and politics in the United States. Hence, conclusions drawn about the opinions of citizens of various faiths—particularly in light of the dynamic character of American religion—must always remain somewhat tentative.

The methodological approach employed in this study reveals a broader epistemological insight. Many scholars of American politics attempt to put distance between themselves and their subjects, either by employing quantitative models aimed at explaining the actions of voters and members of Congress, or by moving to a level of great abstraction. Instead, I sought in part to reduce that distance and understand the world of the religious activists from their own perspectives. There is much to be gained, I think, from an approach that allows those studied some range to move beyond the scholar's categories. I was, quite frankly, astonished at the wealth of information I gained in the interviews with religious lobbyists. But more than this, I felt I gained an understanding of people with radically different perspectives from my own, which proved invaluable in this study.

Research Interviews

Roman Catholic:
  U.S. Catholic Conference
  Dave Connolly (two interviews), one of three lobbyists

  NETWORK—A Catholic Social Justice Lobby
  Catherine Brousseau, Registered Lobbyist,
  Kathleen McMullen, Staff

"Mainline" Protestant:
  National Council of Churches
  Rev. James Hamilton, Director of Washington Office

  Washington Office of the Episcopal Church
  Rev. William Weiler, Director

  Washington Office of the Presbyterian Church
  Rev. Mary Jane Patterson, Director

United Methodist Church, General Board of Church and Society
Rev. Fred Allen, Associate General Secretary for Issue Development and Advocacy

Lutheran Council, Office of Governmental Affairs
Rev. Charles Bergstrom, Executive Director
Martin Sovik, Foreign Affairs Specialist

United Church of Christ, Office for Church and Society
Rev. Gretchen Eick, Policy Advocate

American Baptist Churches USA
Carol Franklin

"Peace" Protestant:
Friends Committee on National Legislation
Edward Snyder, Executive Secretary

Mennonite Central Committee, U.S. Peace Section
Delton Franz, Director

Church of the Brethren, Washington Office
Leland Wilson, Director

Evangelical:
Baptist Joint Committee for Public Affairs
James Dunn, Executive Director

National Association of Evangelicals
Richard Cizik, Issue Researcher

Evangelicals for Social Action
Bill Kallio, Executive Director

General Conference of Seventh Day Adventists
Dr. Gary Ross, Associate Director for Congressional Liaison

Christian Legal Society
Sam Ericsson, Director of the Washington Office and National Coordinator for the Center for Law and Religious Freedom

African Methodist Episcopal Church
Bishop Hurst-Adams, Washington Director

Sojourners Fellowship
Jim Wallis, Founder
Jim Rice, Peace Coordinator
Joyce Holliday, Writer

Fundamentalist:
Moral Majority (Liberty Federation)
Roy Jones, Director of Legislative Affairs

Christian Voice and American Coalition for Traditional Values
Gary Jarmin, Director of Governmental Operations

Concerned Women for America
Michael Ferris, General Legal Counsel

Jewish:
American Jewish Committee
Hyman Bookbinder, Washington Representative

American Jewish Congress
Mark Pelavin, Staff

Union of American Hebrew Congregations—Religious Action Center
Rabbi David Saperstein, Co-Director and Counsel

Coalitions:
IMPACT
Craig Biddle, Director
Richard Houston, Editor

Washington Office on Africa
Randy Nunnelee, Religious Outreach

Washington Office on Latin America
George Rogers

Other:

Bread for the World—A Christian Citizens' Lobby
Stephen Coats, Issue Director

Unitarian Universalist
Robert Alpern, Director, Washington Office

Notes

Chapter 1

1. George Gallup, Jr., "Religion in America, 50 Years: 1935-1985," *The Gallup Report*, no. 236 (May 1985).

2. For some of the most recent studies see especially Robert Booth Fowler, *Religion and Politics in America* (Metuchen, N.J.: Scarecrow, 1985); Robert C. Liebman and Robert Wuthnow, eds., *The New Christian Right* (New York: Aldine, 1983); Paul Weber, "The Power and Performance of Religious Interest Groups," paper presented at the October 1982 meeting of the Society for the Scientific Study of Religion; James Guth, "The Christian Right Revisited: Partisan Realignment Among Southern Baptist Ministers," paper presented at the Midwest Political Science Association, Chicago, 1985; Michael Lienesch, "The Paradoxical Politics of the Religious Right," *Soundings* 66 (Spring 1983): 70–99; Michael Lienesch, "Right-Wing Religion: Christian Conservativism as a Political Movement, *Political Science Quarterly* 97, no. 3 (Fall 1982): 403–25. Emmett H. Buell and Lee Sigelman, "An Army That Meets Every Sunday? Popular Support for the Moral Majority in 1980," *Social Science Quarterly* 66, no. 2 (June 1985): 427–34.

3. There are several reasons why scholars may have underestimated the religious dimension in American politics. First, it could be, as evangelicals and fundamentalists fear, that intellectual elites are not themselves religious and thus are blind, by virtue of unconscious background assumptions, to religious dynamics. Alvin Gouldner, in *The Coming Crisis of Western Sociology* (New York: Avon, 1970), 25–60, persuasively demonstrates the biasing effects of background assumptions in social science research. Second, the weighty modernization literature, which hypothesizes a direct relation between political modernization and secularization, is little help. See especially Brian Wilson, "Return of the Sacred," in *Journal for the Scientific Study of Religion*

18 (Sept. 1979), for a brief review of the secularization literature. Finally, it could be that since religious belief clashes with the spirit of liberal skepticism, many members of the academy have found it difficult to take seriously the apparent religious convictions of many modern citizens.

4. See Paul Lopatto, *Religion and the Presidential Election* (New York: Praeger, 1985); Albert Menendez, *Religion at the Polls* (Philadelphia: Westminister, 1977); E.C. Ladd and Charles Hadley, *Transformations of the American Party System* (New York: Norton, 1975); Fowler, *Religion and Politics*, ch. 3; Seymour Martin Lipset and Earl Raab, "The Election and the Evangelicals," *Commentary* 71 (March 1981): 25–31.

5. See Frank Sorauf, *The Wall of Separation* (Princeton: Princeton Univ. Press, 1976); and Fowler, *Religion and Politics*, chs. 9 and 10.

6. The most thorough of the treatments of religious lobbying are based upon data collected in the 1960s. These include: James Adams, *The Growing Church Lobby in Washington* (Grand Rapids, Mich.: Eerdmans, 1970) and Alfred O. Hero, Jr., *American Religious Groups View Foreign Policy: Trends in Rank-and-File opinion, 1937–1969* (Durham, N.C.: Duke Univ. Press, 1973). Jeffrey Berry included some church groups in his study, *Lobbying for the People* (Princeton: Princeton Univ. Press, 1977); and A. James Reichley included religious lobbying in his discussion of religious political activism in *Religion in American Public Life* (Washington, D.C.: Brookings, 1985), ch. 6.

7. Examples of this tendency include Alfred Hero, *Religious Groups View Foreign Policy*; James Adams, *The Growing Church Lobby*; and A. James Reichley, *Religion in American Public Life*.

8. As examples of the literature demonstrating the supposed lack of public backing for the Christian Right see Emmett H. Buell and Lee Sigelman, "An Army That Meets Every Sunday," and Anson Schupe and William Stacey, "The Moral Majority Constituency," in *The New Christian Right*. Critical studies often employ "feeling thermometer" scales which show that most people do not feel "warm" toward the Moral Majority, but a common flaw is to ignore evidence of public support for facets of the fundamentalists' platform. Another body of literature illustrates the value-laden way in which some scholars approach fundamentalist religion and discount its adherents. Often the constituency represented by fundamentalist groups is viewed as "intolerant," "reactionary," "uneducated," and suffering from "status anxiety." See Seymour Lipset and Earl Raab, *The Politics of Unreason* (Chicago: Univ. of Chicago Press, 1978); Lipset and Raab, "The Election and the Evangelicals;" Karl Patel, Denny Pilant, and Gary Rose, "Christian Conservatism: A Study in Alienation and Lifestyle Concerns," *Journal of Political Science* 12, nos. 1 and 2 (1985): 17–30; and Alan Crawford, *Thunder on the Right* (New York: Pantheon, 1980).

9. Paul Weber's work on religious lobbies, while broader than most treatments, does not concern itself with representational issues. See "The Power and Performance" and also "Examining the Religious Lobbies," *This World*, no. 1 (Winter/Spring 1982): 97–107.

10. Sorauf terms litigation on church-state issues "minoritarian politics." See Sorauf, *The Wall of Separation*.

11. Jeffrey Berry, *The Interest Group Society* (Boston: Little, Brown, 1984).

12. See especially Ladd and Hadley, *Transformations*.

13. Luke Eugene Ebersole, *Church Lobbying in the Nation's Capitol* (New York: Macmillan, 1951).

14. Paul Weber identified seventy-four groups in 1985, and my study revealed at least half a dozen more that were not on his list. See Paul Weber, "The Power and Performance."

15. In surveys of the American public, George Gallup, Jr., reports that nine out of ten Americans express a belief in God and state a religious preference, and a large majority say religion is important in their lives. Americans express more confidence in the church than they do in other institutions of society, including schools, political institutions, business, and the media. Fifty-six percent of those polled in 1984 said they were more reliant on God today than five years ago, and four in ten say their spiritual well-being has improved. Participation in Bible study groups is up, particularly among the young. See George Gallup, Jr., "Religion in America," *The Gallup Report*, no. 222 (March 1984).

16. Ibid.

17. This fact is stressed by Paul Weber, "The Power and Performance."

18. James Madison, "Federalist No. 10," in *The Federalist Papers*, Clinton Rossiter, ed. (New York: New American Library, 1961).

19. This point is stressed by Robert Salisbury in "Interest Groups," *Handbook of Political Science*, Fred Greenstein and Nelson Polsby, eds. (Reading, Mass: Addison-Wesley, 1975), vol. 4.

20. E.E. Schattschneider, *Politics, Pressures and the Tariff* (New York: Farrar and Rinehart, 1942).

21. Jeffrey Berry, *The Interest Group Society*.

22. E.E. Schattschneider, *The SemiSovereign People* (New York: Holt, Rinehart and Winston, 1960).

23. Lester Thurow, *The Zero-Sum Society* (New York: Penguin, 1981), ch. 7.

24. Schattschneider, *SemiSovereign People*.

25. Peter Bachrach and Morton Baratz, "The Two Faces of Power," *American Political Science Review* 56 (Sept. 1963): 632–42.

26. A further variation on this theme is the later work by Lindblom, who argued in *Politics and Markets* (New York: Basic Books, 1977) that in a market economy business groups occupy a privileged position in politics, since their decisions affect the very prosperity of a community or society. Hence, business interests are always weighted more heavily in the decision-making process than other partisans.

27. Mancur Olson, *The Logic of Collective Action* (Cambridge: Harvard Univ. Press, 1965).

28. David Truman, *The Governmental Process* (New York: Knopf, 1951).

29. Thus the Farm Bureau, for example, may thrive because its cheap insurance for members guarantees continued participation, while farmers who oppose its policies may go underrepresented or ignored.

30. Berry, *The Interest Group Society*.

31. Ibid., 66.

32. Jeffrey K. Hadden, *The Gathering Storm in the Churches* (Garden City, N.Y.: Doubleday, 1969), 67.

33. Olson, *Collective Action*, 160.

34. Dean Kelley, *Why Conservative Churches Are Growing* (New York: Harper and Row, 1977).

35. James Q. Wilson, *Political Organizations* (New York: Basic Books, 1973), 60.

36. Weber, "Power and Performance."

37. Richard John Neuhaus, *The Naked Public Square* (Grand Rapids, Mich.: Eerdmans, 1984).

38. Hanna Fenichel Pitkin, *The Concept of Representation* (Berkeley: Univ. of California Press, 1967).

39. See Oliver Garceau, *The Political Life of the American Medical Association* (Cambridge: Harvard Univ. Press, 1941); John Colombotos, "Physicians and Medicine: A Before and After Study of the Effects of Legislation on Attitudes," *American Sociological Review* 34 (June 1969); Harmon Zeigler and Wayne Peak, *Interest Groups in American Society* (Englewood Cliffs, N.J.: Prentice-Hall, 1972); and Grant McConnell, *The Decline of Agrarian Democracy* (Berkeley: Univ. of California Press, 1953).

40. Robert Michels, *Political Parties* (New York: Dover, 1959).

41. Garceau, *Political Life of AMA*.

42. See Colombotos, "Physicians and Medicine," and Zeigler and Peak, *Interest Groups*.

43. Seymour Martin Lipset, Martin Trow, and James Coleman, *Union Democracy* (Garden City, N.Y.: Doubleday/Anchor, 1956).

44. For example, James Adams, *Growing Church Lobby*, reported that at the height of the Vietnam War in 1968, when national representatives of the

major Protestant denominations were calling for a bombing halt, only in one of eight denominations did there appear to be a decent match between the antiwar lobbying of church leaders and survey findings of members' views. Alfred Hero, *Religious Groups View Foreign Policy*, similarly found a gap between the international liberalism of mainline churches and the views of members in the pews—whose collection-plate contributions sustained the Washington offices.

45. See Hadden, *The Gathering Storm in the Churches*, and Harold E. Quinley, *The Prophetic Clergy* (New York: Wiley, 1974).

46. This argument is developed in chapter 5, where I contrast my findings with those of James Reichley, who is the most recent scholar to document the gap between liberal church leaders and lay members. See A. James Reichley, *Religion in American Public Life*.

Chapter 2

1. For a discussion of the pluralism and activism of contemporary American religion see Robert Booth Fowler, *Religion and Politics in America*, ch. 1. The pluralism of American religion is a theme found in a number of historical, theological, and sociological studies. Sydney Ahlstrom, in *A Religious History of the American People* (New Haven: Yale Univ. Press, 1972), documents the extensive denominational pluralism in the colonies and shows how that diversity was central to the experiment in disestablishment for the new nation. Andrew Greeley, in describing the United States as a "denominational" society, similarly views religious pluralism as a key determinate of American exceptionalism. See Andrew Greeley, *The Denominational Society* (Glenview, Ill.: Scott Foresman, 1972). This link between religious pluralism and American exceptionalism is also articulated by Will Herberg, in *Protestant, Catholic, Jew*, rev. ed. (New York: Doubleday, 1955). One theological interpretation of this pluralism is H. Richard Niebuhr's *The Social Sources of Denominationalism* (New York: Meridian Books, 1962), especially p. 6. Niebuhr views denominationalism as Christianity's accommodation to the "caste-system" of society, in which the division of churches closely follows the division of people into "castes of national, racial, and economic groups."

2. Herberg, *Protestant, Catholic, Jew*, 85.

3. Greeley, *Denominational Society*, 116-17. Greeley qualifies his argument by stating that it is unwise to assert that religious pluralism "caused" political pluralism, but he does think that, from the beginning, there has been a strong interactive process going on between religious and political pluralism.

4. Ahlstrom, *Religious History*, 166.

5. Ibid., 200.

6. Reichley, *Religion in American Public Life*, 76.

7. Greeley, *Denominational Society*, 3.

8. See Martin Marty, *Righteous Empire* (New York: Dial, 1970), 35–36.

9. Ibid., 40.

10. Ahlstrom observes that Baptists in particular fought for an end to state establishment, especially in Virginia, where they found allies in Thomas Jefferson and James Madison. See Ahlstrom, *Religious History*, 376.

11. Sidney E. Mead, *The Lively Experiment* (New York: Harper and Row, 1963), 35.

12. Greeley, *Denominational Society*, 3.

13. For an extensive discussion of this revival see Ahlstrom, *Religious History*.

14. Reichley, *Religion in American Public Life*, 73.

15. Ibid., 73.

16. Marty, *Righteous Empire*, 41.

17. As quoted in Reichley, *Religion in American Public Life*, 74.

18. Ibid.

19. Ahlstrom, *Religious History*, documents the tremendous "volunteerist" hyperactivity that characterized the churches of early to mid nineteenth-century America.

20. Marty, *Righteous Empire*, 44–45.

21. Chased out of New York and then Missouri, the Mormons, of course, found their New Israel in Utah.

22. As quoted in Reichley, *Religion*, 191.

23. Ibid., 191–92.

24. Ibid., 193.

25. See Norman H. Clark, *Deliver Us from Evil: An Interpretation of American Prohibition* (New York: Norton, 1976). Clark persuasively demonstrates that, contrary to popular wisdom about the Prohibition era, alcoholism and the influence of the saloon on community life were genuine problems in the nineteenth century and were perceived so by progressives. Moreover, he demonstrates that the Prohibition movement, in fact, did succeed in altering the drinking habits of Americans over the long term.

26. Ibid., 107.

27. For a good discussion of the black church see Fowler, *Religion and Politics in America*, ch. 12.

28. In observing the political utility of religion, Alexis de Tocqueville, of course, went even further in suggesting that religion might be *essential* to the maintenance of a democratic republic. See Alexis de Tocqueville, *Democracy*

in America, Richard D. Heffner, ed. (New York: New American Library, 1956), part 2, book 1, ch. 17, "Influence of Democracy on Religion."

29. The Metropolitan Community Church is a genuinely national church, with congregations in many of the larger cities.

30. Luke Ebersole, *Church Lobbying*, documented sixteen church offices operating in Washington in 1951. In contrast Paul Weber, "Power and Performance," has identified at least seventy-four religious lobbies, and his list does not include several that I found in my interviews.

31. Reichley, *Religion*, 244.

32. See Clark, *Deliver Us From Evil*.

33. See Martin Marty, *Righteous Empire*, 188–220.

34. The National Association of Evangelicals did maintain a Washington office throughout the 1950s and 1960s, but their operation was modest and their focus narrow during those years.

35. For a good summary of the early moves to the capital see Reichley, *Religion*, ch. 5.

36. For a thorough discussion of religious lobbying for the Civil Rights Act see James Adams, *The Growing Church Lobby in Washington*, chs. 1–2.

37. Ibid., 10.

38. Ibid.

39. Ibid., 42–43.

40. James Hamilton, National Council of Churches, Interview, Dec. 1984.

41. See Dean M. Kelley, *Why Conservative Churches Are Growing*.

42. It is an ironic testament to the dynamism of American religion that, while new evangelical churches were meeting in rented school buildings, many established mainline churches were renting space to alternative schools, day-care operations, and the like.

43. For an extremely thorough analysis of the diverse strands of modern evangelism see especially Robert Booth Fowler, *A New Engagement: Evangelical Political Thought, 1966–1976* (Grand Rapids, Mich.: Eerdmans, 1982).

44. George Gallup, Jr., has made a point of charting the religious beliefs of Americans, and what he finds is a strong orthodoxy in the faith of most citizens. See especially "Religion in America, 50 Years: 1935–1985."

45. The American National Election Study includes a "feeling thermometer" question about the Moral Majority, and not surprisingly most respondents did not register a warm reaction. See the 1984 American National Election Study, Center for Political Studies of the Survey Research Center, University of Michigan, Ann Arbor, 1984.

46. One of the reasons why religious cleavages make such an impact on the American party system is that, as Leon Epstein observes, American parties are extremely "porous" and adaptable. Thus leaders of the New Religious

Right have been successful in influencing a number of state Republican party
organizations, in large part because of their ability to galvanize a cadre of
highly motivated partisans to attend caucuses and work in campaigns. See
Leon D. Epstein, *Political Parties in the American Mold* (Madison: Univ. of
Wisconsin Press, 1986).

47. Michael Ferris, Counsel, Concerned Women for America, Interview,
Dec. 1984. "How To Manipulate a Woman," prepared by Concerned Women
for America, P.O. Box 5100, San Diego, CA 92105.

48. The NOW opposition to maternity leave has been widely reported. See
"Women at Work—Still Tough Issues," *The Capital Times* (Madison, Wis.)
April 14, 1986, p. 11. A growing debate is occurring over the wisdom of feminists' preoccupation with the ERA and abortion, to the exclusion of measures
like maternity leave, which are common in Europe. As Sylvia Ann Hewlett
argues in a new book, *A Lesser Life: The Myth of Women's Liberation in
America* (New York: Morrow, 1986), American feminist strategies have not
resulted in the economic advancement of women.

49. As an example see Matthew C. Moen, "School Prayer and the Politics
of Life-Style Concern," *Social Science Quarterly* (Dec. 1984).

50. See Daniel Bell, *The Cultural Contradictions of Capitalism* (New
York: Basic, 1976).

51. Catherine Brousseau, Registered Lobbyist, NETWORK, Interview,
March 1985.

52. Barry Ungar, Counsel, American Jewish Congress, in testimony before
the Subcommittee on Elementary, Secondary, and Vocational Education of
the House Committee on Education and Labor, on H.R. 4996, March 28,
1984.

53. Reichley, *Religion*, 237. Information also obtained from interviews
with Hyman Bookbinder, Washington Representative, American Jewish
Committee, and Mark Pelavin of the American Jewish Congress.

54. Religious Action Center, 2027 Massachusetts Ave., N.W., Washington, D.C. 20036.

55. Rabbi David Saperstein, Co-Director and Counsel, Religious Action
Center of the Union of American Hebrew Congregations, Interview, Dec.
1984.

56. National Jewish Community Relations Advisory Council, *Joint Program Plan*, 1983–84, 443 Park Ave. South, New York, N.Y. 10016, p. 37.

57. Richard Cizik, National Association of Evangelicals, Interview, Dec.
1984.

58. Interview data obtained from James Dunn, Executive Director, Baptist
Joint Committee, and Dr. Gary Ross, Associate Director for Congressional
Liaison, General Conference of Seventh Day Adventists, both in December

1984, and from Sam Ericsson, Director of the Washington Office, Christian Legal Society, March 1985.

59. The seminal document of the young activist evangelicals is *The Chicago Declaration*, Ronald Sider, ed. (Carol Stream, Ill.: Creation House, 1974). See also Richard Quebedeaux, *The Young Evangelicals* (New York: Harper and Row, 1974).

60. Bill Kallio, Executive Director, Evangelicals for Social Action, Interview, March 1985.

61. JustLife, P.O. Box 15263, Washington, D.C. 20003

62. Fowler, *Religion and Politics in America*, 294.

63. "Black Baptists in America and the Origins of Their Conventions," compiled by Sloan S. Hodges, General Secretary, Progressive National Baptist Convention, Inc., 3907 Georgia Avenue, N.W., Washington, D.C. 20011.

Chapter 3

1. See especially Graham Wilson, *Interest Groups in the United States*, (Oxford: Clarendon, 1981).

2. Lester Milbrath, *The Washington Lobbyists*, (Westport, Conn.: Greenwood, 1963), 245.

3. Ibid., 246.

4. Raymond A. Bauer, Ithiel de Sola Pool, and Lewis Anthony Dexter, *American Business and Public Policy*, (New York: Atherton, 1963), 486.

5. These trends are summarized in Jeffrey M. Berry, *The Interest Group Society*, (Boston: Little, Brown, 1984), chs. 2 and 3.

6. David R. Mayhew, *Congress: The Electoral Connection*, (New Haven: Yale Univ. Press, 1972).

7. Richard Fenno, Jr., *Homestyle: House Members in Their Districts*, (Boston: Little, Brown, 1978).

8. Jeffrey Berry, *Interest Group Society*, ch. 6, provides a nice summary of the lobby craft.

9. In my own interviews with congressional aides it was clear that a number of them view lobbyists as extensions of their staffs. Lobbyists, I was told, were useful when they track legislation, provide facts and analyses on the impacts (especially in the member's district or state) of legislation, and work to bring adversaries together for compromise solutions.

10. Dan Evans, Legislative Assistant, Representative Don Bonker, Washington, Interview, March 1985.

11. Most of the individuals interviewed felt that constituent mobilization could work in service of "insider" lobbying. But Alexander Netchvolodoff,

Administrative Assistant to Senator John Danforth, Missouri, felt that reliance on constituent mobilization tempted the groups to take uncompromising positions, and thus worked against the consensus-building process. However, my own analysis is that effective constituent mobilization usually creates a favorable environment in which insider deals can be cut. Whether or not constituent mobilization is always effective, however, is less important for my analysis than that *all* the religious lobbies perceive the necessity to do it.

12. Rabbi Saperstein, UAHC.

13. Not for attribution.

14. Dan Evans, Representative Bonker.

15. "Of Lobbying and Precious Dimensions," *New York Times*, April 8, 1986, p. 12.

16. Thomas Getman, Chief Legislative Assistant to Senator Mark Hatfield, Interview, Dec. 1984.

17. Hyman Bookbinder, Washington Representative, American Jewish Committee, Interview, Dec. 1984.

18. Edward Snyder, Executive Secretary, Friends Committee on National Legislation, Interview, Dec. 1984.

19. Graham Wilson makes the observation that conservative business groups came later to the use of tactics employed by their adversaries, the unions, but used those tactics more effectively, in many cases, when they finally did adopt them. This pattern certainly was followed with respect to the religious lobbies, with the conservative direct-mail groups far more successful than their liberal forerunners in generating pressure on members of Congress. See Wilson, *Interest Groups*.

20. For a good discussion of the marriage between new right direct-mail entrepreneurs and the evangelists of the electronic church, see James Reichley, *Religion in American Public Life*, 319–21.

21. The Moral Majority has not actually gone out of business but is part of the umbrella organization called the Liberty Federation.

22. This information was provided by a Moral Majority official who provided it as background, but not attribution.

23. Moral Majority Report.

24. Gary Jarmin, Director of Government Operations, Christian Voice, Interview, Dec. 1984.

25. Michael Ferris, Concerned Women for America. The organization trumpets the "fact" that they have more members than all the feminist organizations combined.

26. Jarmin, Christian Voice.

27. Ferris, Concerned Women.

28. Jarmin, Christian Voice.

29. Ferris, Concerned Women.

30. Ibid. Dean Kelley provides some corroboration for the assertion that evangelical churches are more successful gaining strong commitments from their members than many mainline congregations. His conclusion is that strict churches are growing because demanding commitments from prospective members is a way of conveying a seriousness about faith. See Dean M. Kelley, *Why Conservative Churches Are Growing*, (New York: Harper and Row, 1972).

31. Ferris, Concerned Women.

32. Jarmin, Christian Voice.

33. Ferris, Concerned Women.

34. Ibid.

35. Whether or not the New Religious Right groups can sustain this constituent support remains to be seen. The Moral Majority is always going through a "financial crisis," and most groups have experienced difficulties sustaining the level of their contributor support.

36. This point is amplified in chapter 5, where I compare lobby policy with member sentiment.

37. Dan Evans, Representative Bonker.

38. Steven Moore, Special Counsel to Senator Lowell Weicker, Jr., Connecticut, Interview, Dec. 1984.

39. Nancy Lifset, Legislative Assistant to Senator Robert Kasten, Wisconsin, Interview, March 1985.

40. Rev. Fred Allen, Associate General Secretary for Issue Development and Advocacy, United Methodist Church, General Board of Church and Society, Interview, Dec. 1984.

41. Not for attribution.

42. Richard Cizik, NAE.

43. Not for attribution.

44. Karl Moor, Subcommittee on Family and Human Services, Committee on Labor of the U.S. Senate, and Legislative Assistant to Senator Jeremiah Denton, Alabama, Interview, March 1985.

45. Cizik, NAE.

46. See my later discussion of Jewish lobbying against the Equal Access Act (ch. 6).

47. Rabbi Saperstein, UAHC.

48. Jewish groups are somewhat unusual in that their grassroots organizations have active local chapters, where members get together face-to-face, in contrast to most direct-mail groups, where membership is impersonal.

49. Stephen Coats, Issue Director, Bread for the World, Interview, Dec. 1984. Other information on Bread for the World was taken from a large file

of monthly legislative updates and issue statements. See also Arthur Simon, *Bread for the World* (New York: Paulist Press, 1975).

50. During the Cambodia crisis, Bread for the World generated so many calls and letters to the White House that President Carter's aides began asking callers if they were members of Bread for the World, according to reports by the organization.

51. Moore, Senator Lowell Weicker.

52. Barbara Thompson, Legislative Assistant to Senator Rudy Boschwitz, Minnesota, Interview, March 1985.

53. Moreover, IMPACT is struggling to develop a clear organizational structure and identity. I sat in on an annual meeting of the IMPACT board, which consisted of leaders of various denominations, and it was clear that leaders still had not defined the relationship between the national organization and state IMPACT organizations, nor had they developed a clear unifying theme for purposes of direct-mail solicitation. This should not detract from the importance of the effort, however, which illustrates my point that all groups feel the need to develop direct constituency contacts.

54. I discuss this theme in chapter 5. National leaders of liberal religious groups tend to be more ideologically consistent (as that is commonly understood) than even somewhat liberal lay members. Thus, church members whose Christian charity makes them sympathetic to hunger issues may find it harder to support other "liberal" issues in IMPACT's agenda.

55. Rev. William Weiler, Director, Washington Office of the Episcopal Church, phone Interview, Dec. 1984.

56. Dan Evans, Representative Bonker's aide, stressed this point in particular in the interview.

57. The Church of the Brethren, for example, has a total U.S. denominational membership of 170,000, yet it supports a Washington staff of five persons, comparable to many of the much larger mainline denominations.

58. These include Sojourners, the Other Side, Rociante, Quixote Center, and such development oriented groups as OXFAM America.

59. Not for attribution.

60. As reported in "The Religion and Society Report," a Gallup study revealed that Roman Catholic sentiment was significantly more dovish on nuclear weapons issues than opinion in other denominations, a finding attributed to lay interpretations of the Bishops' pastoral letter.

61. Rev. Mary Jane Patterson, Director, Washington Office of the Presbyterian Church, Interview, March 1985.

62. Rev. Gretchen Eick, Policy Advocate, United Church of Christ, Office for Church and Society, Interview, March 1985.

63. Ibid.

64. Ibid.

65. Press reports during the Contra debate, for example, indicated that the mail was running against the president's proposal, even though such groups as the Moral Majority attempted to mobilize their constituents in favor of the "freedom fighters."

66. "Witnessing for Peace and Justice in Central America," printed by the American Lutheran Church, Division for World Mission and Interchurch Cooperation, Minneapolis, Minnesota.

67. Bookbinder, AJC.

68. David Connolly, U.S. Catholic Conference, one of two interviews, March 1985.

69. Rabbi Saperstein, UAHC.

70. Bill Kallio, Evangelicals for Social Action.

71. Delton Franz, Director, U.S. Peace Section, Mennonite Central Committee, Interview, Dec. 1984.

72. Catherine Brousseau, NETWORK.

73. Carol Franklin, American Baptist Churches USA, Interview, March 1985.

74. Leland Wilson, Director, Washington Office, Church of the Brethren, Interview, Dec. 1984.

75. Dunn, Baptist Joint Committee for Public Affairs.

76. James Reichley summarizes this evidence in "Religion and the Future of American Politics," *Political Science Quarterly* no. 1 (1986): 40–41.

77. Jarmin, Christian Voice.

78. Ibid.

79. Ibid.

80. "Report Card on Traditional Values," prepared by the American Christian Voice Foundation, Grandbury, Texas.

81. Jarmin, Christian Voice.

82. For example, the *New York Times*-CBS News exit poll in 1984 found that 80% of the white born-again evangelicals voted for Reagan, and perhaps more significantly, 77% voted for a Republican for Congress.

83. George Will, "Pat Robertson's Mustard Seed," *Newsweek*, March 3, 1986.

84. These and other populist characterizations of Republicans by leaders of the Religious Right were said off the record.

85. Jarmin, Christian Voice.

86. George Rogers, Washington Office on Latin America, Interview, March 1985.

87. "Famous Faces Fighting Hard For School Prayer," *Congressional Quarterly Weekly Report*, March 3, 1984, p. 490.

88. Information on the Peace Pentecost obtained from *Sojourners Magazine* and from an interview with Jim Rice, Peace Coordinator, Sojourners Fellowship, March 1985.

89. The Spring and Summer issues (1985) of *Sojourners Magazine* reported widely on the Peace Pentecost and reactions to it.

90. Dan Evans, Representative Bonker.

91. Jeffrey Berry, *Interest Group Society*, 100.

92. Steven Moore, Senator Weicker.

93. Rev. Allen, United Methodists.

94. Rev. Eick, UCC.

95. Not for attribution.

96. Not for attribution.

97. Rabbi Saperstein, UAHC.

98. Roy Jones, Moral Majority.

99. Not for attribution.

100. Bill Tate, Administrative Assistant to Representative Jim Leach, Iowa, Interview, March 1985.

101. Not for attribution.

102. Not for attribution.

103. Mark Popovich, Legislative Assistant, Representative Steve Gunderson, Wisconsin, Interview, March 1985.

104. Rev. Patterson, Presbyterian Church.

105. Rev. Eick, UCC.

106. Stephen Coats, Bread for the World.

107. Alexander Netchvolodoff, Administrative Assistant, Senator John Danforth, Missouri, Interview, March 1985.

108. Ibid.

109. Not for attribution.

110. Rev. Patterson, Presbyterian Church.

111. Rev. Eick, UCC.

112. Martin Sovik, Lutheran Council, Interview, Dec. 1984.

113. Rev. Eick, UCC.

114. "United Methodist Bishops Take Tough Stand Against Nuclear Arms," *Capitol Times*, April 29, 1986.

115. Peter L. Benson and Dorothy L. Williams, *Religion on Capitol Hill: Myths and Realities*, (San Francisco: Harper and Row, 1982).

116. Ibid., 162–63.

117. Mary T. Hanna, "Religious Interest Groups and the Congress," paper presented at the Annual Convention, American Political Science Association, 1982.

118. Barbara Thompson, Senator Rudy Boschwitz.

119. Dr. Gary Ross, General Conference of Seventh Day Adventists.

120. Bookbinder, AJC.

121. Cizik, NAE.

122. Sovik, Lutheran Council.

123. Ferris, Concerned Women.

124. Thomas Getman, Senator Hatfield.

125. Not for attribution.

126. Karl Moor, Senator Denton.

127. Cizik, NAE.

128. Roy Jones, Moral Majority.

129. Connolly, Catholic Conference.

130. "Abortion Issue Weaves an Intricate Web," *New York Times*, April 22, 1986, p. 10.

131. Jones, Moral Majority.

132. Rev. J. Bryan Hehir, as reported in "Abortion Issue Weaves an Intricate Web."

133. Ibid.

134. Brousseau, NETWORK.

135. Randy Nunnelee, Religious Outreach, Washington Office on Africa, Interview, March 1985.

136. Ibid.

137. Ibid.

138. George Rogers, Washington Office on Latin America.

139. Ibid.

140. Michael J. Engelhardt, "The Foreign Policy Constituencies of House Members," Ph.D. diss., Univ. of Wisconsin, 1984.

141. Both quotes were taken from People For the American Way literature.

142. James Reichley, *Religion in American Public Life*, 266.

143. Both statements of church leaders were taken from the now-famous *Reader's Digest* article, "Do You Know Where Your Church Offerings Go," by Rael Jean Isaac (Jan. 1983).

144. Dunn, Baptist Joint Committee.

145. Coats, Bread for the World.

146. Snyder, Friends Committee.

147. Jones, Moral Majority.

148. Ferris, Concerned Women.

149. Rev. Allen, United Methodist.

150. Jarmin, Christian Voice.

151. Jones, Moral Majority.

152. Ibid.

153. Ferris, Concerned Women.
154. Jones, Moral Majority.
155. Nancy Lifset, Senator Kasten.
156. Saul Alinsky, *Rules For Radicals*, (Vintage, 1972), 130.
157. Jones, Moral Majority.
158. Ibid.
159. Ibid.
160. Bookbinder, AJC.
161. Ibid.
162. Rev. Allen, United Methodist.
163. Not for attribution.
164. Berry, *Interest Group Society*, 121.

Chapter 4

1. See Pitkin, *The Concept of Representation*, and *Representation*, Hanna Pitkin, ed. (New York: Atherton), 1969.
2. Pitkin, *The Concept of Representation*.
3. Ibid., 60.
4. Pitkin, ed., *Representation*, 20.
5. Ibid., 20–21.
6. Bookbinder, AJC.
7. Mark Pelavin, Legislative Assistant, American Jewish Congress, Interview, Dec. 1984.
8. Rabbi Saperstein, UAHC.
9. Jones, Moral Majority.
10. Ferris, Counsel, Concerned Women.
11. Jarmin, Christian Voice.
12. Rev. Charles Bergstrom, Executive Director, Office of Governmental Affairs, Lutheran Council in the United States of America, Interview, March 1985.
13. James Hamilton, Director, Washington Office, National Council of Churches of Christ in the USA, Interview, Dec. 1984.
14. Craig Biddle, Director of IMPACT, statement during a meeting of the board, Dec. 1984.
15. Cizik, NAE.
16. Dunn, Baptist Joint Committee.
17. Franklin, American Baptist Churches USA.
18. Dave Connolly, Assistant Director of Government Liaison, United States Catholic Conference, Interview, Dec. 1984.

19. Jeffrey Berry, *Lobbying for the People*, (Princeton: Princeton Univ. Press), 1977.

20. Andrew S. McFarland, *Public Interest Lobbies: Decision-Making on Energy* (Washington, D.C.: American Enterprise Institute, 1976). McFarland does not consider religious organizations as public interest groups because they represent a special interest. Berry, however, rightly observes that religious groups have agendas which surely characterize them in part as public interest lobbies.

21. Connolly, U.S. Catholic Conference (1984).

22. Cizik, NAE.

23. Ibid.

24. Rev. Bergstrom, Lutheran Council.

25. Franklin, American Baptist Convention.

26. Sovik, Lutheran Council.

27. Connolly, Catholic Conference.

28. Rabbi Saperstein, UAHC.

29. Ward Elliott, Professor, Claremont McKenna College, California, statement contained in "Fifteen Theses," nailed to the door of the college chapel.

30. Franz, Mennonite Central Committee.

31. Ferris, Concerned Women.

32. A. James Reichley documents well the ideologically pure liberalism of the mainline leaders, in contrast to the more moderate and diverse laity. See *Religion in American Public Life*.

33. Franz, Mennonite Central Committee.

34. April 1986 Lutheran Council newsletter.

35. Franz, Mennonite Central Committee.

36. April 1986 Lutheran Council newsletter.

37. Rev. Paul Kittlaus, Washington Representative, United Church of Christ, as quoted in "Churches Organize to Tackle Budget," *New York Times*, February 7, 1983.

38. Rev. Joseph Sullivan, as quoted in ibid.

39. Mary Jane Patterson, as quoted in ibid.

40. Ibid.

41. The "seamless garment" metaphor was developed by Cardinal Bernardin in two speeches, one delivered on December 6, 1983, at Fordam University, and the other on March 11, 1984, at Saint Louis University, both of which were printed by the *National Catholic Reporter*. It is a testament to the dynamic nature of current religious thought that some evangelicals draw inspiration from a Roman Catholic intellectual.

42. Ibid.

43. Sovik, Lutheran Council.

44. Franz, Mennonite Central Committee.

45. Michael J. Engelhardt, "Foreign Policy Constituencies of House Members."

46. Not for attribution.

47. Connolly, Catholic Conference.

48. Sovik, Lutheran Council.

49. Cizik, NAE.

50. Franklin, American Baptist.

51. Guest sermon by Namibia pastor at Our Saviors Lutheran Church, Greeley, Colorado, 1985.

Chapter 5

1. Luke Ebersole, *Church Lobbying in the Nation's Capital.*

2. See James L. Adams, *The Growing Church Lobby in Washington;* Alfred O. Hero, Jr., *American Religious Groups View Foreign Policy.*

3. See Harold E. Quinley, *The Prophetic Clergy,* and Jeffrey K. Hadden, *The Gathering Storm in the Churches.*

4. James Reichley, *Religion in American Public Life.*

5. The majority of Lutherans, for example, favored church involvement on civil rights, and more lay Presbyterians favored church involvement in peace issues than opposed it. See Reichley, *Religion in American Public Life.*

6. Ibid., ch. 6.

7. All of the tables referring to ANES data are from the American National Election Study, Center for Political Studies of the Survey Research Center, University of Michigan, Ann Arbor, 1984.

8. Seymour Martin Lipset argues that the American public "rejects" President Reagan's support for fundamentalist issues, which is certainly not accurate on prayer and possibly not on abortion. See Seymour Martin Lipset, "Beyond 1984: The Anomalies of American Politics," *PS* 19, no. 2 (Spring 1986): 222–36. The contention that fundamentalists have little public backing is advanced by Emmett H. Buell and Lee Sigelman, "An Army That Meets Every Sunday? Popular Support for the Moral Majority in 1980."

9. Although a sample of thirty-five respondents is highly suspect, other surveys show the same opposition to school prayer by Jewish citizens.

10. Kristen Luker, *Abortion and the Politics of Motherhood* (Berkeley: Univ. of California Press, 1984).

11. Kokie Roberts of National Public Radio, interviewed on the "MacNeil-Lehrer News Hour," said that on the day of the House vote against the

president's aid package to the Contras the church groups were "the strongest lobby against this package."

12. *Newsweek*, March 17, 1986. Later polls confirm that, despite the president's best rhetorical efforts, the public remains unconvinced of the wisdom of his military support for the Contras. A June *Washington Post*–ABC News poll revealed that 62% of the respondents opposed military and other aid to the Contras, and only 29% favored. As reported in the *Wisconsin State Journal*, "Contra Vote Sends U.S. Into Unchartered Waters," June 29, 1986, Sect. 1, p. 3.

13. These include the American Lutheran Church, the Lutheran Church in America, and the Association of Evangelical Lutheran Churches, soon to be merged into one body.

14. The classic formulation of the nature of mass ideology is Phillip Converse, "The Nature of Belief Systems in Mass Publics," in *Ideology and Discontent*, David Apter, ed. (New York: Free Press, 1964). Converse argued that elites tend to have formulated frames of reference, in which attitudes toward a variety of issues are "constrained" by an overall world view or ideology. In mass publics, especially as education decreases, greater randomness prevails, implying that average folks are not so constrained by logical links in their attitudes toward diverse issues. There is evidence in the material gathered for this study, however, that the religious dimension does in fact order the ideological world of the mass members, but in ways that may seem inconsistent to scholars used to traditional notions of liberal and conservative.

15. Kathleen Murphy Beatty and Oliver Walter, "Religious Belief and Practice: New Forces in American Politics?" paper delivered at the Annual Meeting of the American Political Science Association, Denver, Colorado, Sept. 1982.

16. Beatty and Walter used National Opinion Research Center data from 1972–82. Though potentially dated, such aggregation is useful because it provides some indication of the sentiment in smaller denominations.

17. "Hispanic Catholics Found to Hew to Tradition," *New York Times*, February 9, 1986, p. 14.

18. James Q. Wilson, *Political Organizations* (New York: Basic, 1973), 9.

19. This type of lobby includes the U.S. Catholic Conference, the Episcopal Church, the United Methodist Church, the Presbyterian Church, the Lutheran Council, the United Church of Christ, the Church of the Brethren, the Mennonite Central Committee, the American Baptist Churches USA, the Seventh Day Adventists, and the Union of American Hebrew Congregations.

20. Leaders of older, more stable membership organizations, such as the American Jewish Committee, are probably not as obsessed with financial maintenance as their counterparts in the newer direct-mail groups.

21. Robert Salisbury, "An Exchange Theory of Interest Groups," in *Interest Group Politics in America*, Robert Salisbury, ed. (New York: Harper and Row, 1970).

22. Albert O. Hirschman, *Exit, Voice, and Loyalty* (Cambridge: Harvard Univ. Press), 1970.

23. Coats, Bread for the World.

24. Jarmin, Christian Voice.

25. James Hamilton, National Council of Churches.

26. Coats, Bread for the World.

27. Pitkin, *Concept of Representation*, 221.

28. Berry, *Interest Group Society*, 66.

29. Pitkin, *Concept of Representation*, 221–22.

30. The Moral Majority Report cites a study conducted by Paul C. Vitz, professor of psychology at New York University, titled "Religion and Traditional Values in Public School Textbooks: An Empirical Study." Vitz examined forty secondary textbooks and found an almost complete absence of reference to religion in either past or contemporary American life.

31. Connolly, U.S. Catholic Conference, 1984.

Chapter 6

1. Frank Joseph Sorauf, *The Wall of Separation: The Constitutional Politics of Church and State* (Princeton: Princeton Univ. Press, 1976).

2. House Committee on Education and Labor, "Equal Access Act," Report 98-710, April 26, 1984, page 1.

3. *Brandon v. Board of Education of Guilderland Central Schools*, 632 F. 2d 971 (2nd Cir. 1980), cert. denied 454 U.S. 1154 (1981).

4. *Widmar v. Vincent*, 454 U.S. 263 (1981).

5. House Committee on Ed. and Labor, Report 98–710.

6. Testimony of Patrick Monaghan, general counsel, Catholic League for Religious and Civil Rights, "Hearings on the Equal Access Act," H.R. 2732, before the Subcommittee on Elementary, Secondary, and Vocational Education of the Committee on Education and Labor, House of Representatives, October 18, 19, and 20, 1983, pp. 194–95.

7. "Famous Faces Fighting Hard for School Prayer," *Congressional Quarterly Weekly Report*, March 3, 1984, p. 490.

8. Ibid.

9. The 1984 American National Election Study of the Center for Political Studies at the University of Michigan revealed that school prayer was supported by 69% of all respondents and 83% of all blacks.

10. Rev. Bergstrom, Lutheran Council. See also "Prayer Issue Engulfs Congress as Senate Embarks on Debate," *Congressional Quarterly Weekly Report*, March 10, 1984, p. 538.

11. "Senate Rejects School Prayer Amendment," *Congressional Quarterly Weekly Report*, March 24, 1984, p. 643.

12. Mary T. Hanna, "Religious Interest Groups and the Congress," paper presented at the Annual Convention, American Political Science Association, Denver, Colorado, Sept. 1982.

13. Hearings on H.R. 2732, pp. 232–37.

14. Dan Evans, Representative Bonker.

15. Ibid.

16. Representative Carl Perkins, as quoted in "Two House Veterans Scrap on Issue of School Access," *Congressional Quarterly Weekly Report*, May 12, 1984.

17. Ibid., 1104.

18. Dunn, Baptist Joint Committee.

19. Laurence Tribe, testimony before the Subcommittee on Elementary, Secondary and Vocation Education of the Committee on Education and Labor, House of Representatives, H.R. 4996, March 28, 1984, p. 46.

20. Dan Evans, Representative Bonker.

21. "House Clears Bill Allowing Prayer Meetings In Schools," *Congressional Quarterly Weekly Report*, July 28, 1984, p. 1808.

22. As Matsunaga and Chen report, "Calendar Wednesday" works this way: every Wednesday committee chairs may call up "unprivileged bills for immediate floor action on a committee by committee basis. But since there is no way to entertain all committee requests or ensure immediate House action, the procedure is routinely dispensed with by unanimous consent of House members at the request of the leadership. If a member objects, however, then a ⅔ majority vote must be obtained to avoid the procedure. Perkins's threat, backed by substantial support for his bill, apparently made the price of avoiding a vote on equal access too high for the leadership. See Spark M. Matsunaga and Ping Chen, *Rulemakers of the House* (Urbana: Univ. of Illinois Press 1976), 48.

23. John Baker, "Views of the Wall," in *Report from the Capitol*, published by the Baptist Joint Committee, Sept. 1984, p. 6.

24. Ibid.

25. Senator Mark Hatfield, as reported in the *Congressional Record*, Friday, October 11, 1984.

26. Representative Don Bonker, as reported in the *Congressional Record*, Thursday, October 11, 1984.

27. Ibid.

28. "A Diverse Group Hammers Out Guidelines For Implementing the Equal Access Act," *Christianity Today*, October 19, 1984, p. 52.

29. *Congressional Record*, October 11 and 12.

30. Representative William Goodling, as quoted in the *Congressional Record*, October 11, 1984.

31. Senator Mark Hatfield, as quoted in the *Congressional Record*, October 12, 1984.

32. Dan Evans, Representative Bonker.

33. See especially Aaron Wildavsky and Jeffrey Pressman, *Implementation* (Berkeley: Univ. of California Press, 1973), and Aaron Wildavsky, *Speaking Truth to Power* (Boston: Little, Brown, 1979).

34. Murray Edelman, *Symbolic Uses of Politics* (Urbana: Univ. of Illinois Press, 1964).

35. While Catholic groups supported the equal access legislation, their activities were not central to the analysis employed here; thus, for purposes of brevity and clarity I have excluded them from more detailed treatment.

36. Moor, Senator Denton.

37. Beverley LeHaye, as quoted in Concerned Women for America newsletter, July 1984.

38. Rev. Jerry Falwell, as quoted in *Congressional Quarterly Weekly Report*, May 12, 1984.

39. James Dunn, as quoted in *Congressional Quarterly Weekly Report*, May 12, 1984.

40. Sam Ericsson, Christian Legal Society.

41. See especially Jack Walker, "The Origins and Maintenance of Interest Groups in America," *American Political Science Review* 77 (June 1983): 390-406; and Robert Salisbury, "Interest Representation: The Dominance of Institutions," *American Political Science Review* 78 (March 1984): 64–76.

42. Jones, Moral Majority.

43. Cizik, NAE.

44. Dr. Gary Ross, Seventh Day Adventists.

45. Hearings on H.R. 4996, p. 116.

46. Dunn, Baptist Joint Committee.

47. Cizik, NAE.

48. Evans, Representative Bonker.

49. Ross, Seventh Day Adventists.

50. Bonnie Bailey, 1983 graduate of Monterey High School, Lubbock, Texas, in testimony before hearings on H.R. 2732, p. 35–39.

51. In a Sunday school lecture, which he recorded, Sam Ericsson described the tortuous route of equal access and its eventual success as evidence of the hand of God in human affairs. The title of the tape is quintessential

evangelical: "Equal Access and the Sovereignty of God," Emmanuel Bible Church, Virginia, 1985.

52. Ericsson, CLS.

53. Ibid.

54. Ibid.

55. Nat Hentoff, "Equal Access Lets Teenagers Grow Up," *Washington Post Weekly Edition*, September 24, 1984. Hentoff was particularly impressed with the implications of the inclusion of "political and philosophical" content in protected speech for high school students, which he felt would enhance free speech in many secondary schools.

56. Tribe's testimony was viewed as extremely persuasive to House committee members. Hearings on HR 4996.

57. Ericsson, CLS.

58. Franklin, American Baptist Churches USA.

59. Netchvolodoff, Senator Danforth.

60. Pelavin, AJC.

61. Rabbi Saperstein, UAHC.

62. Saperstein, for example, served as the only Jewish member of IMPACT, an alliance of liberal Protestant groups, and was elected as board chairman for one year.

63. Marc Pearl, testimony in hearings on H.R. 2732, p. 18.

64. Bookbinder, AJC.

65. Hamilton, National Council of Churches of Christ.

66. Richard Neustadt, *Presidential Power*, 2nd ed. (New York: Wiley, 1980).

67. Dean Kelley, *Why Conservative Churches Are Growing*.

68. Dean Kelley, testimony in hearings on H.R. 2732, p. 96.

69. Dean Kelley, testimony in hearings on H.R. 4996, p. 95.

70. James Wood, Jr., "Equal Access: A New Direction in American Public Education," *Journal of Church and State* (Winter 1985): 5–17.

71. The name of the new denomination will be the Evangelical Lutheran Church in America. The variable uses of the word evangelical need explanation. Religious scholars generally use the word "evangelical" to mean an adherence to tenets of Protestant orthodoxy. While many Lutherans doubtless fit this definition, independent evangelical church leaders dispute the extent to which the main Lutheran bodies reflect sufficient orthodoxy and evangelical fervor to warrant the label.

72. Rev. Charles Bergstrom, testimony in hearings on H.R. 4996, pp. 107–9.

73. Ibid., p. 106-7.

74. Rev. Bergstrom, Lutheran Council.

75. Forest Montgomery, as quoted in hearings on H.R. 4966, pp. 121–22.
76. Hearings on H.R. 4996, p. 122.
77. Ibid., pp. 121–22.
78. Ibid.
79. Not for attribution.
80. Not for attribution.
81. Wood, *Journal of Church and State.*
82. Jones, Moral Majority.
83. Jones, as reported in the *Moral Majority Report*, March 1985, p. 7.
84. Rev. Falwell, as quoted in the *Religion and Society Report*, May 1985.
85. Ferris, Concerned Women.
86. Literally, "lifeworld." This implies something even more fundamental than world views.
87. Sam Ericsson, Sunday School lecture.

Chapter 7

1. Carole Pateman argues that direct citizen participation is valuable in itself, because it educates and fosters a public-minded spirit among common people. As I suggest in chapter 5, this "civics education" appears to be a major contribution of the religious lobbyists, who are enlisting direct citizen participation in all levels of government. See Carole Pateman, *Participation and Democratic Theory*, (London: Cambridge Univ. Press, 1970).
2. Bookbinder relayed this story in a meeting of faculty members at the University of Wisconsin, March 1985.
3. Reichley, *Religion in American Public Life.*
4. The American Lutheran Church, to take a representative example, arrives at official policy through a vote of its delegates at annual conventions. Because activist lay members and clergy tend to be the most liberal ones, the thousand delegates, half lay and half clergy, tend to overrepresent that viewpoint. Moreover, the resolutions are drafted by national church officials, who tend to be more liberal still. This pattern repeats itself for the other mainline denominations.
5. Netchvolodoff, Senator Danforth.
6. Jim Wallis, *The Call to Conversion* (New York: Harper and Row, 1982). Jim Wallis draws much inspiration from Bonhoeffer's critique of "cheap grace," the idea that God's grace is merely a blessing and not a challenge to radically change one's life. The term "cheap prophecy" is my own. See Dietrich Bonhoeffer, *The Cost of Discipleship*, rev. ed. (New York: Macmillan, 1963).

7. Reinhold Niebuhr, no doubt, would view many of today's liberal church leaders as naive "children of light." See Reinhold Niebuhr, *Children of Light and Children of Darkness* (New York: Scribner's, 1944).

8. Fowler, *Religion and Politics in America*, ch. 2.

9. Alexis de Tocqueville, *Democracy in America*. See especially vol. 1, part 2, ch. 9; vol. 2, part 1, ch. 5; and vol. 2, part 2, ch. 15.

Appendix

1 See Richard Fenno, Jr., *Congressmen in Committees* (Boston: Little, Brown, 1973).

2 For a discussion of the phenomenological approach, see Richard Bernstein, *The Restructuring of Social and Political Theory* (Philadelphia: Univ. of Pennsylvania Press, 1978), part 3.

Selected Bibliography

Books:

Adams, James L. *The Growing Church Lobby in Washington*. Grand Rapids, Mich.: Eerdmans, 1970.

Ahlstrom, Sydney. *A Religious History of the American People*. New Haven: Yale Univ. Press, 1972.

Alinsky, Saul. *Rules for Radicals*. New York: Vintage, 1972.

Bauer, Raymond A., Ithiel de Sola Pool, and Lewis Anthony Dexter. *American Business and Public Policy*. New York: Atherton, 1963.

Bell, Daniel. *The Cultural Contradictions of Capitalism*. New York: Basic, 1976.

Benson, Peter C., and Dorothy L. Williams. *Religion on Capitol Hill: Myths and Realities*. San Francisco: Harper and Row, 1982. Reprint, New York: Oxford, 1986.

Bentley, Arthur. *The Process of Government*. Bloomington, Ind.: Principia Press, 1949.

Bernstein, Richard. *The Restructuring of Social and Political Theory*. Philadelphia: Univ. of Pennsylvania Press, 1978.

Berry, Jeffrey. *The Interest Group Society*. Boston: Little, Brown, 1984.

———. *Lobbying for the People*. Princeton: Princeton Univ. Press, 1977.

Buzzard, Lynn R., and Samuel Ericsson. *The Battle for Religious Liberty*. Elgin, Ill.: David Cook, 1982.

Cigler, Allan J., and Burdett A. Loomis. *Interest Group Politics*. Washington: Congressional Quarterly, 1983.

Clark, Norman H. *Deliver Us from Evil: An Interpretation of American Prohibition*. New York: Norton, 1976.

Crawford, Alan. *Thunder on the Right*. New York: Pantheon, 1980.

Dahl, Robert. *Who Governs*. New Haven: Yale Univ. Press, 1961.

Ebersole, Luke Eugene. *Church Lobbying in the Nation's Capitol.* New York: Macmillan, 1951.

Edelman, Murray. *The Symbolic Uses of Politics.* Urbana: Univ. of Illinois Press, 1964.

Engelhardt, Michael. "The Foreign Policy Constituencies of House Members." Ph.D. diss., Univ. of Wisconsin, 1984.

Epstein, Leon D. *Political Parties in the American Mold.* Madison: Univ. of Wisconsin Press, 1986.

Eulau, Heinz, and John C. Wahlke. *The Politics of Representation.* Beverly Hills: Sage, 1978.

Falwell, Jerry. *Listen America.* Garden City, N.Y.: Doubleday, 1980.

Fenno, Richard Jr. *Congressmen in Committees.* Boston: Little, Brown, 1973.

——. *Homestyle.* Boston: Little, Brown, 1978.

Fowler, Robert Booth. *A New Engagement: Evangelical Political Thought 1966-1976.* Grand Rapids, Mich.: Eerdmans, 1982.

——. *Religion and Politics in America.* Metuchen, N.J.: Scarecrow, 1985.

Garceau, Oliver. *The Political Life of the American Medical Association.* Cambridge: Harvard Univ. Press, 1941.

Gouldner, Alvin. *The Coming Crisis of Western Sociology.* New York: Avon, 1970.

Greeley, Andrew. *The Denominational Society.* Glenview, Ill.: Scott Foresman, 1972.

Hadden, Jeffrey K. *The Gathering Storm in the Churches.* Garden City, N.Y.: Doubleday, 1969.

Hadden, Jeffrey K., and Charles E. Swan. *Prime Time Preachers: The Rising Power of Televangelism.* Reading, Mass: Addison-Wesley, 1981.

Hanna, Mary T. *Catholics and American Politics.* Cambridge: Harvard Univ. Press, 1979.

Hatfield, Mark. *Between a Rock and a Hard Place.* Waco, Tex.: Word, 1976.

Herberg, Will. *Protestant, Catholic, Jew.* New York: Doubleday, 1955.

Hero, Alfred O., Jr. *American Religious Groups View Foreign Policy: Trends in Rank-and-File Opinion, 1937–1969.* Durham, N.C.: Duke Univ. Press, 1973.

Hewlett, Sylvia Ann. *A Lesser Life: The Myth of Women's Liberation in America.* New York: Morrow, 1986.

Hirschman, Albert. *Exit, Voice and Loyalty.* Cambridge: Harvard Univ. Press, 1970.

Hofstadter, Richard. *Age of Reform.* New York: Knopf, 1956.

Kelley, Dean M. *Why Conservative Churches Are Growing.* New York: Harper and Row, 1972.

Kersten, Lawrence K. *The Lutheran Ethic: The Impact of Religion on Lay-*

men and Clergy. Detroit: Wayne State Univ. Press, 1970.

Ladd, E. C., and Charles Hadley. *Transformations of the American Party System*. New York: Norton, 1975.

Latham, Earl. *The Group Basis of Politics*. Ithaca, N.Y.: Cornell Univ. Press, 1952.

Liebman, Robert C., and Robert Wuthnow, eds. *The New Christian Right*. New York: Aldine, 1983.

Lindblom, Charles. *Politics and Markets*. New York: Basic, 1977.

Lipset, Seymour Martin, and Earl Raab. *The Politics of Unreason*. Chicago: Univ. of Chicago Press, 1978.

Lipset, Seymour Martin, Martin Trow, and James Coleman. *Union Democracy*. Garden City, N.Y.: Doubleday/Anchor, 1956.

Lopatto, Paul. *Religion and the Presidential Election*. New York: Praeger, 1985.

Lowi, Theodore. *The End of Liberalism*. New York: Norton, 1979.

McConnell, Grant. *The Decline of Agrarian Democracy*. Berkeley: Univ. of California Press, 1954.

McFarland, Andrew S. *Public Interest Lobbies: Decision Making on Energy*. Washington, D.C.: American Enterprise Institute, 1976.

Malbin, Michael, ed. *Parties, Interest Groups and Campaign Finance Laws*. Washington, D.C.: American Enterprise Institute, 1980.

Marsden, George. *Fundamentalism and American Culture*. New York: Oxford Univ. Press, 1980.

Marty, Martin. *Righteous Empire*. New York: Dial, 1970.

Mayhew, David R. *Congress: The Electoral Connection*. New Haven: Yale Univ. Press, 1972.

Mead, Sidney E. *The Lively Experiment: The Shaping of Christianity in America*. New York: Harper and Row, 1963.

———. *The Nation with the Soul of a Church*. New York: Harper and Row, 1975.

Menendez, Albert J. *Religion at the Polls*. Philadelphia: Westminister, 1977.

Michels, Robert. *Political Parties*. New York: Dover, 1953.

Milbrath, Lester. *The Washington Lobbyists*. Westport, Conn.: Greenwood, 1963.

Mills, C. Wright. *The Power Elite*. New York: Oxford Univ. Press, 1956.

Neuhaus, Richard John. *The Naked Public Square*. Grand Rapids, Mich.: Eerdmans, 1984.

Niebuhr, H. Richard. *The Social Sources of Denominationalism*. New York: Meridian, 1962.

Niebuhr, Reinhold. *The Children of Light and the Children of Darkness*. New York: Scribner's, 1944.

————. *Moral Man and Immoral Society*. New York: Scribner's, 1960.

Olson, Mancur. *The Logic of Collective Action*. Cambridge: Harvard Univ. Press, 1965.

Ornstein, Norman J., and Shirley Elder. *Interest Groups, Lobbying and Public Policy*. Washington, D.C.: Congressional Quarterly, 1978.

Pateman, Carole. *Participation and Democratic Theory*. London: Cambridge Univ. Press, 1980.

Perkins, John. *Let Justice Roll Down*. Glendale, Calif.: Regal, 1976.

Pitkin, Hanna Fenichel. *The Concept of Representation*. Berkeley: Univ. of California Press, 1967.

————, ed. *Representation*. New York: Atherton, 1969.

Quedbedeaux, Richard. *The Young Evangelicals*. New York: Harper and Row, 1974.

Quinley, Harold E. *The Prophetic Clergy*. New York: Wiley, 1974.

Reichley, A. James. *Religion in American Public Life*. Washington, D.C.: Brookings, 1985.

Salisbury, Robert, ed. *Interest Group Politics in America*. New York: Harper and Row, 1970.

Schaeffer, Frankie. *A Time for Anger*. Westchester, Ill.: Crossway, 1982.

Schattschneider, E.E. *Politics, Pressure and the Tariff*. New York: Farrar and Rinehart, 1942.

————. *The Semisovereign People*. New York: Holt, Rinehart, and Winston, 1960.

Schlozman, Kay Lehman, and John T. Tierney. *Organized Interests and American Democracy*. New York: Harper and Row, 1986.

Sider, Ronald, ed. *The Chicago Declaration*. Carol Stream, Ill.: Creation House, 1974.

Simon, Arthur. *Bread for the World*. New York: Paulist Press, 1975.

Sorauf, Frank J. *The Wall of Separation*. Princeton: Princeton Univ. Press, 1976.

Thurow, Lester. *The Zero Sum Society*. New York: Penguin, 1981.

Tocqueville, Alexis de. *Democracy in America*. Translated by George Lawrence. Edited by J.P. Mayer and A.P. Kerr. Garden City, N.Y.: Doubleday/Anchor, 1969.

Truman, David. *The Governmental Process*. New York: Knopf, 1951.

Wald, Kenneth D. *Religion and Politics in the United States*. New York: St. Martin's, 1987.

Wallis, Jim. *The Call To Conversion*. San Francisco: Harper, 1981.

Wilson, Graham. *Interest Groups in the United States*. Oxford: Clarendon, 1981.

Wilson, James Q. *Political Organizations*. New York: Basic, 1973.

Zeigler, Harmon, and Wayne Peak. *Interest Groups in American Society.* Englewood Cliffs, N.J.: Prentice-Hall, 1972.

Zisk, Betty H., ed. *American Political Interest Groups: Readings in Theory and Research.* Belmont, Calif.: Wadsworth, 1969.

Zwier, Robert. *Born-Again Politics.* Downer's Grove, Ill.: Inter-Varsity, 1982.

Articles:

Bachrach, Peter, and Morton Baratz. "Two Faces of Power." *American Political Science Review* 57, no. 3 (Sept. 1963): 632–42.

Beatty, Kathleen Murphy, and Oliver Walter. "Religious Belief and Practice: New Forces in American Politics." Paper, American Political Science Association, 1982.

———. "Religious Preference and Practice: Reevaluating Their Impact on Political Tolerance." *Public Opinion Quarterly* 48, no. 2 (Spring 1984).

Bellah, Robert. "Civil Religion in America." *Daedalus* (1967).

Brudney, Jeffrey, and Gary W. Copeland, "Evangelicals as a Political Force: Reagan and the 1980 Religious Vote." *Social Science Quarterly* 65, no. 4 (Dec. 1984): 1072–80.

Buell, Emmett H., and Lee Sigelman. "An Army That Meets Every Sunday? Popular Support for the Moral Majority in 1980." *Social Science Quarterly* 66, no. 2 (June 1985): 426–33.

Colombotos, John. "Physicians and Medicine: A Before and After Study of the Effect of Legislation on Attitudes." *American Sociological Review* 34 (June 1969).

Converse, Philip. "The Nature of Belief Systems in Mass Publics." In *Ideology and Discontent,* David Apter, ed. New York: Free Press, 1964.

Gallup, George, Jr. "Religion in America, 50 Years: 1935–1985." *The Gallup Report,* no. 236 (May 1985).

———. "Religion in America." *The Gallup Report,* no. 222 (March 1983).

Guth, James. "The Christian Right Revisited: Partisan Realignment Among Southern Baptist Ministers." Paper, Midwest Political Science Association, 1985.

———. "The Politics of Preachers: Southern Baptist Ministers and the 'Christian Right.'" Paper, Citadel Symposium on Southern Politics, 1982.

———. "The Politics of the 'Evangelical Right': An Interpretive Essay." Paper, American Political Science Association, 1981.

Hanna, Mary T. "Religious Interest Groups and the Congress." Paper, American Political Science Association, 1982.

Lienesch, Michael. "The Paradoxical Politics of the Religious Right." *Soundings* 66 (Spring 1983): 70–99.

————. "Right Wing Religion: Christian Conservatism as a Political Movement." *Political Science Quarterly* 97, no. 3 (Fall 1982): 403–26.

Lipset, Seymour Martin. "Beyond 1984: The Anomalies of American Politics." *PS* 19, no. 2 (Spring 1986): 222–36.

Lipset, Seymour Martin, and Earl Raab. "The Election and the Evangelicals." *Commentary* 71 (March 1981): 25–31.

Moen, Matthew C. "School Prayer and the Politics of Lifestyle Concern." *Social Science Quarterly* (Dec. 1984): 1065–71.

Patel, Karl, Denny Pilant, and Gary Rose. "Christian Conservatism: A Study in Alienation and Lifestyle Concerns." *Journal of Political Science* 12, nos. 1 and 2 ( ): 17–30.

Reichley, A. James. "Religion and the Future of American Politics." *Political Science Quarterly* 101, no. 1 (1986).

Salisbury, Robert. "An Exchange Theory of Interest Groups." *Midwest Journal of Political Science* 13, no. 1 (Feb. 1969): 1–32. Reprinted in *Interest Group Politics in America*, Salisbury, ed.

————. "Interest Representation: The Dominance of Institutions." *American Political Science Review* 78, no. 1 (March 1984).

Schupe, Anson and William Stacey. "The Moral Majority Constituency." In *The New Christian Right*, Liebman and Wuthnow, eds.

Strickwerda, Charles E. "The Churches and Nuclear Arms." Paper, American Political Science Association, 1982.

Walker, Jack. "A Critique of Elitist Theory of Democracy." *American Political Science Review* 60 (June 1966): 285–94.

————. "The Origins and Maintenance of Interest Groups in America." *American Political Science Review* 77 (June 1983): 390–406.

————. "The Mobilization of Political Interest." Paper, American Political Science Association, 1983.

Weber, Paul. "Examining the Religious Lobbies." *This World*, no. 1 (Winter/Spring 1982): 97–107.

————. "The Power and Performance of Religious Interest Groups." Paper, Society for the Scientific Study of Religion, 1982.

Wilson, Brian. "Return of the Sacred." *Journal for the Scientific Study of Religion* 18 (Sept. 1979): 268–80.

Index

Representing God in Washington was designed by Dariel Mayer, composed by Tseng Information Systems, Inc., printed by Thomson-Shore, Inc., and bound by John H. Dekker & Sons. The book was set in Caledonia and printed on 60-lb. Warren's Old Style.